Official
Marimba™ Guide
to Castanet™

OFFICIAL GUIDE TO

marimba™

Castanet™

Laura Lemay

201 West 103rd Street,
Indianapolis, Indiana 46290

To Eric: I'm sorry I forgot your birthday; please accept this dedication in lieu of the new motorcycle I was going to get you.

Copyright © 1997 by Sams.net Publishing

FIRST EDITION

International Standard Book Number: 1-57521-255-2

Library of Congress Catalog Card Number: 96-71499

2000   99   98   97   4   3   2   1

Interpretation of the printing code: the rightmost double-digit number is the year of the book's printing; the rightmost single-digit, the number of the book's printing. For example, a printing code of 97-1 shows that the first printing of the book occurred in 1997.

Composed in AGaramond and MCPdigital by Macmillan Computer Publishing

Printed in the United States of America

Publisher and President:	*Richard K. Swadley*
Publishing Manager:	*Mark Taber*
Director of Editorial Services:	*Cindy Morrow*
Assistant Marketing Managers:	*Kristina Perry, Rachel Wolfe*

Acquisitions Editor
Mark Taber

Development Editor
Fran Hatton

Software Development Specialist
Bob Correll

Production Editor
Mary Inderstrodt

Copy Editors
David Bradford, Fran Hatton, Chuck Hutchinson, Ryan Rader

Indexer
Tom Dinse

Technical Reviewer
Jeffrey Vagg

Editorial Coordinator
Katie Wise

Technical Edit Coordinator
Lorraine Schaffer

Resource Coordinator
Deborah Frisby

Editorial Assistants
Carol Ackerman
Andi Richter
Rhonda Tinch-Mize

Cover Designer
Alyssa Yesh

Book Designer
Alyssa Yesh

Copy Writer
Peter Fuller

Production Team Supervisor
Brad Chinn

Production
Mona Brown, Jennifer Dierdorff, Ayanna Lacey, Shawn Ring

Overview

Contents

Part II Castanet Transmitter   65

Foreward

In early 1996 four members of the team that developed Java decided to leave Sun Microsystems and form a new company to create tools for developers and end users on the Internet.

During 1996 we developed Castanet, a revolutionary mechanism to distribute Java applications. With Castanet, it is possible to distribute large, media-rich, and mission-critical applications over a variety of networks.

Most businesses using Java to develop Internet applications start by creating applets that perform a variety of interactive tasks in the end user's browser. Unfortunately, due to various inefficiencies in the way Java applets are distributed, this quickly becomes cumbersome as the applets get bigger and more sophisticated. With Castanet most of these scalability problems are avoided, and it becomes possible to distribute large, complex, and media-rich applications in Java— without overloading the network or generating unnecessary delays.

Since Castanet's first beta release, many software developers have started distributing powerful applications to their customers using Castanet, to avoid complicated installation and upgrade procedures. Using a sophisticated and incremental protocol, Castanet takes care of automatically updating the end user's application. This means that the end user is never required to download newer versions of the application; the application is automatically kept up-to-date by the Castanet tuner!

Castanet also allows the distribution of applications bundled with very rich libraries. If any of the libraries are already on the user's hard disk, Castanet will not download them again, and thus avoids unnecessary communication overhead. This makes Castanet an ideal mechanism for the distribution of third-party software libraries by independent software developers.

Castanet enables a new generation of exciting applications. The automatic update features of Castanet give developers lots of control over personalization, user feedback, configuration, data distribution, and so on. It won't be long before anything less becomes unacceptable.

I would like to thank Jonathan Payne, Sami Shaio, Josh Sirota, and Senthil Supramaniam for devoting so much of their time to building Castanet. Also many thanks go to the rest of the Marimba engineering team: Rob Currie, Maurice Balick, Car Haynes, Klaas Waslander, Brigham Stevens, Aron Hall, Will Gordon, Kris Farren, and Carlos Aguayo.

Special thanks go to Laura Lemay for writing this definitive reference guide for Castanet programmers and end users. Thanks for all the late nights, and sorry for all last-minute changes. This book will be an indispensible tool for many Castanet developers.

Have fun,

Arthur van Hoff
Chief Technology Officer
Marimba Inc.

Acknowledgments

To Marimba, for asking me to write this book and for being so helpful while it was being written, and especially to Maurice Balick, Sami Shaio, Arthur van Hoff, Jonathan Payne, and Josh Sirota for answering silly questions.

To all the nice folks at Sams.net for tolerating my oddities, and particularly to Mark Taber and Fran Hatton, without whom these books would not A. exist, B. be as good as they are.

To all the things that kept me sane during the writing of this book: Mary Toth (the uber-assistant), Mountain Dew, grande-skim-lattes, the WeLL, the Barnes & Noble in Redwood City, CA, www.amazon.com, www.cdnow.com, www.minds.com, www.stim.com, www.salon1999.com, www.motorcycle.com. And Eric, of course.

About the Author

In just two years, Laura Lemay has gone from being an overworked, overstressed technical writer to being one of the most popular overworked, overstressed computer book authors in the country. A confessed nerd, she lives in Northern California with a boyfriend, two cats, eight computers, too many motorcycles, and enormous electric and Internet bills. She has written several incarnations of *Teach Yourself Web Publishing with HTML* and *Teach Yourself Java in 21 Days*, and is the series editor for the *Laura Lemay's Web Workshop* books, all published by Sams.net. She also writes a monthly column on HTML for *Web Techniques Magazine* and hosts the Web Tech conference on Electric Minds (`http://www.minds.com/`).

If she had any spare time, she would probably spend it trying to catch up with her e-mail. Visit her Web site at `http://www.1ne.com/lemay/`.

Tell Us What You Think!

As a reader, you are the most important critic and commentator of our books. We value your opinion and want to know what we're doing right, what we could do better, what areas you'd like to see us publish in, and any other words of wisdom you're willing to pass our way. You can help us make strong books that meet your needs and give you the computer guidance you require.

Do you have access to CompuServe or the World Wide Web? If so, then check out our CompuServe forum by typing `GO SAMS` at any prompt. If you prefer the World Wide Web, check out our site at `http://www.samspublishing.com`.

Note

If you have a technical question about this book, call the technical support line at (317) 581-3833.

As the publishing manager of the group that created this book, I welcome your comments. You can fax, e-mail, or write me directly to let me know what you did or didn't like about this book—as well as what we can do to make our books better. Here's the information:

Fax: 317/581-4669

E-mail: `newtech_mgr@sams.mcp.com`

Mail: Mark Taber
          Sams.net Publishing
          201 W. 103rd Street
          Indianapolis, IN 46290

Introduction

1996 was the year Java took over the world—or so it seemed, from the amount of attention that was given to Sun's language for creating secure, cross-platform applications on and off the Internet. Everywhere you looked, it seemed, there were books, magazines, news articles, announcements of Java products, conferences, and organizations all about working with Java. Although the excitement has faded somewhat, Java companies are still being formed and Java programmers are still at the top of recruitment lists.

During the Java craze, huge numbers of small startup companies sprang up, dedicated to working with Java. Marimba is one of those companies, formed in February of 1996 by four founding members of the original Sun Java team. Marimba's goal, as stated on their home page, is to "provide the tools and infrastructure for creating a new breed of network-managed applications for consumers and businesses." The implicit goal for Marimba is that they're building on the strengths and success of Java to create a whole new way of creating and distributing applications. In many ways, Marimba is taking Java beyond flashy but pointless Web-based applets to the next step, where Java can really begin to fulfill it promises and live up to—or even exceed—the hype.

Marimba's first two products are *Castanet,* a mechanism for creating and distributing applications over the Internet, and *Bongo,* a presentation builder that allows you to create Java applications and interfaces without knowing a whole lot of Java code.

Castanet is the focus of this book. Castanet is made up of two major parts: the Castanet Tuner, which you install on your desktop system and use to locate and subscribe to software *channels,* and the Castanet Transmitter, which broadcasts or publishes those same channels so that tuners can locate them. Once you've downloaded a channel using a tuner, all updates and changes to that channel—new code features, new information, new data—become available and are downloaded automatically.

This book covers all aspects of Castanet, including installing and using both the Castanet Tuner and Transmitter, as well as full coverage of actually developing Castanet channels. Regardless of the interest you have in Castanet—from the user, administrator, or developer side—this book will provide ample information for getting started with Castanet.

The Official Guide

What does the "Official Marimba Guide" mean? It means this book was written with the cooperation and input of the actual Marimba engineers. Unlike other books you might find on the subject, the *Official Marimba Guide to Castanet* is the only book with the Marimba stamp of approval.

Also available is the *Official Marimba Guide to Bongo*, which covers Marimba's tool for creating presentations and user interfaces. Although you don't need that book to understand Castanet (the two products and the two books can work equally well independently of each other), there might be some overlap with topics in this book that are explained in more detail in the Bongo book. I'll point these out as they occur throughout the book.

This book covers the features of the 1.0 versions of the Castanet Tuner and Castanet Transmitter software, as well as the procedures for developing channels for Castanet. However, because this book was written before the final version of the software was shipped, there might be very minor differences between the descriptions and pictures in this book and the actual software that you will install and use. These differences should not interfere at all with the procedures in this book or prevent you from using any part of the Castanet technology.

How To Use This Book

Is this book for you? Probably. If you've picked up this book in a store and read this far, you'll most likely be able to use at least some part of this book. Regardless of whether you're just curious about the Castanet technology, if you want to know how to use the tuner or the transmitter, if you've been told to get Castanet up and running for your organization, or if you really want to create your own Castanet channels, there's something in this book for you.

This book is split into 14 chapters and four parts (including appendixes). Each part provides a different view of the Castanet technology; you can start at the beginning and progress through learning about using the tuner, installing and administering the transmitter, and creating your own channels.

Part I: "An Introduction to Castanet" provides a general overview of the Castanet technology. This will explain what Castanet is all about and why it's really cool.

Chapter 1: "Castanet Tuner" covers Castanet from the user side—installing and using the Castanet Tuner to subscribe to and use Castanet channels.

Chapter 2: "Installing and Configuring the Tuner" explains just that—how to get the tuner installed, configured, and running on your system.

Chapter 3: "Using the Tuner" describes the various things you can do with the Castanet tuner and with channels. If the tuner can do it, you'll learn about it here.

Part II: "Castanet Transmitter" moves to the other side of the network and describes how to set up and use the Castanet Transmitter to publish and distribute channels.

Chapter 4: "Installing and Configuring the Transmitter" explains how to install and set up the transmitter on your own system.

Chapter 5: "Installing and Broadcasting Channels" shows how to make channels available on the transmitter you just installed, including how to set up the channel directory and create channel properties.

Chapter 6: "Transmitter Administration and Performance Tuning" explains how to fine-tune the transmitter for performance after you've got it installed and running. It also explains basic transmitter administration and the various forms of log files the transmitter creates.

Part III: "Developing Channels" takes you from Castanet software user to Castanet software producer. In this section you'll learn how to create your own channels, from HTML pages, from applets, all the way up through using Java to create sophisticated updateable channels.

Chapter 7: "How Channels Work" describes, well, how channels work. In this chapter you'll get a more in-depth view of the Castanet update process—how channel data moves from your development directories to the transmitter and eventually to the tuner—and learn about channel feedback and security.

Chapter 8: "Building Simple Channels" provides an overview of how to put together a channel from an HTML Web site or an applet, and describes how to publish and use that channel.

Chapter 9: "Creating Presentations and Channels with Bongo" moves to the next level of channel development: creating presentations with the Castanet Bongo tool.

Chapter 10: "Creating Application Channels" describes how to create full-fledged Castanet channels in the Java language, including how to interface those channels to Bongo presentations and to convert existing Java applications into channels.

Chapter 11: "Managing Updates and User Information" describes the methods and procedures to use in your Java channels for managing automatic updates (to both running and non-running channels) and for saving local state files.

Chapter 12: "Creating Transmitter Plug-Ins" describes how to create programs for the transmitter side of the technology that can receive channel feedback and customize the contents of a channel.

Chapter 13: "Inside WordSmith" provides a walkthrough of a more complex channel that uses many of the features described in previous chapters.

Chapter 14: "An Overview of the Marimba Classes" provides a high-level overview of the Java classes available for developing presentations and channels as part of the Marimba packages.

An Introduction to Castanet

Castanet
Tuner

Greetings! Welcome to the *Official Marimba Guide to Castanet* and to the Castanet technology. We'll start out in this chapter with a general overview of Castanet: what it's used for, why it's a good idea, what its various parts are, and how they interact. Regardless of how you intend to use Castanet—if you're just interested in what it's all about, if you're going to use it in your own organization, or if you're planning on developing software for use with Castanet—this is a good place to start.

What Is Castanet?

Castanet is, most simply, a mechanism for the distribution of software—that is, to make it easier and faster for individuals and organizations to get software from one place to another. Castanet takes advantage of the power and flexibility of the Internet and of Sun's Java language to create a framework that revolutionizes how traditional applications are distributed and makes it possible to create entirely new kinds of applications as well.

Whereas most software distribution is based on a publishing metaphor—the developer creates and publishes a piece of software, which is purchased, installed, and used by some number of individuals—the Castanet model is based more closely on a broadcasting metaphor. Consider the production of a television show. Television producers create their product (the show), and when it's complete, they broadcast that product to the audience over satellite, cable, or regular TV airwaves. The audience, in turn, uses their television sets to receive that product.

Castanet works in a similar way. Organizations create software *channels*—applications and their data—and make them available on the Internet using a *transmitter*. Users who are interested in that channel then use a *tuner* to locate various Castanet transmitters on the Internet and download and use channels contained on those transmitters. Figure 1.1 shows how this works.

Note

Although Castanet uses the broadcasting metaphor, it doesn't actually "push" data over the Net the way Pointcast and similar "netcasting" technologies do. The language and the metaphor is the same, but the technology is different. You'll learn more about this as the book progresses.

A *channel* is usually a Java application and its data. Because channels are written in Java, Castanet can take advantage of the strengths of the Java language, including

● Java programs are platform-independent; the same executable file can run on many different platforms. This means that you need to write a Java channel only once, and that channel can be available on any platform on which the tuner runs.

● Channels written in Java run without complicated installation procedures. To run a Java channel, you just download it and it runs. There is no need to run a setup script or wizard to make sure everything is installed and updated and registered, nor do you have to reinstall it every time there's a new version.

● Channels take advantage of the Java applet security model, which Web browsers use to make sure Java applets do not harm a user's system. Channels have most of the same restrictions as applets do in this respect.

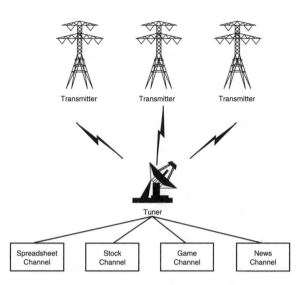

Figure 1.1. Subscribing to channels using the tuner and the transmitter.

The Castanet model builds on the strengths of Java and of applets, but also adds several other new features that make Castanet channels more flexible and powerful than simple applets. Those new features and advantages are described in the next section.

Note

For this first release, Castanet supports only applications written in Java. In future releases, there will be mechanisms in place for using platform-specific applications (written in C, C++, or some other native language) as channels with Castanet.

On the client side, you use the Castanet Tuner, a Java application that runs in the background on your desktop machine. (Figure 1.2 shows a tuner window with several channels subscribed.) From the tuner, you can subscribe to, download, and launch channels—and view lists of channels on transmitters. (*Subscribing* to a channel is similar to bookmarking a Web page; it means you're interested in running that channel and getting updates when that channel has changed. More about this later.) The Castanet Tuner is available for Windows 95, Windows NT, and Solaris, and is contained on the CD that comes with this book. It is free for personal use; contact Marimba if you're interested in using it inside a company. Chapters 2 and 3 of this book describe how to install and use the tuner.

Note

Marimba can be reached at http://www.marimba.com/.

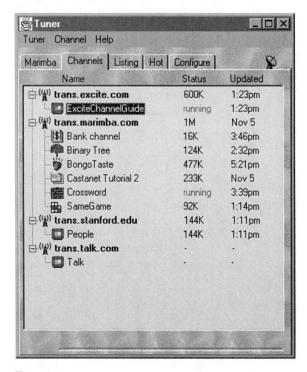

Figure 1.2. *The Castanet Tuner.*

On the server side is the Castanet Transmitter, which broadcasts software channels. (*Broadcasts* isn't exactly the right term here, as the transmitter does not send any data out without a request from a tuner; *makes channels available* would be a better expression.) The transmitter, like a Web server, can be configured in different ways to prevent overloading the machine on which it runs or for remote administration. The Castanet Transmitter is also available for Windows 95, Windows NT, and Solaris. A trial version which allows a limited number of connections is available on the CD for this book. You can purchase a more flexible Castanet Transmitter from Marimba.

In addition to the tuner and the transmitter, Castanet also offers the Castanet Proxy and the Castanet Repeater, which allow more efficient tuner connections through a firewall and easy mirroring of a transmitter's channels, respectively. The section titled "Castanet Repeaters and Proxies" discusses more about these products.

Castanet's Advantages

Despite the broadcast-influenced, tuner-transmitter-channel metaphor, the Castanet model might seem very similar to that of the World Wide Web—and in many ways, it is. Like surfing the Web with a browser and downloading Web pages with embedded Java applets, users use tuners to visit transmitters and to download Java channels. And, in fact, the protocol that the tuner and the transmitter use to communicate is based on and compatible with the HTTP protocol. There are, however, several significant differences between the Web model and the Castanet model that make Castanet more generally useful than either the Web or traditional software publishing:

- Persistence
- Automatic updates
- Less reliance on network speed and bandwidth
- The capability to save state or properties on the local system
- Channels are actual applications

Channels Are Persistent

When you visit a Web site with a Web browser, the data on that Web site (HTML, images, Java applets, and so on) is downloaded to your local system and displayed. That information is stored temporarily on your local disk in the browser's cache. Depending on how large your cache is and how often you browse the Web, that information might be deleted in a matter of hours. So the next time you visit that same Web site, the browser often has to go through the process of redownloading everything. For complete Web sites or Java applets, this process can be very tedious, particularly on slower connections. You're always guaranteed to get the latest and greatest updated information—but if it takes too long to download, it might not be worth it.

With Castanet channels, after you've used the tuner to subscribe to a channel, that information remains on your local system until you explicitly remove it. Also, you can run or view that channel as often as you want to, much in the same way you would an application you installed from a floppy or from a file you downloaded from the Web. The channel's data will never be deleted to make room for other channels, as might happen with a browser cache.

Although Castanet channels are usually Java programs, you can also create channels that are made up of HTML pages, images, and other typical Web page content; in other words, you can create a channel that contains the entire contents of a Web site. Because all the data for that channel is downloaded at once and stored on the local disk, it's quick to display, quick to read, and can be accessed again and again without the need to reload.

Channels Are Automatically Updated

Probably the most significant difference between a Castanet channel and either a Java applet or a program downloaded and installed in the more traditional manner is that a software channel also has the capability to update itself on a regular basis. Each channel that you subscribe to using the tuner has a preferred update schedule—some channels might need to be more frequently updated than others—and each time a channel comes due for updating, the tuner will recontact the transmitter and see if new information is available. If there is indeed an update to be made, the tuner will download and install that new data into the channel on the local disk.

An update to a channel can involve changes to an application or simply new information that the channel might need to know. (For HTML channels, for example, that might include updated files or new pages.) Updates are small and incremental, so they occur quickly, often in the background. Updates can be made to channels that are running and active on the user's system, without the need to quit the application or reboot the machine. And, in cases where there's a network problem or some other unforeseen difficulty with the updating process, the channel will revert to its original state; it's impossible for an aborted update to leave a channel in a state where it doesn't run.

What automatic updating means is that once you've subscribed to the channel, the version of the channel you have is guaranteed to always be the latest version. For HTML channels, that means you always have the most current version of the Web site on your local disk. You don't have to install anything. You don't have to worry about which version of a program you have. Updates happen on the fly, quietly, in the background.

If you're administering the software for a large organization, automatic updates mean that you don't have to worry about making sure that all your users are running the same version of a particular software package—or that it'll take enormous amounts of time and resources to try and upgrade the organization.

If you're a software developer, automatic channel updates mean that all your users will always have the most recent version of your software; there's no need to support older versions. It means that you can get bug fixes and new features out to customers faster than ever before.

In addition to the basic version control aspects of channels, updates also allow you to create channels that rely on frequently changing data. Because updates can happen as frequently as every few minutes, you could create, for example, news channels that update to include breaking stories, a weather channel to give you the current weather forecast for your area, calendar channels that give you the cartoon of the day, or puzzles that change on a frequent enough basis to remain interesting.

Channels Rely Less on the Network

One of the major stumbling blocks of creating complex Web sites and Java applets is the typical speed of a user's network connection. Most people on the Internet at large do not have very fast network connections at all (usually modem connections at speeds of 28.8 or slower), and even in organizations where the internal network is heavily used, it's easy to become impatient with the amount of time it takes to download the program or information that you need.

Castanet uses several techniques to reduce the amount of downloading time and the bandwidth a channel needs. When you initially subscribe to a channel, it might take some time for that channel to download, depending on the size of the channel and the speed of the connection. But after it's downloaded, it's stored persistently on the local disk so you can reuse it over and over, or run it even when you're not connected to the network.

Each update to a channel does require another network connection. But updates involve only the channel information that has changed from the old version to the new version—which makes updates much smaller, and therefore much more quickly downloaded, than the original channel.

The channel structure itself can also help with reducing downloading time. With Web pages and Java applets, the Web browser makes separate network connections for each Web page, each image on the Web page, each Java applet, and each supporting class and file the applet needs. For very complex Web pages or applets, this can mean dozens or even hundreds of individual network connections. And because each network connection takes a few seconds just to start up, that's not a very efficient way for the browser to behave. Channels, in comparison, are a collection of files. A single channel (or update to a channel) can contain hundreds of files, but the tuner makes only one network connection for each channel or update. Also, channel files and libraries are shared between channels. So, for example, if you create multiple channels that all use the same library (to draw graphics for example), the tuner will only need to download one copy of that library. All the other channels will automatically use the one copy of the library and not download extra copies each time.

Finally, the tuner can be configured to allow updates only at a certain time or to prevent updates from being made too often (or at all). You could, for example, make updates only at night when you aren't working on your system, or make updates once a day in one fell swoop as opposed to whenever they need to be made. You can even turn off automatic updating altogether—and only update channels manually when you're dialed into your ISP and have some time to kill. The Castanet Tuner can be configured at what time and frequency updates are to occur.

Channels Can Save State

Java applets that run in Web browsers are constrained by a set of security restrictions that prevent those applets from unauthorized use or damage to the local system on which they run. In particular, applets are not allowed to run any local programs, to link to any native libraries (DLLs), or to connect to systems on the Internet other than the Web server where they came from. In addition, applets are not permitted to read or write files to the local system in any way, which prevents an applet from, deleting files or sending private information back to the applet's author. This last restriction has been the most debated among applet developers because it prevents an applet from saving any kind of state whatsoever—for example, a user's position in a game, or files they might have created inside an applet for a spreadsheet, a drawing program, or a word processor. Workarounds exist—state can be saved to the applet's server instead, and the applet or the page could be written to uniquely identify a user—but for the most part, the inability to save state has limited the overall usefulness of applets.

Channels use much of the same security restrictions as applets do, with the restriction on reading and writing local files somewhat eased; when you subscribe to a channel, that channel is given a special data directory on your local disk, and it is allowed to read files from and write files to that one directory (but nowhere else on the system). Channels can only access their own directories; they cannot touch other files for other channels. This simple change in the security policy opens up a whole new realm of options to channel developers.

Note

In addition to easing the basic applet security restrictions, future versions of Castanet will offer the ability for channels to be authenticated (require a password) or digitally signed (or both). This will not only allow channels to have a greater variety of features, but also allow channels to be written in languages other than Java. Stay tuned!

Channels Are Real Applications

Unlike Java applets, which run inside a Web page and are constrained by the Web browser, Castanet channels run as real applications, on the desktop, the same way other applications do. This means channels don't need a heavyweight Web browser to run the same time they're running. It also gives channels more flexibility for interface design; channels run in their own windows, which can have menu bars and dialogs.

Developing Channels

If you're a software developer or a Webmaster and you've read this far, your next question is most likely, "How do I create my own channels?" You have several options in this realm; in this section I'll summarize those options. Part III of this book, "Developing Channels," describes more about all aspects of channel development.

Castanet supports four basic kinds of channels: HTML, applet, application, and presentation channels. For each of these channels, you develop the content and then "publish" the channel on a transmitter. The publishing process is managed by a tool called Castanet Publish.

Easiest to create are HTML and applet channels. For each of these kinds of channels, you don't need to modify the original source in any way. All you need to so is set a few parameters using a configuration file or Castanet Publish itself, and then publish the channel. The Castanet Transmitter handles everything else.

Application channels are written in Java using your favorite Java development tools. In order to take advantage of live updates and other Castanet features, your channel classes must implement several Marimba interfaces. If you have a basic understanding of Java and of Java's AWT (the Abstract Windowing Toolkit), you should not have any difficulties learning how to develop channels. See Part III of this book for more.

The final kind of channel is called a *presentation.* Presentations are a special kind of channel developed using a Marimba tool called Bongo. Bongo is a sort of user-interface builder for Java; you can use it to position and link together various user-interface elements (called widgets) as well as create your own elements. Bongo presentations can then be used alone as channels or together with Java classes to form channels.

You'll get a quick taste of Bongo in Chapter 9, "Creating Presentations and Channels with Bongo." A companion to this book, *The Official Marimba Guide to Bongo,* by Danny Goodman, describes Bongo in lurid detail if you're interested in learning more.

Castanet Repeaters and Proxies

The primary components of the Castanet Technology are the Castanet Tuner (for subscribing to, downloading, and updating channels) and the Castanet Transmitter (for making channels available on the Net to tuners). For special purposes such as firewall installations and very popular or high-load transmitters, Marimba also provides Castanet repeaters and proxies.

Repeaters

For especially large sites or popular transmitters, Castanet offers transmitter *repeaters.* Repeaters are used to mirror a channel across multiple transmitters. As with extremely popular Web or FTP sites, it is possible for a channel to become so popular that its transmitter becomes overloaded with connections. Creating mirror sites—copying the contents of one site to a different machine on the network, and accepting connections at any of those sites—

distributes the load on the one transmitter to multiple systems, offering scalability of a single transmitter as high as you need it to be and reducing the load on any single transmitter. (Figure 1.3 shows a general model for how mirrors work.) In addition, if mirrors are located in different geographical locations, they can provide better performance for users at those locations. For example, a Japanese user of a channel in the United States could instead tune into a repeater transmitter in Japan, making the connection times faster and reducing the amount of traffic across intercontinental networks.

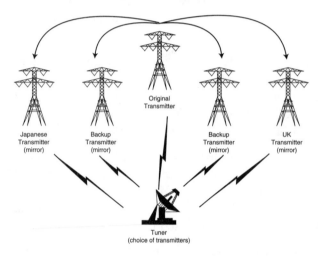

Figure 1.3. *Mirror sites.*

Currently, the problems of mirroring a Web or FTP site are similar to those of keeping software up to date at a number of sites; you have to coordinate the contents of the primary site with those on the mirror, which can involve administrative nightmares (keeping track of which files are now or have changed, and updating only those files), or routinely bundling up the entire server and shipping it to the mirror (involving long download times). You'll also, of course, need administrators on each mirror to oversee the update process. This can result in the mirrors being not quite as up to date or robust as the primary server, which reduces the usefulness of the mirror site.

This is obviously a task for which the Castanet model for channels and updates is ideal. Castanet repeaters make it easy to distribute channels to multiple sites and to keep the data coordinated between the primary transmitter and the repeater. A repeater is effectively both a tuner and a transmitter at the same time. The repeater subscribes to channels on a primary transmitter, so that all the data in the channel on the repeater's site is up to date at all times. The repeater also then transmits its channels to other tuners, and those tuners subscribe to and download channels from the repeater as if they were the primary transmitter. (See Figure 1.4.)

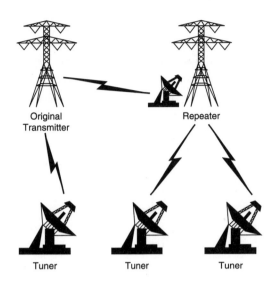

Original Transmitter

Repeater

Tuner   Tuner   Tuner

Figure 1.4. *How repeaters work.*

In addition to simply mirroring a channel's content, repeaters also allow automatic redirection of incoming connections from one transmitter to an available repeater. When a tuner makes a connection to a transmitter, therefore, the transmitter can pass on that connection automatically to a less-loaded repeater or to one closer to the original tuner. If the new repeater becomes unavailable or is itself overloaded with connections, the tuner can recontact the original transmitter for another repeater. All this is transparent to the user with the tuner, and it provides a seamless mechanism for transmitting channels to one user or to millions.

The Castanet repeater is an add-on to existing transmitters; the repeater simply provides the capability for two transmitters to talk to each other. You will have to purchase each transmitter (the primary and each mirror) independently. The Castanet Repeater is not yet available, so I won't cover it in this book; contact Marimba or visit `http://www.marimba.com/` for more details about purchasing and using the Castanet Repeater.

Proxies

The final part of the overall Castanet system I'll mention in this chapter is the Castanet Proxy. A proxy server is, generically, a program that acts as a network liaison between one set of systems and another, typically on organizations that have firewalls. For the World Wide Web, for example, a browser running on an internal network would make HTTP requests to an HTTP proxy server, which would in turn pass those requests out to the Internet at large and then pass the data back to the internal network. This allows the network administrator to control access to the Internet from inside a network, and, in turn, to control access to the network from the Internet.

Figure 1.5 shows how this works: The systems in the lower half of the figure are on an internal network (intranet)—for example, for a corporation or a university, and include computers running Web browsers or computers running Castanet tuners. Whenever a connection is made from one of those systems to a system on the Internet (the systems in the upper half of the figure, which include Web servers or Castanet transmitters), the request is routed through the proxy server (in the middle). The proxy server also passes the data back from the Internet systems back to the systems on the internal network.

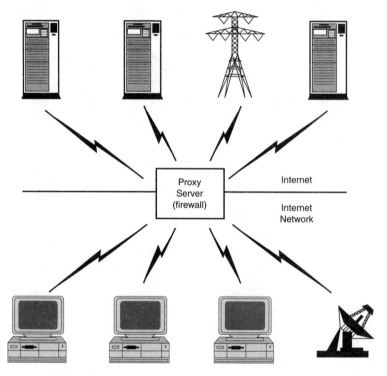

Figure 1.5. *Proxy servers and firewalls.*

The problem with proxy servers is that because all connections between an internal and external network must run through the proxy server, that tends to create a bottleneck in that proxy. To reduce the bottleneck, an additional feature of proxy servers is the capability to cache popular data on the proxy server itself. If, for example, multiple requests are made for a single popular page on a Web site from inside a firewall, the proxy server keeps a local copy of that page in the local cache to reduce the number of connections outside the firewall. The proxy would, of course, have to occasionally check the original server to make sure the page hadn't changed and update things accordingly.

Castanet proxies provide both these features for channels: The capability to use tuners to access transmitters through a firewall and to store channels on a local system to reduce network traffic through the firewall. Although you could use a standard HTTP server for accessing transmitters (as the Marimba connection protocol is compatible with HTTP), you would not get the caching effect that the Castanet Proxy provides. If your organization uses a firewall and you expect many of your users to take advantage of the Castanet technology, you should look into installing a Castanet Proxy.

As with the Castanet Repeater, Castanet proxy servers are not yet shipping, so I won't cover their use in this book. Contact Marimba or visit `http://www.marimba.com/` for more details.

Where Castanet Is Now

At the time I write this, the 1.0 versions of Castanet and Bongo are about to be released. Although this book was written and tested on earlier beta versions of Castanet and Bongo, it has been reviewed for completeness by the Marimba team and should reflect the final versions with only minor differences.

Currently, the 1.0 version of Castanet supports a basic framework for developing and using channels written primarily in Java. Future versions of Castanet will build on that framework and extend it to channels written in any language, to include security mechanisms for authenticated channels, to allow channels to be digitally signed, and to provide billing for channels or for updates. In addition, the current version of Castanet works with the 1.02 JDK (Java Developer's Kit); future versions will include support for the newly released 1.1 JDK and its many features.

I'll point out where new features of Castanet are planned or where changes will most likely occur throughout this book.

Summary

Castanet was created to solve the problems of traditional software distribution, installation, and maintenance. Traditionally, a software developer publishes a product on floppies or CD-ROMs, and users have to install that product on their own systems before they can use it. Each new version of the product has to be independently installed. Shipping software as a downloadable file from an FTP or Web site makes it faster for products to reach the hands of customers, but it still requires the user to actually take the time to install the product.

Java applets solve the installation problem; you just download the applet and run it. But applets have their own limitations, the most obvious being that they're not stored on the local disk except for a temporary cache.

Castanet provides the next step in software distribution: a transparent system by which software is distributed in the form of channels, and users automatically receive that software (have it downloaded and installed) by subscribing to it over a network. After a channel has been subscribed to, users continue to receive updates to that channel over the Internet quietly in the background, guaranteeing that they have the latest version of the channel at all times. Channels have all the advantages of Java applets—being up to date all the time, can run in multiple environments and have built-in security to prevent malicious behaviors—while retaining the persistence and the capability to write local files of the conventional application.

In this chapter, you got a basic overview of how Castanet works and why it's useful. Throughout this book, you'll learn how to install and use the Castanet Tuner and Castanet Transmitter to use and publish channels. In the last part of this book you'll learn about developing your own channels for use with tuners and transmitters. Read on to learn more!

two

Installing and Configuring the Tuner

In the last chapter, you learned that the Castanet framework has two parts: the tuner, to receive software on your desktop, and the transmitter, to make software available on the Internet to tuners. For the next couple of chapters we'll focus on how to install and use the Castanet Tuner, and how to use it to download, run, and update software channels available all over the Internet.

Before you can use the tuner, you have to install it. That's what this chapter is for: getting the tuner installed and configured on your system so you can start exploring channels.

Before You Start

Before you install the tuner, there are several other things you will need to have ready, or information you should have available. Make sure you can answer all these questions before going on:

- Do you have a working connection to the Internet? This can be a simple modem dial-up connection, or a direct connection through work or school. You should already be able to run Internet programs such as Netscape or FTP.

- Do you have the right kind of computer and operating system? The Castanet Tuner system requires a Windows 95 or Windows NT 4.0 system with at least 8MB of RAM, or a Solaris 2.4 or higher system with at least 16MB of RAM.

Note

By the time you read this, a version of the Castanet software for the Macintosh might be available. (It was not available when we went to press.) Check with Marimba's home page (`http://www.marimba.com/`) if you're interested.

Several other unsupported ports of the Marimba software are also available for other UNIX systems such as Linux and FreeBSD. See `http://www.marimba.com/products/unsupported.html` for more details.

The Castanet Tuner does not currently on run Windows 3.1.

- Do you have enough free disk space? Marimba recommends that on all systems you have at least 10MB of free disk space for the Castanet Tuner; this includes space for the software itself and for subscriptions to an average number of channels. If you subscribe to a large number of channels, you'll most likely need more disk space available.

- Do you know where on your local system you're going to install the software? For Windows 95 or Windows NT, the default location for all the Marimba software is `C:\Marimba`. For UNIX, you can install the Castanet Tuner anywhere on your disk you want to.

- Do you have a Web browser available? The Marimba documentation and help files are available as Web pages (and as a channel from Marimba's transmitter). You will need a Web browser such as Netscape or Internet Explorer to view these pages.

- Are you accessing the Internet from behind a firewall? (Many companies and organizations have their Internet connection set up in this sort of configuration.) If so, you will need to contact your system administrator or support organization for the host name and port number of your Web server (HTTP) proxy.

Note

If you're behind a firewall and Netscape or Explorer works just fine, this information might also be available to you in the configuration menus for your browser. See Options | Network-Proxies | View in Netscape or View | Options | Connection | Settings in Internet Explorer for this information.

Note

The Castanet Tuner does not support firewalls that use the SOCKS proxy. Future versions of the tuner will include SOCKS support.

● Is your organization running a Castanet proxy? If so, you will need the host name and port number of that proxy (which might or might not be the same as the host name and port number of the HTTP proxy). Ask your system administrator for details.

● Are you upgrading from a previous version? If you've been using a beta version of the tuner, you don't have to go through this installation process. You can simply update the tuner software using the Tuner | Update Tuner menu item.

If you must reinstall the software from scratch, make sure you've removed the old versions of the tuner software before installing the new one. In Windows, choose Add/Remove Programs from the Control Panel, choose Castanet Tuner from the list, and click Remove. On Solaris, simply delete the old tuner directory. See the section titled "Uninstalling (Removing) the Tuner" at the end of this chapter for more details.

Installing the Software

Next, install the software from the tuner installer. There are two places you can get the installer software:

● On the CD-ROM that comes with this book.

● From Marimba's site at http://www.marimba.com/.

You'll need to download the installer software for your system and put it somewhere on your local disk so you can run it.

For Windows, the installer is an executable archive called Tuner1_0.EXE. On UNIX, the installer is a compressed tar archive called tuner1_0_tar.Z.

Windows 95 and Windows NT 4.0

To install the Castanet Tuner on Windows 95 or NT 4.0, first quit all running Windows programs and double-click the installer file. Windows will load the installer wizard for Castanet.

Note

> If you're installing the software from the CD-ROM that came with this book, you can find the tuner installer in the directory Marimba and then in the subdirectory for your platform (Win95, WinNT, or Solaris), for example, Marimba\Win95\Tuner1_0.EXE.

The Castanet Tuner wizard will lead you through the process of installing the tuner software, including letting you read and agree to the license agreement. The first step is to choose a directory to install the software into. (The default is C:\Marimba, as shown in Figure 2.1.)

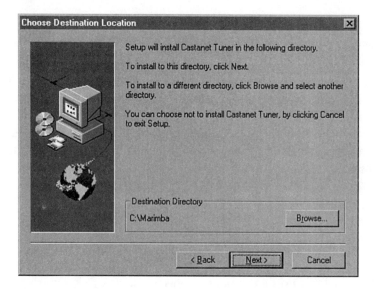

Figure 2.1. Choosing an installation directory.

The next step is to choose a directory for channels. (See Figure 2.2.) This is the directory in which downloaded channels will be stored; the default is C:\Windows\ for Windows 95 or C:\WinNT\ for Windows NT. Your channels directory should be local to your system (don't install it on a network disk) and should not be shared by other people.

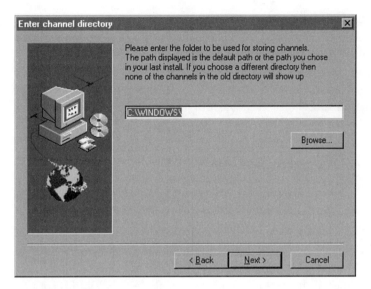

Figure 2.2. *Choosing a channel directory.*

After the Castanet files have been installed, you are asked if you want to have the tuner start automatically when you reboot. This will guarantee that the tuner software is available whenever your computer is running. Choose Yes to have the setup program modify your system to start the tuner on reboot.

Finally, you'll be asked if you want to finish the installation. If you choose Yes, continue on to the section on "Configuring the Tuner." You can also choose No, in which case the setup program will exit. (If you do choose No, when you start the tuner for the first time you'll be asked to configure it, so there's no penalty for waiting until later.)

Solaris

To install the Castanet Tuner on a Solaris system, use the following steps:

1. The Castanet Tuner installer will put the tuner files into a directory called `castanet`. You'll want to copy the tuner installer file to the location where you want your `castanet` directory to exist (for example, `/usr/local` or `/home`).

   Note that the tuner software might update itself from time to time, so the directory partition you install it into should be writeable and, preferably, a partition on the local disk (as opposed to a mounted partition).

Note

At this time, the Castanet Tuner is designed to be run by a single user on a single machine. You should install the tuner software as the same user who will be running the tuner software, and the partition you install the software on should be accessible by that user. This means you should not install the tuner software as root if you are not going to run it as root. Future versions will work better on multiuser systems.

2. Copy the compressed installer file to your chosen location and decompress it:

```
cp tuner1_0_tar.Z /usr/local/
cd /usr/local/
uncompress tuner1_0_tar.Z
```

3. Finally, use the `tar` command to extract all the tuner files into that directory:

```
tar xvf tuner1_0_tar
```

The actual tuner executable is contained in the directory `castanet/tuner/bin/`. You might want to put that directory into your execution path so that you can easily start the tuner. If, for example, you were using the C Shell, this command would put the tuner directory into your execution path:

```
set path=($path /usr/local/castanet/tuner/bin)
```

You can delete the tuner installer file when you're finished with the installation:

```
rm tuner1_0_tar
```

Configuring the Software

After the tuner is installed, you'll have to configure it before you can use it. The tuner will lead you through the configuration process the first time you start it.

If you're using Windows, the tuner was launched as part of the initial installation process. If you didn't start it at that time, you can start it now via the Start menu. (See Figure 2.3.)

If you're using Solaris, start the tuner with the `tuner` command from any prompt, like this:

```
/usr/local/bin/marimba.tuner/tuner.solaris/bin/tuner
```

If you've put the tuner directory into your execution path, you should just be able to type `tuner` to start it.

On both Windows and Solaris, the tuner will start and display an opening screen. From here, most of the steps are the same on Windows and on Solaris.

The first step in the configuration is to personalize your tuner. The User Information window is shown in Figure 2.4.

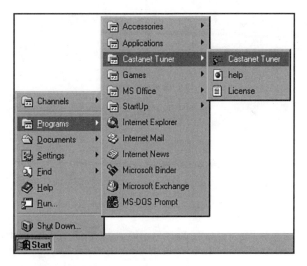

Figure 2.3. *Starting the tuner.*

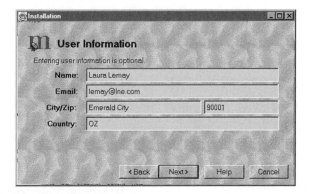

Figure 2.4. *The User Information window.*

User information is entirely optional; the only thing it's used for is to identify you to Marimba. Channels will not be able to extract this information. If you don't want to reveal any of this information, you don't have to enter it.

If you're on Solaris, the next window, shown in Figure 2.5, is the Update Mailcap File window. The .mailcap file, stored in your home directory, is used to configure applications that use MIME to understand how to process different kinds of files. In this case, it's used by your Web browser so that you can launch channels from inside a browser. Choose the Update button to update the Mailcap file.

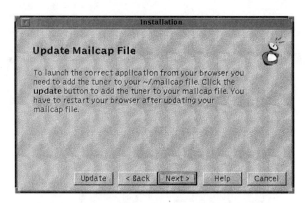

Figure 2.5. *The Update Mailcap File window.*

If you're in Windows, the next window (shown in Figure 2.6) is the Internet Connection window. This window allows you to specify your network connection, which determines how often the tuner will attempt to update channels. (It'll try less often on slower connections.) A direct connection is the sort of connection you have through work or school; it includes a T1, T2, ISDN, frame-relay, or other high-speed connection. A modem connection is exactly what it sounds like; you get your Internet connection through a 14.4Kbps or 28.8Kbps modem by dialing up to your ISP (Internet service provider). Choose the button that best describes your Internet connection.

The No Internet Connection option is a red herring; you won't be able to proceed with the configuration if you choose this option. (In future versions, this might result in something useful.) If you're trying to install and run a tuner locally (for example, trying to run a tuner and a transmitter on the same machine for testing), use Direct Connection instead.

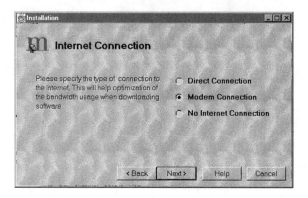

Figure 2.6. *Internet Connection information.*

If you choose Modem connection, the next window (shown in Figure 2.7) allows you to choose the dialup server you use. These servers are set up using the Dialup Networking Wizard for Windows; you should already have your modem connection configured in order to set up the tuner. Note that for a modem connection you will have to enter the user name and password for your network connection so that the tuner can connect to your ISP without needing you to be there.

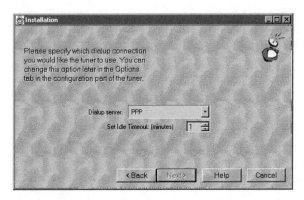

Figure 2.7. Dialup server information.

The next window for both Solaris and Windows is the Proxy Configuration window (shown in Figure 2.8). Use this window only if you're accessing the Internet through a firewall. (You can skip this window if you have a regular Internet connection.) You should already have found out the information about your HTTP proxy server from your system administrator; enter the host name of your proxy server and the port number that proxy runs on. You can also use this window to configure your tuner for use with a Castanet proxy; contact your system administrator to see if you're running a Castanet proxy server.

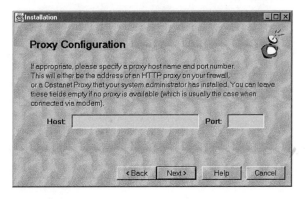

Figure 2.8. Proxy configuration information.

Note

If you're using Windows, note that because of restrictions in Java, you can enter only a host name here, not an IP address. On Solaris you can use either the proxy's host name or its address.

Note

The screen shown in Figure 2.8 might also have fields for the user name and password. If your HTTP proxy is the sort that requires you to enter this information to access the proxy (Gauntlet is one of these), this is where you should enter this information.

After you enter data on the first four windows, the tuner will try to contact Marimba to see if there are any updates available. You can skip the update by choosing the Skip button; otherwise, choose Next.

Note

If you choose Skip, you can update the tuner at any time while its running by choosing Tuner | Tuner Update (more about this in the next chapter). The tuner will also try to update itself on a regular basis.

If your configuration is correct, the tuner software will update itself. (See Figure 2.9.)

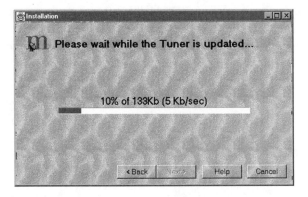

Figure 2.9. The Castanet Tuner updates itself.

When the update is complete (if any updates need to occur), you're finished installing and configuring the tuner and you can begin exploring channels. Choose the Finish button to launch the tuner itself and bring up the tuner window (shown in Figure 2.10).

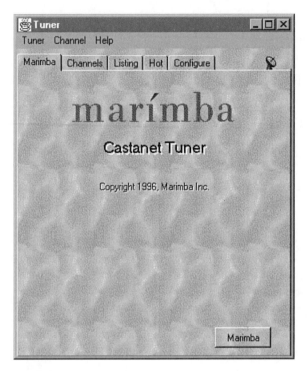

Figure 2.10. *The main tuner window.*

Troubleshooting

Most problems installing the tuner result when the tuner update occurs and then usually because the tuner cannot contact Marimba's site on the Internet. Check to make sure your Internet connection is running by starting up a Web browser and seeing if you can connect to http://www.marimba.com/. If that site is inaccessible but you can reach other sites on the Internet, try updating the tuner again later. If you cannot access any sites on the Internet, something is wrong with your Internet connection.

If you're inside an organization with a firewall, your proxy information may be incorrect. Double-check with your system administrator (or, if your browser is running, with the configuration information there) to make sure you have the right proxy address and port. You can use the Back buttons in the installer to back up to the window for the HTTP proxy.

If starting the tuner results in I/O errors, make sure that the directory you installed the tuner into is writeable; the tuner needs to be able to write to that directory for updates.

On Solaris, you might run into errors if you are running the tuner as a different user than the one who installed the tuner. The tuner must be installed and run by the same userid, and that user must have write access to the tuner's directories.

For other problems, consult Marimba's list of Frequently Asked Questions at `http://www.marimba.com/developer/faq.html`. There's also a channel called Marimba Forum at `trans.marimba.com`, which contains discussion on all the Marimba software. And, finally, the page at `http://www.marimba.com/developer/support.html` contains information about getting support for all parts of the Castanet software.

Uninstalling (Removing) the Tuner

In the unlikely case that you would want to remove the tuner software from your system, you can use these instructions to do so. One reason you might want to do this is to reinstall the software from scratch on a clean system, or to upgrade the tuner software from an earlier beta to the new 1.0 version.

On Solaris, uninstalling the software is easy. Just make sure the tuner isn't actually running and then delete the directory the software is stored in (for example, `/usr/local/castanet/tuner`). You'll also need to remove the `.marimba` directory from your home directory if you want to also delete the currently installed channels.

To remove the Castanet Tuner software on Windows, choose Add/Remove Programs from the Control Panels window and select Castanet Tuner from the list of programs. (The example in Figure 2.11 shows a beta version of the tuner; your list might have another version to uninstall.) Finally, choose Add/Remove to start the uninstall process.

Note

If you're upgrading from a beta version of the tuner, the Castanet uninstall program will delete the actual tuner software but leave your downloaded channel directories intact. If you're deleting the 1.0 version of the tuner that came with this CD, the uninstall program will delete everything: the software, the channels, and any other tuner information contained on your disk.

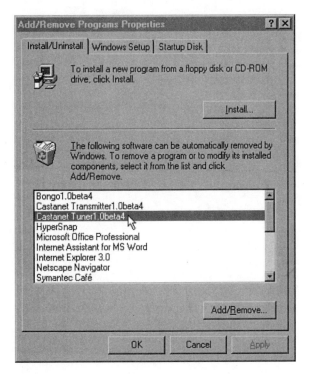

Figure 2.11. Uninstalling the tuner.

Summary

After finishing this chapter, you should now have the Castanet Tuner installed and running on your system, ready to start downloading and running channels. Continue on to the next two chapters to learn how to use the tuner and to explore the wide variety of channels available to you on the Internet.

CHAPTER three

Using the Tuner

With the Castanet Tuner installed, now you can use it to tune into Castanet Transmitters on the Internet, and download and use various channels contained on those transmitters. In this chapter, you'll get a feel for how to use the tuner to do basic tasks, including how to manage channels. You'll also learn how to start channels from outside the tuner, including from the desktop and from inside a Web page.

Starting the Tuner

If you don't have the tuner already running on your system, here's how to start it. Marimba recommends that you run the tuner in the background all the time, so that channels can be automatically updated at regular intervals. (Running the tuner itself all the time does not significantly impact system resources.)

To start the tuner from Windows, navigate through the Start menus (Start | Programs | Castanet Tuner | Castanet Tuner; see Figure 3.1):

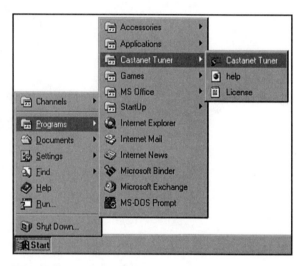

Figure 3.1. *Starting the tuner.*

In Windows, the tuner is running when the tuner icon appears on the right side of the task bar (see Figure 3.2), even if the tuner window does not appear on the desktop or in the task bar. Double-clicking the tuner icon in the task bar causes the tuner window to display on the screen.

The Tuner icon

Figure 3.2. *The Tuner icon.*

To start the tuner in Solaris, use the tuner command from any UNIX prompt. If the tuner directory is not in your execution path, you'll have to use the full path name of the tuner (in this case, the tuner software has been installed in the /usr/local/ directory):

```
/usr/local/castanet/tuner/bin/tuner
```

Quick Start: The Basics

Want to get started as fast as possible? Read this section for the bare-bones details of how to use the Castanet Tuner.

Castanet channels are broadcast from Castanet Transmitters. To subscribe to a channel—that is, to download that channel to your system—you point the Castanet Tuner to the transmitter that contains that channel.

When you first start up the Castanet Tuner, the default transmitter you'll have available to visit is Marimba's transmitter at `trans.marimba.com`. Choosing the Listing tab will show you that transmitter and the listing of channels available on that transmitter. (See Figure 3.3.)

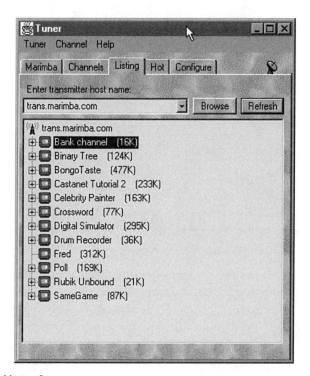

Figure 3.3. *The channel listing for* `trans.marimba.com`.

Each line of that listing is a different software channel. To subscribe to it, double-click the channel. That channel will then be downloaded and stored on your local disk. So, for example, to subscribe to the SameGame channel, double-click its icon. SameGame is a game with a set of tiles; you can remove groups of tiles of the same color by double-clicking them. You get points based on how many adjoining tiles you remove. It's very addictive. Watch out!

The tuner will switch panels from the Listing panel to the Channels panel, download that channel, and start it. Figure 3.4 shows the Channels panel after subscribing to the SameGame channel.

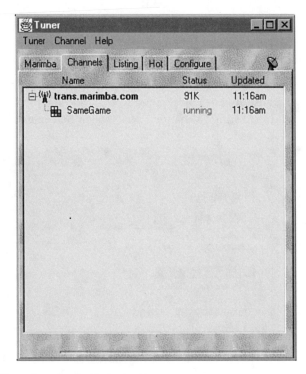

Figure 3.4. *The SameGame channel, subscribed to in the tuner.*

Note that whereas the Listing panel shows you all the available channels on a transmitter, the Channels panel shows you the channels you are currently subscribed to and the transmitter where you got them from. You can switch between those two panels to subscribe to new channels or launch channels you've already downloaded.

After you've subscribed to a channel, that channel will remain loaded and stored on your hard drive; you don't have to download it all over again every single time. You can start and stop a channel just as you would any other program installed on your system; just double-click on its icon in the Channel panel to start it.

After they have been subscribed to, channels will update automatically as new data becomes available on the transmitter. Different channels will update at different times; a news channel, for example, might update every few minutes, whereas a channel for a word processor or other sophisticated application might update only when there are significant changes to be made. Channels will update automatically, in the background, as long as the tuner is running, or you can manually update a channel by choosing the Update menu item.

To get rid of a channel, you can either unsubscribe to it (which removes the channel files but not its saved state) or remove it altogether. Both Unsubscribe and Remove are menu items in the Channel menu, as shown in Figure 3.5.

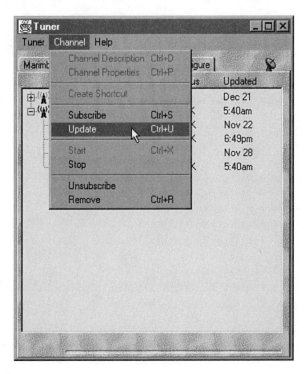

Figure 3.5. *The Channel menu.*

Got it? Read the rest of this chapter for more details on how to use the tuner to explore transmitters and channels.

Exploring Transmitters

Channels are located on transmitters, similar to the way that Web pages are located on Web sites. To explore channels, therefore, you must first find a transmitter and get a listing of the available channels from that transmitter.

The Listing Panel

The Listing panel is used to point the tuner to a particular transmitter, show the channels available on that transmitter, and subscribe to those channels. You can get to that Listing panel by choosing the Listing tab or selecting Listing Page from the Tuner menu. Figure 3.6 shows the listing for the transmitter located at trans.marimba.com.

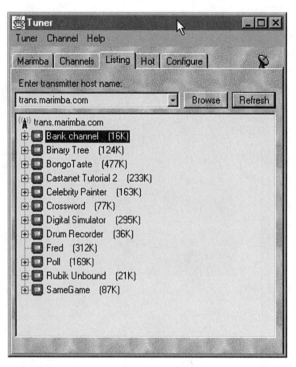

Figure 3.6. *The Listing panel.*

Each channel in the listing has a name, a channel size, and a channel description. The channel size determines how long it will take for that channel to initially download, depending on the speed of your connection.

Note

> After you've subscribed to a channel once, you won't have to download it again as you would for an applet or a file on a Web page. If there are updates to that channel, they'll be downloaded as they are needed, but those are usually much smaller than the initial channel. Keep that in mind before becoming nervous about the size of a channel.

The channel description contains information about the channel. The channel description can be as simple as the author's name, or it can include more information about the channel itself so that you can get an idea of what the channel is for before downloading it. You can read channel descriptions by choosing the plus sign to the left of each channel, and hide the channel description by choosing the minus sign. (See Figure 3.7, which shows the channel description for the Digital Simulator channel.)

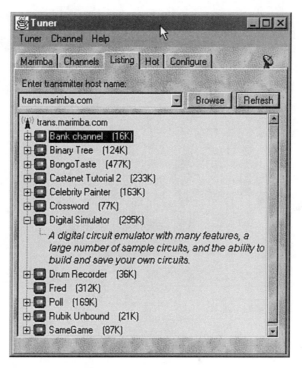

Figure 3.7. *Channel descriptions.*

There are two buttons to the right of the transmitter name: Browse and Refresh. Browse is used to examine the list of channels in a Web browser. Choosing the Browse button starts up your Web browser and displays the listing of channels as a Web page, including each channel's description. (See Figure 3.8.) You can then print that page or bookmark it to visit later. (You'll learn more about using channels from a browser in "Other Ways of Using Transmitters and Channels," later in this chapter.)

Note

In Windows, the Browse button will launch your default Web browser. In Solaris, your browser must already be running for Browse to work.

The Refresh button is used to make the tuner contact the transmitter for a new list of channels, just in case new channels have been added since the last time you looked at that transmitter.

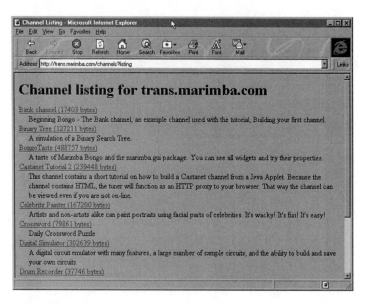

Figure 3.8. *Channel listing in a browser.*

Tuning into Different Transmitters

The `trans.marimba.com` transmitter that you get when you start up the tuner isn't the only transmitter you have available to explore. A Castanet Transmitter can be located on any site on the Internet; all you have to do is point your tuner at a transmitter to view or subscribe to the channels available on that transmitter.

To tune into a new transmitter, type its name into the transmitter name field (the one marked "Enter Transmitter Host Name" on the Listing panel, shown in Figure 3.9) and press the Enter or Return key. The tuner will contact that transmitter and give you a list of the channels that transmitter broadcasts.

Some transmitter names have a number after them—for example, `trans.havefun.com:5282`. The number is the network port on which that transmitter is located and is important; don't forget it! Your tuner might not be able to get a listing from a transmitter if you leave the number off.

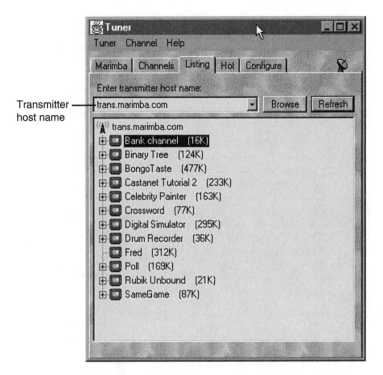

Transmitter host name

Figure 3.9. The transmitter name field.

Note

Transmitter names generally begin with the prefix `trans`, as in `trans.marimba.com` or `trans.excite.com`. However, transmitters can be located on any site on the Internet, including Web or FTP sites. Don't let the transmitter name fool you.

If the transmitter name you listed does not exist (for example, if you misspelled the name), you'll get an Unknown Host error at the bottom of the tuner screen. Make sure you've spelled the host name correctly and that there is indeed a transmitter installed on that host and port number.

The field containing the name of the transmitter is actually a pull-down menu that contains all the transmitters you've ever visited. You can choose from that list to get a list of channels from any of those transmitters. (Figure 3.10 shows an example of a few transmitters.)

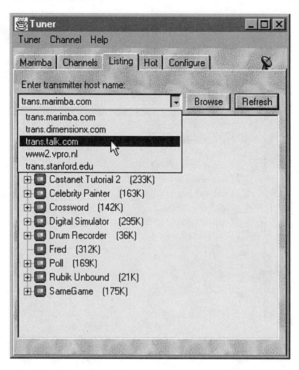

Figure 3.10. *Choose from a list of transmitters.*

Once you've subscribed to a channel on a transmitter, you can also get a listing of that transmitter by double-clicking the transmitter name in the Channels panel (more about this later).

The Transmitter Hotlist

Where can you find other transmitters? Often you can find them much the same way you find Web sites—through friends, Web pages, advertisements, or even other transmitters. One of the easiest ways, however, is to use the transmitter hotlist. Choose the Hot tab in the tuner to see a listing of available transmitters that Marimba has designated as having good channels. Figure 3.11 shows an example listing.

Choosing any of the transmitter icons in the Hot panel tells the tuner to switch to the Listing panel and to contact that transmitter for a list of channels.

The Register button in the top-right corner of this panel gives you information on registering your own transmitter for use in the hotlist. See Chapter 6, "Transmitter Administration and Performance Tuning."

Figure 3.11. *The transmitter hotlist.*

Working with Channels

Use the Listing panel in the tuner to explore different transmitters and get a listing of the channels available on those transmitters. Then, double-click a channel to subscribe to it. The tuner will switch to the Channels panel, and then download and run the channel you've just subscribed to. Then, from the Channels panel, you can get a listing of the channels you're currently subscribed to and maintain those channels. From the Channels panel, you can

● Subscribe, unsubscribe, or resubscribe to channels

● Start or stop channels

● Update channels

● Remove channels

Figure 3.12 shows a sample Channel panel, with multiple channels from multiple transmitters available. The status column shows the current status of a channel, whether it is subscribed to or not, whether it is running or not, and any interim status (whether or not the channel is downloading, launching, or stopping, for example). It'll also show the word error if there was a problem downloading or updating the channel, with the actual error as a tooltip. (Move your mouse over the channel name; the error will appear in a little pop-up window.) Errors usually result because a connection to the transmitter could not be made but sometimes because there's an actual error in the channel.

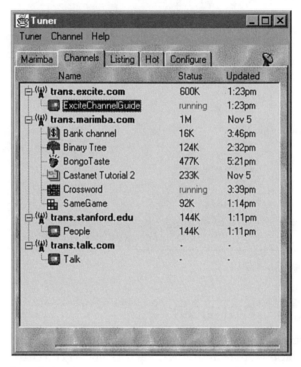

Figure 3.12. *The Channels panel.*

Subscribing and Unsubscribing to Channels

To subscribe to a channel, start at the Listing panel with a transmitter listing and double-click the icon for the channel you want to subscribe to (or, select the name of the channel and choose Subscribe or Start from the Channel menu). The tuner will switch to the Channels panel and begin downloading the channel from the transmitter. As the download progresses, the tuner will keep you updated on the progress of the channel both in the Channels panel itself and in the status bar at the bottom of the window. (See Figure 3.13.)

When the channel has fully downloaded, it will appear in the Channels panel.

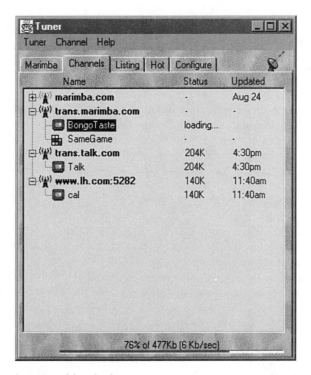

Figure 3.13. *Channel in the process of downloading.*

Note

Channels are stored on your local disk. In Windows, you had the option of where to install those channels; by default on Windows 95, they're stored in c:\Windows\.marimba\; on Windows NT, in c:\WINNT\.marimba\. On Solaris, channels are stored in your home directory, in the .marimba directory. Inside the channel directory, channels are organized by transmitter name, and each channel has its own directories for channel files and for data. Note that the channel files are actually stored in a special database-like format so they can be shared between channels; if you browse the channel directories, chances are you won't find anything useful. Most of the time you won't need to know this; channels will simply work as you expect when you launch them from the tuner.

Quick Subscription Using the New Channel Panel

If you already know the name of a channel and the transmitter it is located on (for example, if someone told you to check out a cool new channel), you can use the New Channel menu item from the Tuner menu (see Figure 3.14) to quickly subscribe to that channel. New Channel brings up the panel shown in Figure 3.15.

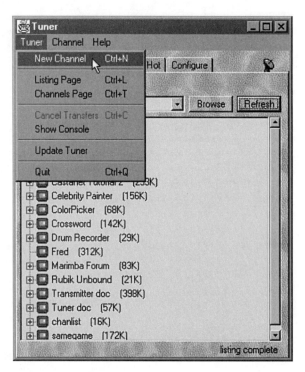

Figure 3.14. *New Channel from the Tuner menu.*

From this panel, you can enter the name of the transmitter (and the port number, if necessary), and the name of the channel. Choosing Subscribe takes you to the Channels panel, where the channel is subscribed to, downloaded, and run.

If you know the name of the transmitter but not the name of the channel, you can enter the name of the transmitter into the field marked Transmitter and choose the List button. The tuner will switch to the Listing panel and display the channels available on that transmitter just as if you had entered the name of the transmitter here.

Figure 3.15. *Subscribing to new channels.*

Starting and Stopping Channels

The first time you download a channel, that channel will also start running, so you can see what it is you've downloaded. Channels run in their own windows, just like regular applications.

To stop a channel from running, you can quit it from that channel's menu bar or use the close box, just as you would any other application. In addition, you can select that channel from the tuner's Channels panel and choose the Stop menu item.

To restart a channel, double-click its icon in the Channels panel, or select it and choose Start from the Channel menu.

Note

There are also other ways to start channels, including from the Start menu and from shortcuts in Windows. You'll learn about these later in this chapter in the section titled "Other Ways of Using Transmitters and Channels."

Updating Channels

Probably the niftiest feature of channels is that the tuner will update them automatically if there is new information available for that channel on the transmitter. New information for a channel can be anything from something as simple as a new quote in a quote-of-the-day channel, to an updated database of books for a library channel, all the way up to an entirely new revision of the channel itself. The Castanet Tuner keeps track of updating the channels you are subscribed to, whether or not they are currently running; you never have to do anything to make sure any of your channels is up to date.

There are two ways to update channels:

● You can let the tuner update all your channels automatically, in which case you don't have to do anything at all (although you can configure the tuner to update your channels more or less often or turn off updating altogether; see "Controlling Updates" for more information). The tuner must be running for automatic updates to occur.

● You can update a channel manually at any time.

To update a channel yourself, select that channel from the Channels panel and choose Update from the Channel menu. The tuner will contact that channel's transmitter, check for new information, and download and install it if there is any.

Note

The tuner is smart about updates. A channel becomes updated only if the new data on the transmitter can be fully downloaded. If an update is aborted either because of a network failure or because you stopped an update in the middle, the old version of the channel will continue to work. There will never be a point where a channel is in an in-between state and cannot run. And, if an update is interrupted for any reason, the tuner will pick up where it left off, rather than restarting from the beginning every time.

Note that in the Channels panel, the Updated column shows when the channel was last updated.

Channel Properties

On the Listing panel in the tuner, you can get some summary information about a channel by selecting the plus sign to the left of the channel name. Once you've subscribed to a channel, however, there are several other properties you can examine.

To display a channel's properties, select the channel from the Channels panel and choose Channel Properties from the Channel menu. A window similar to the one shown in Figure 3.16 is displayed. (This one is for the SameGame channel.)

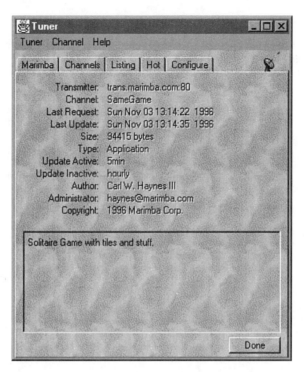

Figure 3.16. *Channel properties.*

Channel properties include information about the channel and its transmitter, when it was last updated, its current size, the type of channel it is (application, applet, presentation, HTML), and how often that channel should be updated. Finally, it also includes information about the author and the administrator of the channel (which can be different people).

Unsubscribing and Removing Channels

What if you've played with a channel and decided you don't like it any more? You can do one of two things: You can unsubscribe from that channel, or you can remove that channel.

To unsubscribe from a channel, select that channel's name from the Channels panel and choose Unsubscribe from the Channel menu. The channel will continue to be listed in the Channels panel, but both its status and updated column will be empty. (See Figure 3.17.)

Unsubscribing from a channel means that the channel is no longer active; it will not be updated by the tuner, and the files that make up that channel are deleted from your hard drive. Unsubscribed channels, however, continue to be listed in the tuner and in the Start menu, and any data or information you have saved along with that channel will also continue to exist. After you've unsubscribed from a channel, you can resubscribe to it at any time, and the tuner will de-download the channel's files and let the channel pick up where it left off. Unsubscribing to channels is useful for channels that you use infrequently; the tuner won't tie up your network connection updating these channels, and you won't need to set aside disk space to store them.

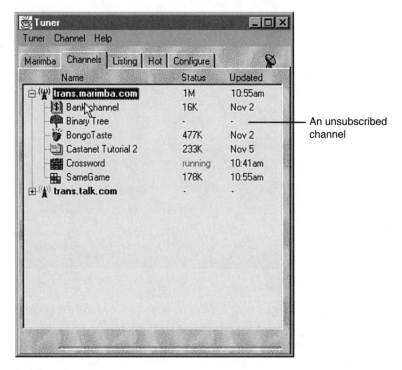

Figure 3.17. An unsubscribed channel.

Removing a channel is how you get rid of a channel altogether. To remove a channel, select its name from the Channels panel and select the Remove item from the Channel menu. Removing a channel deletes the channel from your tuner, removes all its files from your hard drive, and deletes any data you may have saved with that channel.

Caution

Use Remove only when you truly never want to use a channel ever again; to get it back, you'll have to go back to that channel's transmitter and redownload it.

Using HTML Channels

In Castanet, most of the channels you download and use will be based on Java applets, applications, or presentations created using Bongo. They'll run in their own windows on your desktop. HTML channels are a special kind of channel that look and act just like a normal Web site—except it is downloaded and stored on your local disk as a whole, rather than page by page.

HTML channels are subscribed to and updated exactly in the same way that regular channels are, so that new data on a Web site is always available on your local system for browsing. Contrast this with the "normal" way of viewing Web sites, where you must revisit and redownload all the data on a Web page each time to see any new information.

After you've subscribed to and downloaded an HTML channel, you use your default Web browser to view that HTML channel. There's a catch, however; because HTML channels are managed through the tuner instead of through a regular Web server, you have to configure your browser in a special way in order to view them.

To view HTML channels in your browser, set up your browser such that the Castanet Tuner is your HTTP proxy. Then, each request the browser makes to a Web page in an HTML channel can be redirected to the channel stored on your local disk (or passed back out to the Web at large for Web sites that are not HTML channels).

To configure Netscape to view HTML channels, select Options | Network Preferences | Proxy, choose Manual Proxy Configuration, and click the View button. A window similar to the one shown in Figure 3.18 will appear.

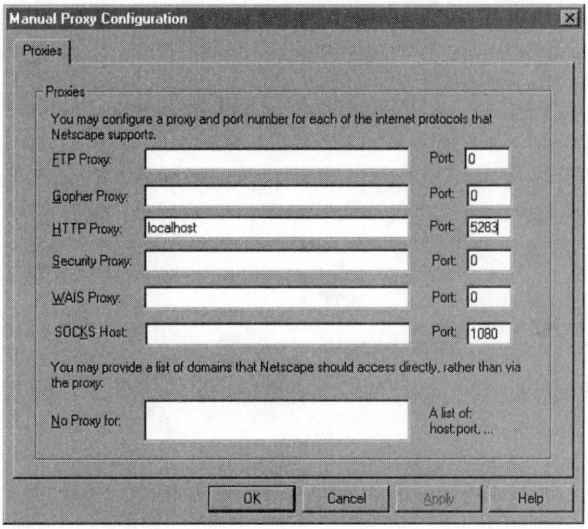

Figure 3.18. *Proxy configuration in Netscape.*

The line marked HTTP Proxy should have the host name `localhost`, and the port should be `5283` (as shown in Figure 3.18). If your HTTP proxy had been set to some other value, you might want to mark down that proxy and port in case you end up removing the tuner at some later date.

To configure Internet Explorer to view HTML channels, select View | Options | Connection, choose "Connect Through a Proxy Server," and click the Settings button. Figure 3.19 shows the window that appears.

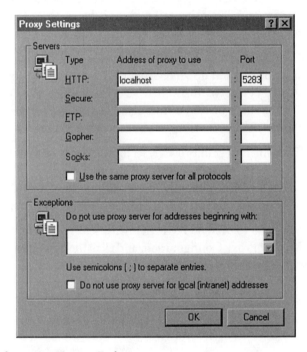

Figure 3.19. *Proxy configuration in Internet Explorer.*

As with Netscape, the line marked HTTP Proxy should have `localhost` as the host and `5283` for the port. If you've already got values for that line, you'll want to save those in case you need them at a later time.

Note that setting the HTTP proxy of the browser to be the tuner will not interfere with your normal Web browsing of pages that are not HTML channels. As long as the tuner is running each time you use your Web browser, requests to the Internet at large will be passed on by the tuner.

This is true even if your organization uses a firewall and you were required to have a host and port in your HTTP proxy configuration of your browser. As long as the tuner has been configured to use your organization's HTTP proxy, Netscape will still work even when configured in this way.

Note

If you find that your browser has suddenly stopped working—that it can't find any hosts or tries to save all the pages you access—make sure the tuner is running, or reset your proxy information back to its original state.

After your browser has been correctly configured, you should be able to launch HTML channels from within the tuner, and view and navigate them inside your browser. Note that on Windows, if your browser isn't running when you launch an HTML channel, your default browser will start up automatically. On Solaris, you must have a browser running ahead of time to be able to launch HTML channels from the tuner.

Note

Obviously, setting up the tuner as a proxy is not the most ideal solution for browsing HTML channels. Marimba is exploring other options for browsing these channels for later versions of the Castanet software.

Controlling Updates

Updates to channels happen automatically. Each channel has an update interval that determines how often the tuner tries to update that channel. (For example, a channel to display news headlines or stock data would update fairly frequently, whereas a game or spreadsheet channel might not update very often at all.) As long as the tuner is running, the tuner will attempt to update each channel at its proper time by contacting the transmitter and checking for new data.

If you have a slow or intermittent network connection, you might not want the tuner to spend a lot of time doing updates. Or, you might want to have the full bandwidth of your connection for more important work during the day.

You can configure the tuner to update channels only at certain times of the day or not to update automatically at all. To configure tuner updates, choose the Configure tab from the tuner (and the Loading tab, if the Loading panel is not already displayed).

The Loading panel contains two drop-down lists: one for the time automatic updates can occur and one for the frequency of those updates.

The first menu (shown in Figure 3.20) determines the time of day you would like updates to occur. For example, if you use the network a lot during the work day, you might want to restrict updates to nonworking hours so you can have the full network bandwidth for your own work. Or, you might want to turn off automatic updates altogether (in which case you'll have to update each channel automatically to make sure it gets all its new information).

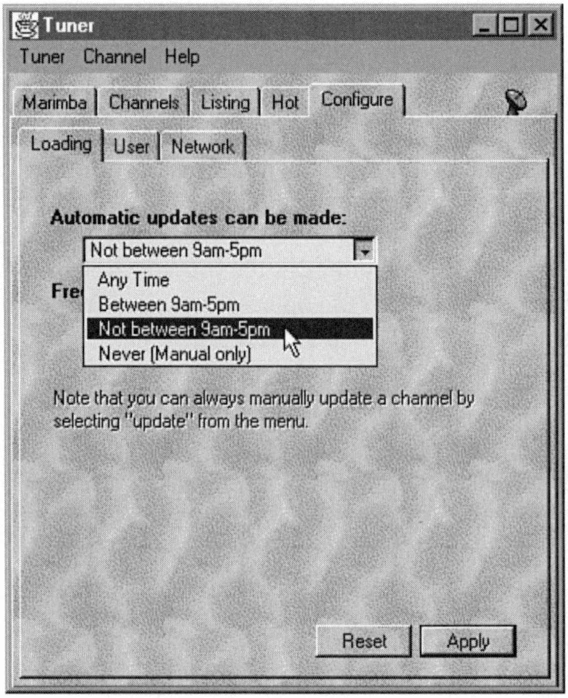

Figure 3.20. Update times.

Tip

> If you have Internet software that automatically dials your ISP each time you attempt to make a network connection, you might want to choose Never to prevent the tuner from dialing your ISP for you at unexpected times. Keep in mind that if your tuner does dial your ISP for you, you can configure it to disconnect itself after being idle for some time. Choose the Configure panel and then the Network subpanel to change the configuration for your connection.

The second menu on this panel (shown in Figure 3.21) determines how often updates can be made. By default, updates are made every 15 minutes if you have a direct connection or once an hour if you have a modem connection. If you set the defaults to update more often, updates are made as often as the channels you have subscribed to need them. By limiting the frequency of updates, however, you can prevent the tuner from making too-frequent network connections and potentially slowing down your machine or your network.

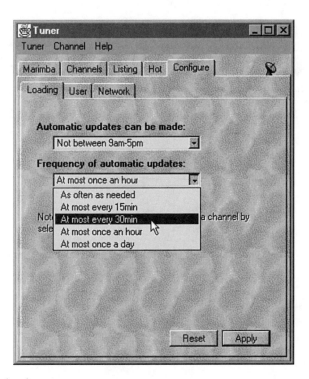

Figure 3.21. *Update frequency.*

Interrupting Tuner Downloads

When a tuner is downloading a channel, updating that channel, or getting a listing of channels from a transmitter, the satellite dish on the top-right corner of the tuner will animate, and the status of the connection will appear along the bottom of the screen. (See Figure 3.22.) If you want to interrupt any of these connections for any reason (perhaps the network is being unbearably slow or has stopped working altogether, as networks are sometimes prone to do), you can stop the download in one of two ways:

● Choose Cancel Transfers from the Tuner menu.
● Press Ctrl+C on the keyboard.

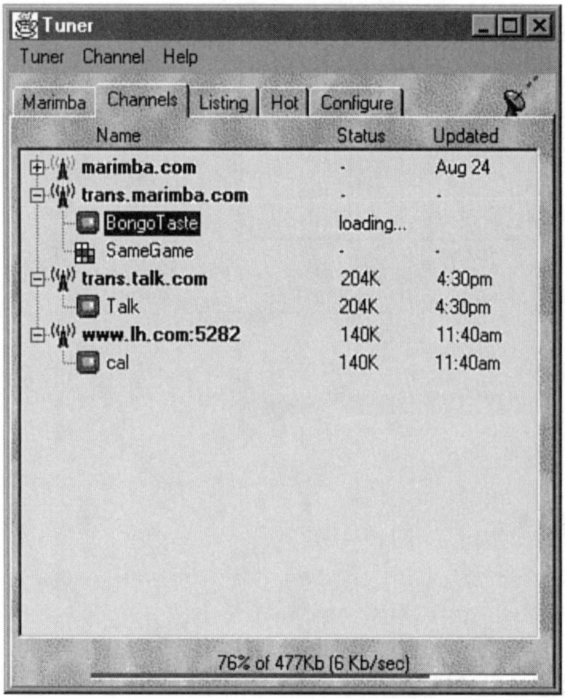

Figure 3.22. Tuner in the process of downloading a channel.

Note

If you stop downloading a channel in the middle of subscribing to it, that channel will still appear in the Channels panel. The next time you try to run that channel, it will restart the downloading process. If you try downloading it again within a few minutes, the download will begin where it left off, rather than restarting again from scratch (a useful feature for when you have a flaky network connection as well; if you keep trying eventually the full channel will get downloaded).

If you interrupt an update in the middle of downloading, the channel will revert to its original state. Castanet is designed so that interrupting an update in the middle will never break what you already have.

Other Ways of Using Transmitters and Channels

Although the Castanet Tuner is your primary interface for exploring and using channels, there are several other ways you can browse and use Castanet Transmitters and channels, including browsing transmitters and launching channels from a Web browser, and accessing channels from the desktop.

Exploring Transmitters and Channels Using a Web Browser

You can use your Web browser instead of the tuner to explore a transmitter's channel listing and to subscribe to and launch channels from that browser.

You've already seen one way to do this. If you enter a transmitter name in the field at the top of the Listing panel in the tuner, you can then choose the Browse button to see a listing of that transmitter's channels.

Outside of the tuner, if you know the name of the transmitter you want to browse, you can use the name of that transmitter in your browser as if it were a Web site. (For example, to contact the transmitter at `trans.marimba.com`, use the URL `http://trans.marimba.com/`.)

In either case, the browser will display a listing of the available channels on the transmitter as a Web page, with each channel as a link. (See Figure 3.23.) Clicking the links downloads and subscribes you to the channel (if it's not yet subscribed to).

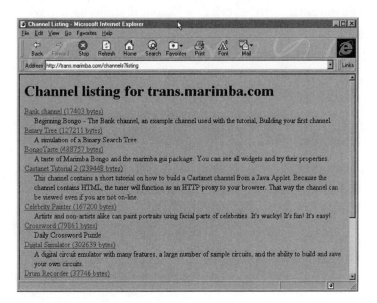

Figure 3.23. *Transmitter listings in browsers.*

Note

> With Netscape, clicking a channel link will launch the tuner as a helper application automatically. If you're using Internet Explorer, you'll need to configure that browser by hand to launch the tuner when you select a link to a channel. To do, this, select View | Options | Programs and select the File Types button. From the File Types window, choose New Type, and enter `Marimba Channel` into the "Description of Type" field, `.chn` into the "Associated Extension" field, and `application/marimba` into the Content Type field. Then, click the New button. A New Action window will appear; enter `Open` into the Action field and then use the Browse button to navigate to the location of the tuner. (By default, it's in `C:\Marimba\Castanet Tuner\Tuner.exe`.) Choose OK all the way back up to browser to finish.

Note that because you can get access to a transmitter and a channel in this way, you can also create links to channels in your own HTML Web pages—for example, to create a list of cool channels for others to browse. Just link to the channel using an `<A>` tag, the same way you would any other link, where the destination URL is the name of the transmitter, the name of the channel, a question mark, and the word `start`. For example, to link to the SameGame channel on Marimba's transmitter, use HTML code something like this:

```
Warning! <A HREF="http://trans.marimba.com/SameGame?start">The SameGame
channel</A> is extremely addictive!
```

Launching Channels from the Desktop

In Windows, you can launch channels from outside the tuner itself through the use of the Start menu or with shortcuts. On Solaris, you can start or subscribe to channels from the command line.

Channels in the Start Menu (Windows only)

When the tuner is installed, the installer program adds an item to the Start menu for channels. That menu contains all the channels you have subscribed to, arranged by transmitter. (See Figure 3.24.) To launch a channel, simply select its name from the Channel menu.

Note that channels are only removed from the Start menu when you actually remove them; an unsubscribed channel will continue to appear in the start menu.

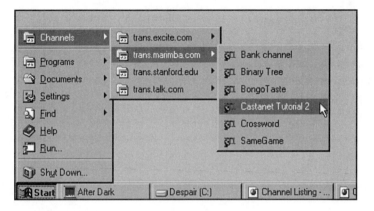

Figure 3.24. Start menu channels.

If you don't want channels to be added to the Start menu when you subscribe to them, you can turn off this option in the tuner by choosing the Configure panel and then the Options panel. Deselect the checkbox for "Add Subscribed Channels to Start Menu."

Channel Shortcuts (Windows only)

You can also create shortcuts to channels, put those shortcuts on your desktop or in folders on your hard disk, and launch channels from those shortcuts.

To create a shortcut, go to the Channels panel in the tuner and select the channel you're interested in. Then choose Create Shortcut from the Channel menu. The shortcut to that channel will appear on the desktop (see Figure 3.25); you can then drag and drop it anywhere you want.

Figure 3.25. Channel shortcuts.

Channels from the Command Line (Solaris Only)

On Solaris, you can start channels from the UNIX command line, which allows you to create aliases or menu items for those channels. To start a channel from the command line, you must know the name of the transmitter and the name of the channel. If the channel name contains spaces, substitute underscores for those spaces (for example, My_Cool_Channel for "My Cool Channel").

Then use the tuner command to start the channel, like this:

```
tuner -start transmitter channelname
```

If the tuner isn't running, the tuner will start. If the tuner is running but the channel has not yet been subscribed to, the tuner will download the channel and run it. If the tuner is running and you've already subscribed to that channel, the tuner will just start it. If you get an error when you try to launch the channel, make sure you're using all the same upper- and lowercase letters as the actual name of the channel, and watch out for those spaces.

You can also use the tuner command to stop a channel, like this:

```
tuner -stop channelname
```

Other Tuner Features

This last section is a catch-all for the other tuner features that didn't fit anywhere else.

Updating the Tuner

Just as channels are updated automatically, the tuner itself is also a form of channel and can be updated when there is new information (new features or fixes) available at Marimba.

The tuner will attempt to update itself once a week. (There won't necessarily be changes to be made every week, of course, but that's how often the tuner will check back to Marimba.) As with channels, however, you can always update the channel manually by choosing Update Tuner from the Tuner menu. The tuner will exit and display the Tuner Update box shown in Figure 3.26.

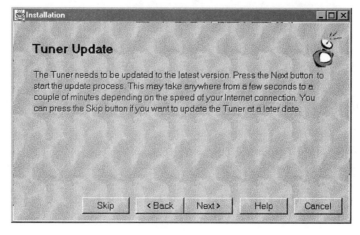

Figure 3.26. *The Tuner Update box.*

Choose the Next button to update the tuner, or Skip to skip updating this time. Note that the tuner always contacts Marimba's site for updates, so even if you use your tuner exclusively on an internal network, you will need an external Internet connection to successfully update the tuner.

Changing the Configuration Information

When you installed the tuner initially, you entered information about you and your network. You can change that information at any time by selecting the Configuration tab from the tuner and then selecting any of the subpanels on this window. See the previous chapter for information on the information contained in these tabs.

Getting Help

As you explore various aspects of the tuner, you might notice various Help buttons in various windows. In addition, the tuner itself has a Help menu with various items. (See Figure 3.27.)

Selecting any Help button or any of the items in the Help menu brings up the online help for the tuner. Most of the Help files for the tuner are written as Web pages and stored on Marimba's Web site as both regular pages and as a channel. (The channel is called Tuner doc; it's contained on trans.marimba.com.) When you choose a Help item, the tuner launches your default browser and displays the relevant Help file—either the local version, if you've subscribed to the Tuner doc channel, or the version stored on Marimba's Web site.

For more immediate help, Marimba provides a number of discussion lists and groups. The Marimba Forum channel from trans.marimba.com provides a forum in which you can post questions and comments and get help from both Marimba folk and others who are using the technology. For support and help over e-mail, consult the page at http://www.marimba.com/developer/support.html for information about discussion and support lists.

Java Console

Some channels might make use of a text console to display messages, information about the channel, or, most often, errors and debugging information. If a channel you've subscribed to prints these messages, they will appear in the Tuner's Java console. You can display this console by selecting Show Console from the Tuner menu. Figure 3.28 shows the console.

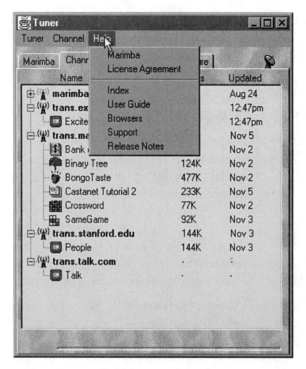

Figure 3.27. *The Help menu.*

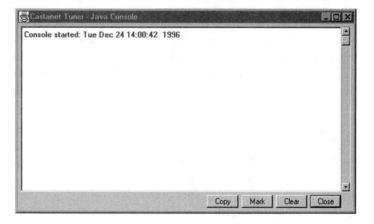

Figure 3.28. *The Tuner's Java console.*

Note

The Java console is most useful to developers working on creating new channels. It would be unusual for a channel to intentionally print output to the Java console.

Tuner Extensions and CD-ROM Files

Some special kinds of channels may require you to do extra work in order for you to be able to run channels that use local libraries and channels that read files from CD-ROM.

The former are channels that require you to install special software on your machine before you can run them, similar to how Netscape uses plug-ins to extend the features of the browser. That special software, called an extension, is usually specific to your system, so it cannot be automatically downloaded as part of the channel itself. Usually a channel that uses these kinds of extensions will let you know the first time you run it how to get those files and how to install them so you can use the channel.

The most important thing to keep in mind about tuner extensions is that those files that you download and install yourself are not subject to the security constraints that normal channels have — so those files can do just about anything they want to your system. Make sure before you install tuner extensions that you trust the company or organization that has made them available and that you understand what the extensions will be used for; you are responsible for the safety of your system.

The second kind of special channel is one that reads files contained on a CD-ROM — for example, you might have a very sophisticated game channel that stores its very large images and video files on a CD-ROM to save on downloading time. If you run across this kind of channel, you'll have to not only purchase the CD-ROM, but you'll also have to specially configure your tuner to use that CD-ROM.

By default, channels aren't allowed to look at any files on your local system other than in one specific directory. This includes examining the disk in your CD-ROM drive. However, using the option in Figure 3.29, which you can get to from the Configure panel and the Options panel under that, allows the channel to make an exception for the CD-ROM. Generally it's a good idea not to enable this option until you run into a channel that actually needs it.

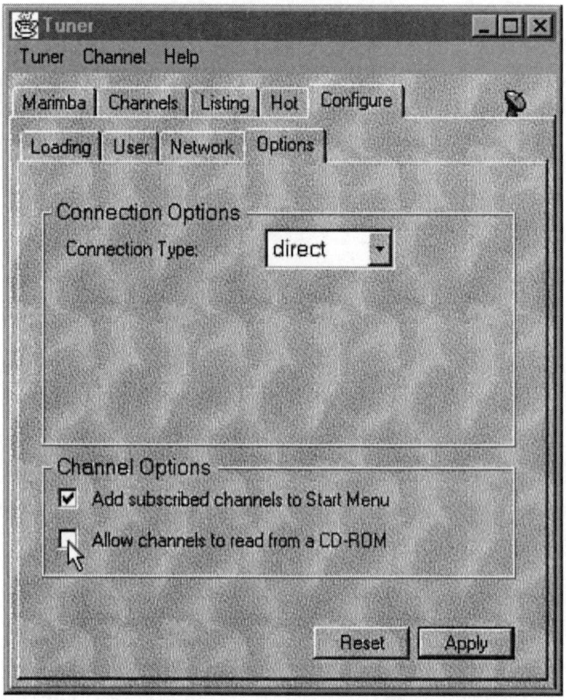

Figure 3.29. *Allow the tuner to read from the CD-ROM.*

Finding Channels

Looking for new transmitters and channels to play with? There are a number of places you can look:

- The tuner Hotlist, described earlier in this chapter, is a great place to start looking for channels.

- The transmitter at `trans.havefun.com:5282` is a public transmitter for channels developed by various people around the world.

- Excite, the popular search engine, has a terrific channel guide at `trans.excite.com`.

- Gamelan, known mostly for their very complete resource for Java, has a section for transmitters and channels at `http://www.gamelan.com/`. They also run a Gamelan channel at `trans.gamelan.com`.

- Marimba's Web site has a Channel of the Week page at `http://www.marimba.com/channels/` with reviews and links to interesting channels.

Quitting the Tuner

The tuner is designed to run all the time on your system so that it can keep your channels up to date and so that it can serve as a proxy for your Web browser (assuming you've set your browser up to view HTML channels).

On Windows, the tuner is running as long as the tuner icon appears in the task bar. Closing the tuner window using the close box hides the tuner but does not quit it; by double-clicking the tuner's icon, you can make the tuner visible again.

To actually quit the tuner, use the Tuner | Quit menu item (shown in Figure 3.30). The tuner will be relaunched if you start it by hand, if you start any subscribed channels, or if you reboot your system and the tuner has been configured to start when the system starts.

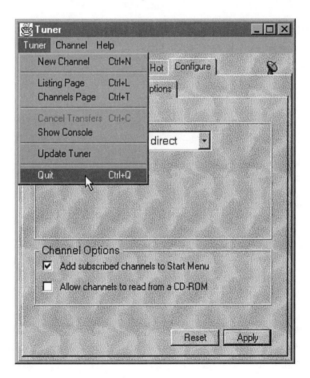

Figure 3.30. *Quitting the tuner.*

Keyboard Shortcuts

Many menu items in the tuner have keyboard shortcuts, which you can use in place of selecting the menu item itself. Table 3.1 shows a summary of those shortcuts.

Table 3.1. Tuner keyboard shortcuts.

Menu Item	Shortcut
New Channel	Ctrl+N
Listing Page	Ctrl+L
Channels Page	Ctrl+T
Channel Description	Ctrl+D
Channel Properties	Ctrl+P
Subscribe	Ctrl+S
Update	Ctrl+U
Start	Ctrl+X
Remove	Ctrl+R
Cancel Transfers	Ctrl+C
Quit	Ctrl+Q

Summary

The Castanet Tuner is used on your local desktop to download, launch, and manage various channels stored on various Castanet transmitters on the Internet. It also keeps those channels up to date and lets you visit transmitters to download new channels. Throughout this chapter you've learned how to use the tuner to do all these things: to find new channels, to subscribe to and run those channels, to update them once you've subscribed to them, and to unsubscribe to them or remove them when you've had enough. You also learned how to use channels in conjunction with a Web browser—both to view HTML channels and to create links to real channels from inside a Web page.

Congratulations on finishing Part I! You now know nearly everything there is to know about the Castanet Tuner. In Part II, we'll move to the transmitter side of the process, and you'll learn how to install and use the transmitter as well as how to publish channels.

Castanet Transmitter

four

Installing and Configuring the Transmitter

The Castanet Transmitter is the other half of the Castanet technology. The transmitter is the tool that makes channels available on the Internet for tuners to subscribe to. If you develop your own channels or support channel developers, you'll need to install a Castanet Transmitter on an Internet-accessible system and then publish your channels on that transmitter.

In the next three chapters, you'll learn all about installing and administering the Castanet Transmitter, as well as how to add and maintain channels. (You'll learn how to actually write the channels in Part III.)

Before You Start

As with the installation for the tuner, let's first go through and make sure you've got the ingredients to install everything successfully.

● Make sure you have the right system requirements. For Windows you'll need a Windows 95 or Windows NT 4.0 system with at least 8MB of memory and 10MB of free disk space. For Solaris you'll need to be running Solaris 2.4 or higher with 16MB of RAM and 10MB of free disk space (again, more if you've got lots of channels).

Note

Currently, Marimba supports transmitters on these platforms only. However, several other unsupported ports of the Marimba software are also available for other UNIX systems such as Linux and FreeBSD. See `http://www.marimba.com/products/unsupported.html` for more details.

● Make sure the system you install the transmitter on is accessible to the Internet at large. (Or, if you're publishing channels for intranet use only, your transmitter should be accessible to those systems inside your network that will be using it.)

For either Internet or intranet use, you will need the fully qualified host name of that machine (that is, starting with the system name and including the domain name). Transmitters often have a name with the prefix "trans" (for example, `trans.marimba.com`). You can set up a DNS alias (CNAME) for your transmitter to follow this convention.

Note

Keep in mind that transmitters should be accessible to tuners 24 hours a day, 7 days a week. If your only connection to the Internet is a dial-up PPP or other part-time connection, you might want to locate an ISP that supports transmitters for your channels rather than install your own transmitter.

● You can install the transmitter for personal testing use on a system without a network connection (for example, if you want to make sure your channels are working before installing them somewhere else). On Windows, however, you will need to use the Network control panel to make sure that the TCP/IP Protocol is installed, and that DNS is disabled.

● Pick a port number that the transmitter will run on. By default, the transmitter runs on port 80. This enables Web browsers to get a channel listing from your transmitter (Web servers typically run on port 80.) If you already have a Web server running on port 80, you'll need to pick another port number. Conventionally, transmitters run on port 5282 when they can't run on port 80. If your transmitter is running on a firewall system, you'll have to open access to the transmitter's port so that tuners can get to it.

Note

On Solaris, if you do not have access to root (superuser), you will have to install the transmitter on a port number higher than 1024. (5282 will do just fine.)

● Choose a directory to store channels in. This directory is usually separate from the transmitter software itself. On Windows, it's typically `C:\Marimba\Transmitter`; on UNIX, it can be anywhere you want it to be. Note that for best transmitter performance, channels should be located on a local disk (as opposed to one mounted over a network).

● Do you have a Web browser available? The transmitter documentation and help files are available as Web pages (and as a channel from Marimba's transmitter). You will need a Web browser such as Netscape or Internet Explorer to view these pages.

Installing and Configuring the Transmitter

After you've assembled or found out all the information from the last section, you can install the transmitter software on the system that will serve as your transmitter. There are two places you can get transmitter software:

● On the CD-ROM that comes with this book.

● From Marimba's Web site at `http://www.marimba.com/`.

Note

The transmitter contained on the CD-ROM for this book is a limited version that only allows five unique users per hour to connect to the transmitter. (Each of those users can make unlimited connections, but once the limit is reached, new users will be turned away.) This version is intended for testing the software; if you're creating channels for public consumption, you'll want to look into using the commercial version of the transmitter, which allows 100 unique users per hour (or more, for additional cost).

For Windows, the transmitter is an executable file called `Trans1_0.EXE`. On Solaris, there are two transmitter installation files, both compressed `tar` archives. The first, `transmitter1_0_pgk_tar.Z`, is intended for use with the `pkgadd` program and can only be run installed as root. The second, `transmitter1_0_tar.Z`, can be unarchived anywhere and can be used by any user on the system.

Skip to the section that describes the installation for your system.

Installation of Windows

To install the transmitter on Windows 95 of Windows NT, first quit all running Windows programs (particularly the Castanet Tuner, if it's running), and double-click the installer file. Windows will load the transmitter installer wizard.

Note

> If you're using the transmitter installer from the CD-ROM that came with this book, you can find the transmitter installer in the directory `Marimba` and then in the subdirectory for your platform (`Win95`, `WinNT`, or `Solaris`)—for example, `Marimba\Win95\Trans1_0.EXE`.

The Castanet Transmitter installer wizard will lead you through the installation, including choosing an installation directory. (See Figure 4.1.)

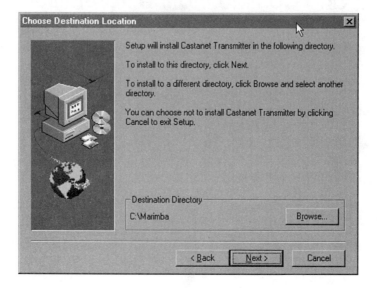

Figure 4.1. *Choosing an installation directory.*

By default, the transmitter software is installed into `c:\Marimba` (also the default location for the tuner). You can install it anywhere on the system where you have disk space available.

After all the transmitter files have been installed, you are asked if you would like to have the transmitter start automatically when you reboot. Because the transmitter should be available to tuners that may want to access it at any time during the day or night, it's a very good idea to choose Yes for this option so you don't always have to remember to start up the transmitter when the system reboots. If you choose No, you can add a shortcut to the transmitter to the StartUp folder later; see Chapter 6, " Transmitter Administration and Performance Tuning" for details.

After the installation process is finished, skip to "Configuring the Transmitter" to finish getting the transmitter up and running.

Installation on Solaris with pkgadd

The preferred method of installing the transmitter on Solaris is with the `pkgadd` program (part of the standard Solaris operating system). You will, however, need to be root to run `pgkadd`. If you do not have root access on your system, skip to the next section, "Installation on Solaris Without `pkgadd`."

Before you can run `pkgadd` to install the transmitter, you'll need to uncompress and un-`tar` the installation archive file into some temporary location (for example, `/tmp`). These lines do just that:

```
mkdir /tmp/trans
cp transmitter1_0_pkg_tar.Z /tmp/trans
cd /tmp/trans
uncompress transmitter1_0_pkg_tar.Z
tar xvf transmitter1_0_pkg_tar
```

The contents of the `tar` archive will be extracted and installed into the directory `/tmp/trans`. Then, run `pkgadd` with that directory as an argument:

```
pkgadd -d /tmp/trans
```

You'll get a message similar to this one:

```
The following packages are available:
  1  MRBtrans      Marimba Transmitter
                   (sun4) 1.0beta2

Select package(s) you wish to process (or 'all' to process
all packages). (default: all) [?,??,q]:
```

Choose 1 and press Return.

You'll be asked to agree to a user agreement, and then the install script will ask you to choose an installation directory:

71

```
First, choose a directory to install the transmitter binaries, and
    the Java Virtual Machine.  This normally would go somewhere under
    /opt.  This is called the "package base directory."

Enter the package base directory [/opt/MRBtrans]:
```

Packages, under Solaris, are traditionally installed in the /opt directory, but you can install the transmitter software anywhere you have room—for example, /usr/local or /export/home.

In the next step you're asked to choose a channels directory, which is used to store the channels that you've published on your transmitter. It should not be the same directory as your transmitter software; if you have to upgrade the transmitter, you don't want to overwrite all your channels. Choose some other directory for channel use. For best performance, that directory should be located on a local disk (as opposed to one mounted over the network). Here I chose the directory /usr/local/channels:

```
Please select the transmitter's channel directory.  This is the directory
that stores the channels that the transmitter broadcasts.  For optimal
performance, this directory should be located on a local file system.
There must be more than enough free disk space to store the data for all
channels.

Enter the transmitter channel directory: /usr/local/channels
```

The next two steps are to enter the fully qualified host name of the transmitter's system and the port number on which the transmitter will run. Keep in mind that if you already have a Web server running, you'll need to use some port other than 80—5282 is the traditional alternative port number. In this example I've used trans.1ne.com as the host name of my server, and 5282 for the port.

```
Enter the fully-qualified host name [.]: trans.1ne.com

Enter the port number [80]: 5282
```

Note

The host name you use for the transmitter must already be an existing host name for that site. (If it doesn't exist, your tuner won't be able to connect to that system.) Typing it here will not modify your network setup to include that name, so make sure you choose a name that already exists.

The last couple of steps involved setting a transmitter password and a list of trusted hosts for publishing to this transmitter. You can use these options to restrict who can publish to this transmitter.

The first option is the transmitter password. If you set a transmitter password, you can restrict who has access to publishing on this transmitter. (You can also control access to individual channels, but you'll learn about that in Chapter 5, "Installing and Broadcasting Channels.") You don't have to set a transmitter password if you don't want to.

Note

If you'll be publishing channels from the same system on which the transmitter is running, you cannot set a password to restrict transmitter access (or rather, you can set one, but it won't be used). The password only applies to people publishing the channels from remote systems; the transmitter is open to anyone running on that same system.

The list of trusted hosts is also used to restrict access to the transmitter. Only host names that you enter in this list will be allowed to publish to the transmitter — regardless of whether or not they have a password. Use localhost to restrict publishing access to the same machine the transmitter runs on, or don't enter any hosts to allow open access to the transmitter.

Note

You can always change the password or list of hosts later, so don't worry about getting it right this time.

Enter the password at the prompt, and then each host name at each individual prompt, with a return to stop entering host names:

```
Please specify a password and a list of trusted hosts.  These will be
    required in order to create, putback, and delete channels on this
    transmitter.  If no hosts are specified, then any host may perform a
    putback.  To restrict access to only this host, list either this
    host's name, or "localhost".

Enter a password:  [?,q]

Enter a trusted host name (blank line to finish): localhost
Enter a trusted host name (blank line to finish):
```

If all goes well, the transmitter software will be installed and you'll be returned to the "Select package(s) you wish to process" prompt. Choose q to quit the installation.

To start and run the transmitter, skip ahead to "Starting the transmitter from the command line."

Installation on Solaris Without pkgadd

If you don't have access to root on your system or can't stand the pkgadd interface, you can install the transmitter software by hand.

The installation archive for this purpose is called transmitter1_0_tar.Z (not transmitter1_0_pkg_tar.Z). Copy that archive to your chosen installation location and decompress it:

```
cp transmitter1_0_tar.Z /usr/local/
cd /usr/local/
uncompress transmitter1_0_tar.Z
```

73

Then use tar to extract the files from the archive.

```
tar xvf transmitter1_0_tar
```

Note

In this example, I've installed the transmitter in the same location that I installed the tuner in Chapter 2; both products will end up located in the /usr/local/castanet directory.

Once you're done, you can delete the tar archive:

```
rm transmitter1_0_tar
```

Go on to the next section to finish setting up the transmitter.

Configuring the Transmitter

If you installed the transmitter on Windows or on Solaris without using pkgadd, the next step is to configure it so that it can run. The transmitter comes with a configuration program built in; all you have to do is start it to step through the process.

Note

If you installed the software using pkgadd, you've already configured the transmitter for basic operation, so you can skip this section. However, should you ever need to reconfigure the transmitter to have different values, you can use the procedures described in this section.

To start the transmitter on Windows, navigate through the Start menu to the transmitter program. (See Figure 4.2.)

To start the transmitter on Solaris, run the transmitter program contained in the transmitter directory hierarchy. For example, if you had installed the transmitter software into /usr/local/, you'd start the transmitter with this command:

```
/usr/local/castanet/transmitter/bin/transmitter
```

On both Windows and Solaris, the transmitter displays an initial window. Choose Next to proceed to the first configuration screen.

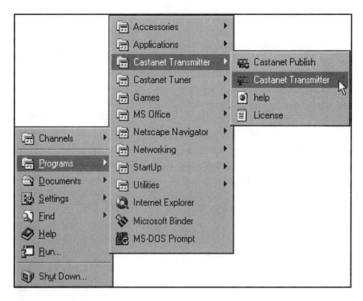

Figure 4.2. *Starting the Castanet Transmitter.*

Setting the Transmitter Directory

This first screen, shown in Figure 4.3, is used to set the transmitter's channel directory.

Figure 4.3. *Transmitter Root Directory.*

The root directory is used to store all the channels that are available on the transmitter. It should not be the same directory as your transmitter software; in case you have to upgrade the transmitter you don't want to overwrite all your channels. Choose some other directory for channel use. For best performance, that directory should be located on a local disk (as opposed to one mounted over the network).

On Windows, the default channel directory is at `C:\Marimba\Transmitter` (note that this is different from the default install directory, which is `C:\Marimba\Castanet Transmitter`). On Solaris, you can put the channel directory anywhere you'd like (for example, `/usr/local/channels` or `/usr/local/castanet/transmitter_channels/`).

Setting the Transmitter Host and Port

Choose Next to go to the next screen: the Transmitter Host and Port window, shown in Figure 4.4.

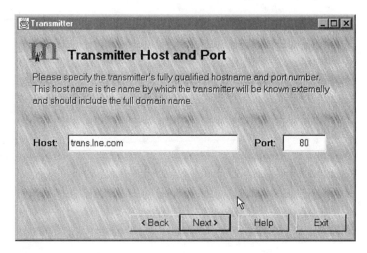

Figure 4.4. Transmitter Host and Port.

In this window, enter the fully qualified host name of the transmitter and the port number on which it runs. (A fully qualified host name is one that ends with your domain name—for example, `trans.marimba.com` or `trans.mysite.org` as opposed to just `trans` or `www` or some other shorter host name.) If you're installing the transmitter on a system without a network connection, for local testing you can use localhost as the transmitter name.

Also enter the port number which the transmitter will run on. On Solaris, if you're using a port number less than `1024`, you must be running this configuration program as root; otherwise you're restricted to port numbers over `1024` (for example, `5282`). Keep in mind that although the default port is `80`, if you already have a Web server on that port you'll have to choose a number other than `80`.

Setting Transmitter Access Control

The next screen, shown in Figure 4.5, is for controlling access to who can publish on this transmitter. It includes setting a password and defining a list of trusted hosts.

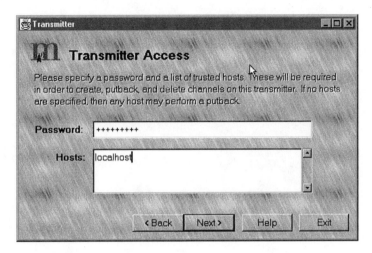

Figure 4.5. *Transmitter Access.*

First, enter the transmitter, if needed. If you set a transmitter password, you can restrict who has full access to publishing on this transmitter. The transmitter password is similar to a root password for this transmitter; anyone who has the transmitter password has full access. (There are also channel passwords, for publishing specific channels; you'll learn about these in Chapter 5.) You don't have to set a transmitter password if you don't want to.

Second, enter a series of host names (again, fully qualified host names) of systems that are allowed to publish or update channels on a transmitter. If you have a separate system for channel development, for example, you might put the name of that system here. Use localhost for the host the transmitter is installed on, or leave this field blank to allow any system that can access your transmitter to publish channels on that transmitter.

Setting Publish Notification

Choose Next to move on to the Publish Notifications screen (shown in Figure 4.6). The address shown in the e-mail address window is a special address at Marimba to let them know when you've published a channel. If you don't want to tell Marimba about new channels or you're inside a firewall and cannot send mail to the Internet, delete this address and leave that field blank.

Note

The picture shown in Figure 4.6 is actually labelled Putback Notifications; Putback is the previous name of the Publish tool. They are the same thing.

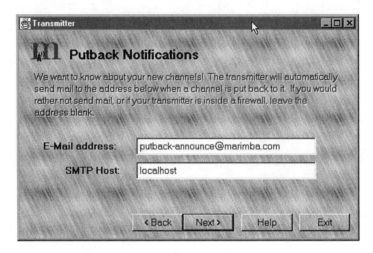

Figure 4.6. *The Publish Notifications screen.*

If you do leave the address in place, fill in the SMTP field with the name of your mail host. This is often the same mail host where your e-mail program checks for mail.

Confirmation

The last screen is simply a confirmation of the basic properties for the transmitter. (The Advanced button is used to set advanced properties of the transmitter; you'll learn about these properties in Chapter 6.) Choose the Launch button to start the transmitter actually running. The window shown in Figure 4.7 will appear after the transmitter is active and running on the system.

When the transmitter is running, a transmitter icon will appear in the task bar. (See Figure 4.8.) You can show the transmitter window at any time by double-clicking that icon.

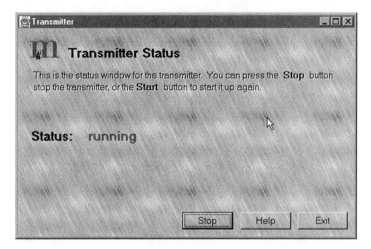

Figure 4.7. A running transmitter.

Figure 4.8. The icon for a running transmitter.

Testing a Running Transmitter

You can test to see if the transmitter is working at this point by starting up a tuner and connecting to the transmitter from the Listing panel using the transmitter name you entered in the configuration. (Don't forget the port number if it was something other than 80!) Use the localhost for the name of the transmitter if you're running both the transmitter and the tuner on a local system with no network connection. You won't get a channel listing (you haven't published any channels yet; you'll do that in the next chapter) but the status bar in the lower right should say "Listing Empty." (See Figure 4.9.)

If you get no response from the transmitter or a Connection failed error, make sure the transmitter name you're using actually does point to that system and that the system is reachable over your network. If it is reachable, make sure the transmitter is running and that it's running on the port that you think it's running on. If you're still having problems, make sure that you don't already have something running on the port where you installed the transmitter (for example, a Web server), which would prevent the transmitter from replying, and change the port for the transmitter if necessary.

If you're using a system without a network connection, make sure that you've disabled DNS (using the Network Control Panel, double-click the entry for TCP/IP and switch to the DNS panel), and that you've used localhost as the name of the transmitter in the transmitter configuration and as the name of the transmitter in the tuner.

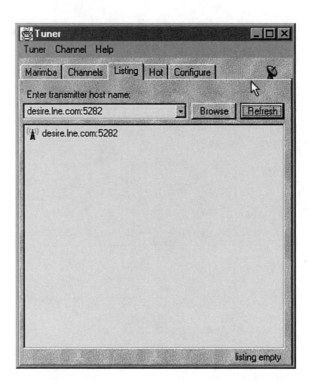

Figure 4.9. *Running the transmitter (no channels yet).*

What Gets Installed, and Where

On Windows, the transmitter installer creates two directories. The main software directory, typically `C:\Marimba\Castanet Transmitter`, contains the main transmitter software. The second is the transmitter's channel directory where channels are stored; that directory is typically `C:\Marimba\Transmitter`. Both these locations can be changed via the installation or configuration programs.

After you configure the transmitter, that configuration information is stored in a file called `properties.txt` in the transmitter's channel directory. You can edit its directory using your favorite text editor or using the configuration tool; you'll learn more about configuring the transmitter in Chapter 6.

If, during the Windows installation, you agreed to let the transmitter start up when you reboot the machine, a shortcut to the transmitter program is stored in the Start menu. To prevent the transmitter from being started on reboot, choose Start | Settings | Taskbar | Start Menu Programs, and then click Remove. Navigate to the StartUp folder, click Castanet Transmitter, and choose Remove.

On Solaris, if you install the software using pkgadd, several things are installed for you:

- The main transmitter software is installed into /opt/MRBtrans/, or into the directory you chose for the pkgadd base directory.
- The transmitter's channel directory is created for you.
- Your transmitter configuration information is stored in a file called properties.txt in the transmitter's channel directory. You can edit that file with a text editor, or modify its values using the transmitter GUI program.
- A script for starting and stopping the transmitter is located in /etc/init.d.
- Basic transmitter configuration is stored in /etc/transmitter.conf.
- Your rc files are modified to start the transmitter when the system boots.

If you install the transmitter without pkgadd, the transmitter software is installed into the location where you expanded the tar archive. After you run the configuration program, your transmitter's channel directory is created and the configuration information is stored in a properties.txt file in that directory.

Uninstalling the Transmitter

There might be cases wherein you'll want to remove the transmitter software from your system—for example, to reinstall a new version of the transmitter or to "decommission" a former transmitter system.

To remove the Castanet Transmitter from Windows, choose the Add/Remove Programs from the Control Panels, and select the transmitter from the list. (See Figure 4.10, which shows an old transmitter beta being removed.) Finally, choose the Add/Remove button to remove the software. You'll be asked if you want to remove the transmitter's channel directory in addition to the regular software.

There are two ways to remove the transmitter from Solaris, depending on whether you installed it using pgkadd or used the regular installation. If you used pkgadd to install the software, you can use the pkgrm command to remove it. Simply type pkgrm alone at a UNIX prompt. You must be root to run pkgrm.

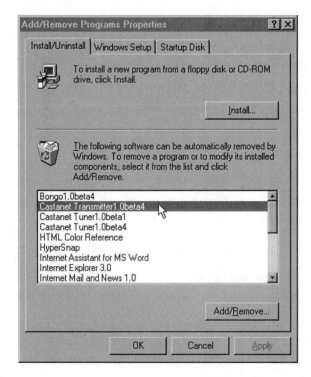

Figure 4.10. *Uninstalling the transmitter.*

The `pkgrm` command will give you a list of the install packages; one of those will be the MRBtrans package. Choose its number and verify that that's the package you want to remove; the `pkgrm` program will then remove that package and all its supporting files. You'll be asked if you also want to remove the transmitter's channel directory.

If you used the regular transmitter installation (the one without `pkgadd`) to install the transmitter, you can simply remote the `castanet/transmitter` directory to uninstall the transmitter. You may also want to remove the transmitter's channel directory if you want to remove all traces of the transmitter from your system.

Getting Help

The documentation for the transmitter is available as a set of HTML Web pages, both on Marimba's Web site and as a channel (called "Transmitter doc" from `trans.marimba.com`). Choosing any of the Help buttons from the transmitter administration tool will bring up those help files in your browser (on Windows, your default browser will be launched to view the files; on Solaris, you'll need to have your browser already running).

Summary

In this chapter you installed the transmitter and configured it for basic use by a tuner. In the next chapter you'll complete the process: You'll add some channels that then become available to tuners that can access that transmitter.

five

Installing and Broadcasting Channels

So now you have a transmitter up and running on your transmitter site. And that transmitter is transmitting nothing, which is about as useful as a TV or radio station broadcasting nothing but static. The next step, then, is to publish one or more channels on that transmitter for tuners to subscribe to.

This chapter describes channel publishing from the transmitter administrator's point of view, where a channel has already been written and is ready to go. In many cases—if you're in a small organization, for example, or doing this on your own time—you'll be both channel developer and transmitter administrator. If that's the case here, you'll get an idea of how channel publishing works and how to use Castanet Publish. Later in this book, in Part III, you'll learn more about constructing channels.

How Channel Publishing Works

The first thing to understand about channel publishing in Castanet is that channel publishing is not at all like Web publishing, even though the Castanet Transmitter and a Web server have similar purposes.

With Web publishing, you're placing HTML files and images and other media on a Web server. Usually you don't have to do anything other than put them in the right place—you can copy the files, or FTP them, or use a special HTML editor that will let you "save to" the server. As long as the Web server can find your files, those files are considered published. (See Figure 5.1.) It's a very simple process.

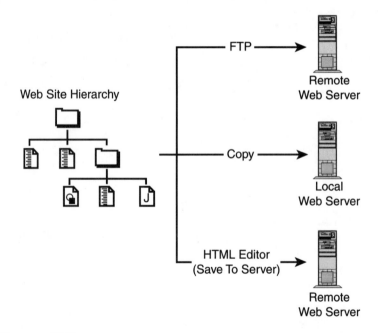

Figure 5.1. *Web server publishing.*

With Castanet channels, the process of publishing is much more deliberate. To publish channels on a transmitter, you run a program called Castanet Publish, which not only copies the files from your internal development directory to the final directory where the transmitter can find them, but also enables you to configure other properties of the channel such as its name and how frequently it will be updated. (See Figure 5.2.) You *must* run Publish to accomplish this; copying the files will not work.

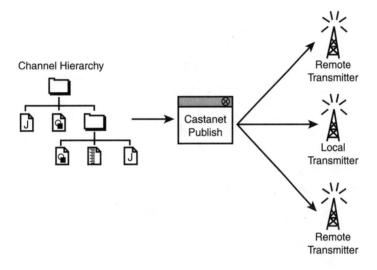

Figure 5.2. *Channel publishing using Castanet Publish.*

Note

Castanet Publish used to be called Castanet Putback. If you see references to *channel putback* or to the *putback* command, keep in mind putback and publish are the same thing.

You also use the Publish tool when you have updates to a channel; whenever you change something that you want to be propagated out to your users, you run publish. The Publish tool will figure out the differences between your old channel and the new one, and the next time a tuner asks for an update to a channel, those differences—and *only* those differences—will be downloaded and installed. At every step in the channel-publishing process, you'll be using the publish tool.

This chapter will tell you how to use it.

Starting the Publish Tool

Castanet Publish comes with the Castanet Transmitter, and it is installed in the same directory as the transmitter software.

To start Castanet Publish on Windows, navigate through the Start menu to the publish program. (See Figure 5.3.)

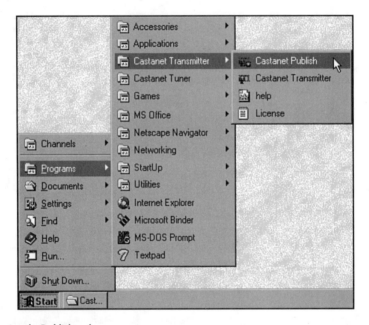

Figure 5.3. *Starting the Publish tool.*

To start the Castanet Publish tool on Solaris, run Publish from the command line:

```
/opt/MRBtrans/castanet/transmitter/publish
```

On both Windows and Solaris, the Publish tool will launch and display an opening screen. Choose Channels to display the Channels Under Development screen (shown in Figure 5.4).

Note

This screen looks rather empty because you haven't published any channels yet. Keep reading.

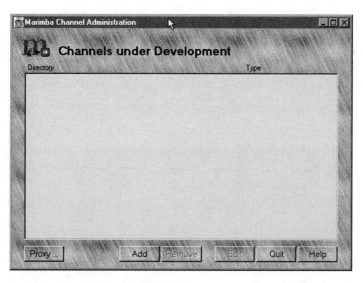

Figure 5.4. *The main Channels Under Development screen.*

From here you can add and remove channels as well as modify their properties so that they behave differently.

Quick Start: Publishing a Sample Channel

Let's run through a quick example so you can get a feel for how the Publish tool works. We'll use, as an example, one of the sample channels that comes with the Castanet Transmitter.

The Castanet sample channels are installed in the main transmitter software directory, in a directory called `channels`. For example, on Windows, if you installed the software in the default location, they would be located in `C:\Marimba\Castanet Transmitter\channels`. On Solaris, again, if you used the default installation, they would be in `/opt/MBRtrans/castanet/transmitter/channels`. The channels in these directories are all set up and ready to go—all you have to do is use publish to make them available on your transmitter.

We'll use the Crossword channel. Make note of the directory path to that channel, particularly if you've installed the software in locations other than the defaults.

Switch to the Publish tool. At the Channels Under Development screen, choose Add to add a new channel. The Add/Create a Channel screen appears. Type in the pathname to your channel directory, on Windows starting from the disk letter (`C:` or `E:`) and in Solaris from the root directory (`/`). So, for example, Figure 5.5 shows the pathname to the Crossword channel in Windows.

Note

The directory you type in here is the local development directory for your channels, not the channel directory for the transmitter itself. The publish tool will create and manage that directory. This directory is where the publish tool should get your files from.

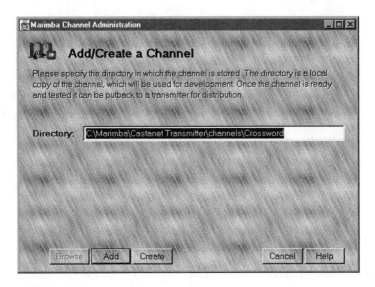

Figure 5.5. Add a channel using Castanet Publish.

Choose Add to add the channel to the list of channels the Publish tool manages. The screen returns to the Channels Under Development screen, with the path to the Crossword channel listed (as shown in Figure 5.6).

Usually at this point, the next step would be to define the channel's properties. Because this is an example channel for Castanet, the properties have already been set for this channel.

There is one property panel you will need to fill out, and that's the transmitter panel. Choose Edit to open the property panels, and the Transmitter tab to see the transmitter properties (if they are not already visible). Figure 5.7 shows the Transmitter properties panel:

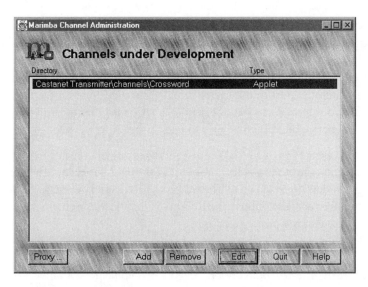

Figure 5.6. *The Crossword channel added to the listing.*

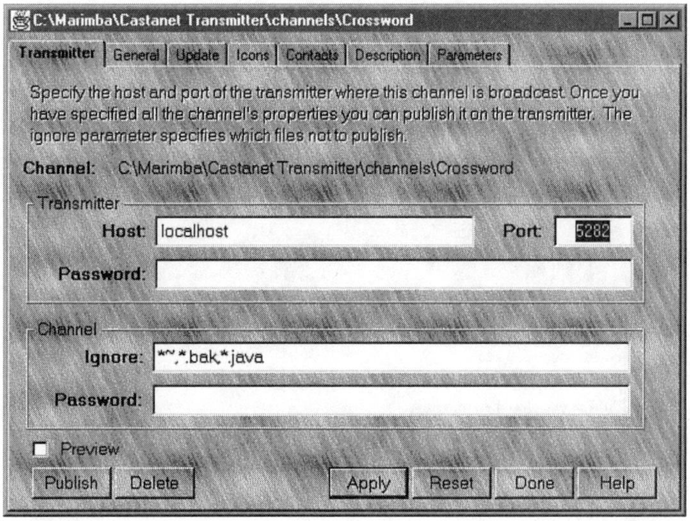

Figure 5.7. *Transmitter properties.*

For this channel, the channel and the transmitter are running on the same system, so the transmitter host name will be localhost (you can also do your channel development on another host on the network, and then publish it using the Publish tool to a remote transmitter). The two other things you'll need to check for in this example are the port number (it should match the port number you actually installed the transmitter on—here I've used 5282), and, if your transmitter has one, you'll also need to enter the transmitter password. After you enter or change the values, be sure to click either Apply or Done to make sure the values are saved.

You can examine the other possible properties for this channel to see what sort of values those properties can have (we'll cover all the properties in detail later on in this chapter), and then the final step is to actually publish the channel. To publish the channel, you'll use the Publish button from any of the properties panels.

Note

Make sure the Preview box is not checked when you choose Publish. You'll learn about previews later.

The Publish tool will switch to the Publish window, generate the necessary property files for publishing, and publish the channel. Figure 5.8 shows the result when the publish occurred successfully.

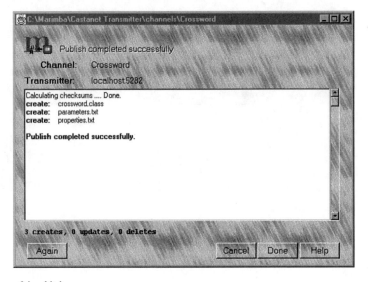

Figure 5.8. *A successful publish.*

The last step is to test to see if the publish did actually occur. You can do this by getting the channel listing for your transmitter from a Castanet Tuner. So, for example, Figure 5.9 shows the channel listing from my transmitter, which shows the Crossword channel successfully published and available.

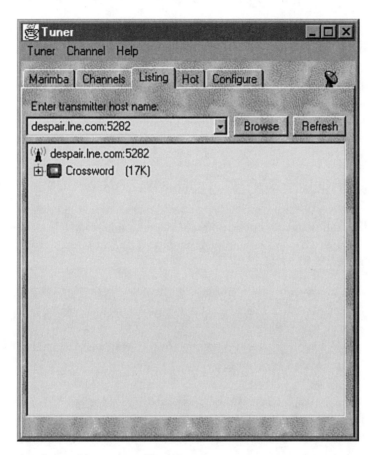

Figure 5.9. *Transmitter listing with new channel in place.*

What happens when you need to update the Crossword channel? All you have to do is make the changes in your local development directory, start up Castanet Publish, double-click the channel you want to update, and click on the Publish button. You don't have to define the channel's properties all over again, unless you want to change any of them; just choose Publish to accomplish the update.

And that's it! You've just published your first channel. Although the startup process may be somewhat longer for a brand new channel, after you've got it configured in the publish tool it's easy to keep updating it.

Continue through the rest of this chapter to learn about the publish tool in greater detail.

Using the Publish Tool

You use Castanet Publish to publish a channel—in other words, to move it from a local development directory to its final location in the transmitter directory. You must use the publish tool to do this; simply copying the files over will not work. You can use the publish tool on the same system as the transmitter, or from any other system on your network (or on the Internet at large, for that matter) for remote publishing.

Adding and Creating Channel Directories

The first step to publishing a channel is to add that channel's development directory to the channel list inside Castanet Publish. To add a local channel to that list, choose the Add button from the Channels Under Development window. The Add/Create a Channel screen appears. (See Figure 5.10.)

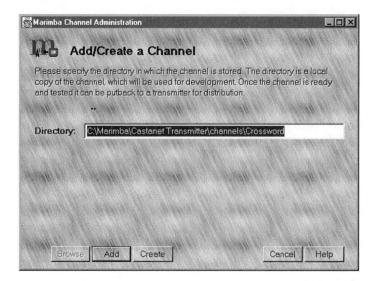

Figure 5.10. *Add a channel.*

Enter the full pathname of the local channel-development directory, using the pathname conventions of the local system (back slashes on Windows, forward slashes on UNIX).

Note

By the time you read this, Castanet Publish will most likely have a Browse button you can use to locate your channel directory, so you won't have to type it by hand.

Note

Keep in mind that the directory name you choose is that of your local channel-development directory (where the channel source comes *from*), not the transmitter root (where the channels are published *to*). The Publish tool will create the directories it needs on the transmitter root; you don't need to create anything by hand in that directory.

Choose either Add or Create to add the channel to the Channel Development list. Add is used to add channel directories that already have configuration files—most are typically directories for channels that have been published before. For new channels, most of the time you'll use Create instead.

Note

The Create button is somewhat misleading; if the channel directory you enter in the Directory field already exists on your hard drive and has files in it, Create will not overwrite that directory. It'll simply add it to the list.

You can also add a channel directory to the channel list before you even do any work to develop that channel. This will create that directory and set the initial properties of the channel. By creating a channel directory in publish before you start working, the publish tool will know all about the channel and its properties by the time you're ready to publish it, and the publishing process will be simple.

Setting the Publish Proxy

If you're using the Publish tool across the boundaries of a firewall—for example, if your development machine is on an internal network and your transmitter is on the firewall—you'll most likely need to specify proxy information for the Publish tool so that you can publish channels.

To enter proxy information for the Publish tool, select the Proxy button from the main Channels Under Development screen. The Proxy screen will appear (shown in Figure 5.11).

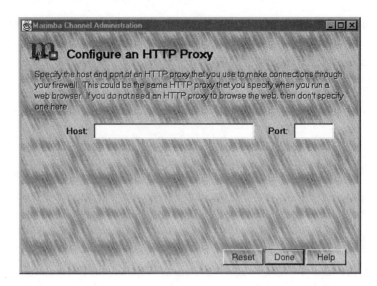

Figure 5.11. *Publish tool proxy information.*

Enter the host name and port for your firewall HTTP proxy information. This is often the same value you would use for a Web browser to access systems outside the firewall; check with your firewall administrator if you're not certain what to put here.

Getting Help

As with the Castanet Tuner and Transmitter, online help is available for most aspects of Castanet Publish through the Help button on each screen. The help files for publish are a set of Web files contained on Marimba's Web site or as a channel. (It's part of the transmitter documentation.) Choosing the Help button takes you to the help for that item in your Web browser (in Windows, it launches your default Web browser; in Solaris, that browser must already be running).

Creating or Modifying Channel Properties

When you have an entry for your local channel, you can create or modify the properties of that channel.

Channel properties include everything from the transmitter on which to publish the channel to the description of that channel, its parameters, the frequency of its updates, and other information. A lot of the information you create as channel properties shows up in the Channel Properties panel in the tuner.

You can create and edit the properties for a channel even if that channel doesn't yet exist, although you will need to create a directory for that channel and have it listed in the Channels Under Development window. Channel properties are stored in a file called `properties.txt` in your channel development directory. You can set up the properties for a new channel before you ever start developing that channel.

Note

> Because channel properties are stored in a text file, you can always create or edit that file by hand (for example, to set up a property template). Some properties, however, must be set by Castanet Publish itself.

To create or edit the properties for a channel, either double-click that channel's entry in the Channels Under Development list, or select a channel and choose Edit.

The Channel Properties screens will appear. You have several panels of properties to choose from (note the tabs across the top of the screen); each of these panels is described in the next couple of sections.

After you're done modifying properties on any panel, choose the Apply button to save those properties and then the Done button to return to the Channels Under Development window. (Choosing Done will also save all the properties for you.)

Transmitter Properties

Transmitter properties are the values the publish tool will need to actually publish the channel on a transmitter. Figure 5.12 shows the Transmitter Properties panel.

This panel is divided into two sections: Transmitter properties and Channel properties. The Host and Port fields in the transmitter section indicate the transmitter on which to publish this channel. So you could, for example, develop a channel on any system on the network and then publish that channel to a transmitter on another system. In the example shown in Figure 5.12, the channel-development directory and the transmitter are on the same system, so the host is localhost (it could also be the name of the transmitter itself; `localhost` is a useful shortcut). The port number must be the same as the port number you're running the transmitter on; `80` is the default. Here I've got my transmitter running on port `5282`.

Use the password field in the transmitter section to specify the password for that transmitter, if the transmitter has been set up to require a password. Note that if you're running publish on the same system as the transmitter (that is, you've used localhost as the transmitter name), you have full access to the transmitter and all its channels.

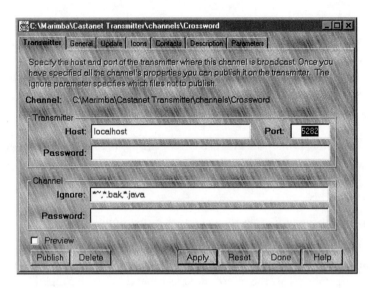

Figure 5.12. *The Transmitter Properties panel.*

The Ignore field in the channel section is for files in the development directory that are not to be included in the final channel package. You can use wildcards to exclude classes or filenames. So, for example, the default files to ignore are backup files (files ending with ~ or with .bak) and Java source files (files ending with .java). You can also include subdirectories in this list: for example, an SCCS directory that contains files under source-code control or a testing directory for local tests. The goal here is to exclude files in your channel-development directory that are not part of the channel itself.

Caution

Do not include *.txt in the Ignore field, because each channel has files called properties.txt and parameters.txt to define its properties and parameters. Ignoring all files ending with *.txt will also ignore these files, and your channel won't show up when you publish it.

The password field in the Channel section is used for a password specific to this channel. The difference between the transmitter password and the channel password is in access: If you have the transmitter password, you can publish any channel to that transmitter; if all you have is the channel password, you can only publish that one channel. Usually you'll enter either the channel password or the transmitter password, but not both (if you enter the channel password, you don't need the transmitter password.)

To create a password-protected channel, include the transmitter password, if any, and also include the initial channel password. After you publish the channel for the first time, the channel password will be stored on the transmitter and can be used to update that channel without also needing to know the transmitter password.

To change the password of a password-protected channel, you'll have to delete that channel from the transmitter, and then republish it with the new password.

Note

This somewhat awkward procedure for changing the password will be improved in a future release.

General Channel Properties

The general channel properties are the properties that tell the tuner how to launch and handle your channel—for example, which Java class file contains the starting code for the rest of the channel. Figure 5.13 shows the General Channel Properties windows.

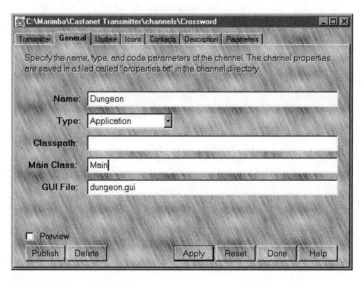

Figure 5.13. *The General Channel Properties panel.*

The Name field is the name of the channel as it will appear in the tuner. Be sure and choose a distinctive name for your channel (something better than MyChannel, for example), so that users of that channel have some idea what it is. (You can add a longer description of it in another property.)

The Type pull-down menu determines what kind of channel this is. You have four choices for the types of channels you can create, each of which gives you different options for other properties: Application, Applet, Presentation, and HTML.

An application is, as you might expect, a channel application written in Java. If you choose application from the Type menu, you'll have the fields shown in Figure 5.13 to fill in. Those fields include

- The Classpath field, which indicates the directories or `.zip` files in which the tuner should look for Java classes relating to this application. Classpath directories are subdirectories of the channel's main directory; if you've stored all your Java class files in the channel directory itself, you can leave this blank. If you've packaged your class files into a zip archive, use the name of that archive here. Separate multiple directories or filenames with a colon—for example, `classes:classes/classes.zip`.

- The Main Class field, which contains the name of the primary application class (the one to run first). In this field, the class should appear without the `.class` extension; for example, if your main application is called `Main.class`, you'll want to just put Main in this field.

- The GUI File field is used to indicate a presentation file for this application. Presentation files, which have a `.gui` extension, are created using Castanet Bongo (which you can learn more about in Chapter 9, "Creating Presentations and Channels with Bongo," and in *Official Marimba Guide to Bongo,* also published by Sams.net.)

The second type of channel you can create is an applet—or rather, you can use a Java applet written to work inside a Web page as a channel. Choosing Applet as the type of channel you're creating brings up a number of new fields (shown in Figure 5.14).

The names of many of these fields correspond to the values of the `<APPLET>` tag inside an HTML file, and include

- The Code field is the name of the main applet class (the one you would usually name in the `CODE` attribute of the `<APPLET>` tag), minus the .class extension. So, for example, if your main applet class was `DataBaseApplet.class`, you'd enter `DataBaseApplet` here.

- The Code base field is the location of your channel classes, relative to the channel directory itself, and is identical to the value of the `CODEBASE` attribute in the `<APPLET>` tag. Otherwise, it's similar in use to the Class path field.

- The Width and Height fields are the width and height of the applet, in pixels. You must include values here for the width and height of the applet.

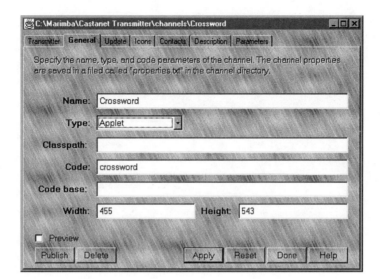

Figure 5.14. *Applet properties.*

The third kind of channel you can configure is a Presentation channel. Presentation channels are channels created with the Marimba Bongo application (you'll learn a little about Bongo in Chapter 9; the *Official Marimba Guide to Bongo* contains the definitive guide to creating presentations with Bongo). The only new value you'll need to enter here is the name of the Bongo .gui file for the main presentation—for example, `Headlines.gui` or `Calendar.gui` or `SomeOtherPresentation.gui`. Note that unlike the Java class files for applications and applets, for presentations the main presentation file must have the `.gui` extension.

The final type of channel in the pop-up menu is an HTML channel. For HTML channels, you'll need to enter the name of the topmost home page for the channel—typically `index.html`. The value of class path is ignored for HTML channels, as any applets contained in those channels are indicated using `<APPLET>` tags.

Frequency of Updates

The Update panel is for update properties—that is, how often tuners will check back to see if there are updates. There are two states a channel can be in during which updates can occur: active and inactive. An active channel is one that's actually up and running on a user's system, and an inactive channel is one that's subscribed to, but not currently running. For each channel state you can choose an update interval and a Data available action.

The update intervals fall in frequencies of every few minutes, hourly, daily, weekly, and never for active channels, or less frequently (hourly, daily, weekly, or never) for inactive applets. (See Figure 5.15.)

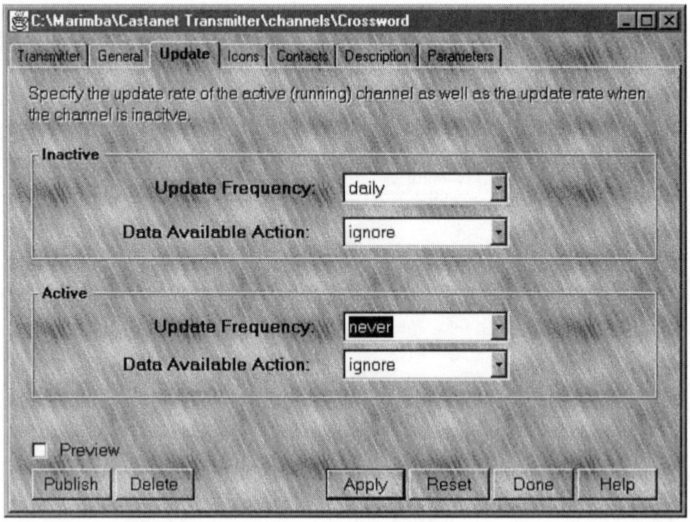

Figure 5.15. *Update frequency properties.*

Keep in mind that the update frequency is not how often you update your own channel; you can update it more or less frequently than you set in these properties, with no penalties or problems. What these values do determine is how often the tuner will check back to the transmitter to see if there is new information to download.

Choose the update interval for both the active and inactive states for the channel. Be sure and choose a realistic update interval—just because you can force an update every few minutes does not mean you should. Excessive updates put a load on the tuner, on your transmitter, and on the network between the two. Try and choose a reasonable update interval for each channel state.

The values for the Data Available Action drop-down lists affect how the channel will react to an update—for example, if it will ignore the new data until the channel is started or restarted, to start up or restart the channel altogether, or to perform even more complex procedures. You'll learn more about these when you start developing your own channels.

Channel Icons

When your channel is subscribed to by a tuner, several icons are used to identify that channel on the desktop itself and inside the tuner. Use the icon properties to customize those icons. (If you don't indicate any special icons, the default icons will be used.) Figure 5.16 shows the icon properties.

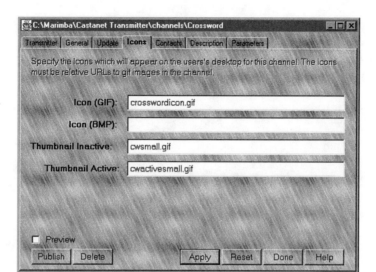

Figure 5.16. *Channel icon properties.*

The values for each of these fields are pathnames to image files relative to the channel directory (for example, `icon.gif` or `icons/active.gif`). The four values are as follows:

● Icon (GIF): This is a large icon (64 pixels square), representing the channel. (For example, in Solaris, this icon will be used as the desktop icon when the channel is iconified.) The file given must be in GIF format; it'll be converted into BMP format for Windows.

● Icon (BMP): This BMP-format icon is the same as the GIF version, but is used only on Windows if the GIF version doesn't look right.

● Thumbnail Inactive: Inside the tuner, each channel has a small icon in the channel listing. The inactive icon is displayed when the channel is subscribed to, but not running. The thumbnail icon should be in GIF format and 16 pixels square.

● Thumbnail Active: Same as the previous icon, except it's displayed when the channel is running. Active icons are often red versions of the inactive icons. This one is also in GIF format and 16 pixels square.

Channel Contact Information and Descriptions

The next two panels are for optional channel contact information and a channel description. Both of these are used by the tuner to help the reader figure out what the channel is for and who to contact if they have difficulties with it.

The Contacts panel (shown in Figure 5.17) is used to indicate the author or the administrator of the channel. (They might very well be the same person.) The author would be the person to contact for bugs in the channel itself; the administrator would be the person to contact if updates have stopped or if a transmitter has become inaccessible.

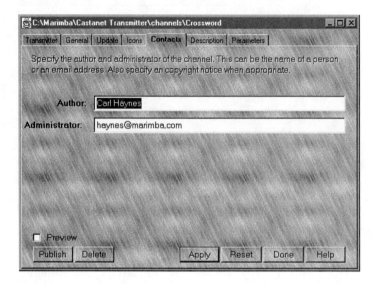

Figure 5.17. Channel contacts.

Enter the name and e-mail address of both the channel's author and administrator in the fields on this page and progress to the Description panel.

The Description panel, shown in Figure 5.18, continues the information from the previous page and includes fields for copyright information (if necessary) and a general description of the channel.

Copyright information is used to legally identify the copyright holder of the channel, which may not be the same person or entity that authored the channel. If you've written a channel that's in the public domain (all free use and unrestricted for any purpose), you might want to specify that here.

The channel description is used to describe the channel in as much detail as you'd like. This is your chance to explain what the channel is for and why it's useful. This information appears in the tuner in the Listing panel (see Figure 5.19), as well as in the page that appears when you use a browser to explore a transmitter. As with the channel contact information, both the channel description and the copyright information are optional.

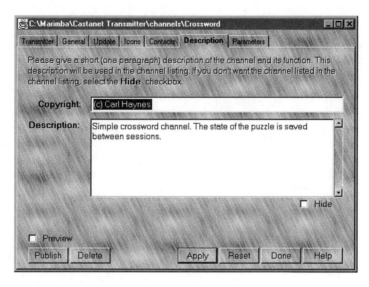

Figure 5.18. *The channel description.*

Hidden Channels

One other option in the Description panel deserves mentioning: The small checkbox in the corner marked "Hide." (See Figure 5.20.)

If you select this box and then publish the channel, that channel will be "hidden." Hidden channels do not show up in the listing of transmitters on a channel, nor do they appear if you browse a transmitter with a Web browser. However, if you or anyone else knows the name of the channel, they can still subscribe to it directly using the New Channel menu item in the tuner.

Hiding channels can be useful for testing to see whether a channel is working correctly without letting regular visitors to the transmitter know it is there. You can publish a hidden version of the channel, test it extensively, and then publish it again with the hidden option turned off to make it available for public use.

You could also use the hidden option to restrict access to a channel—just give out the name to those you want to be able to subscribe to it. Hiding channels, however, is a form of "security through obscurity"—that is, it isn't very secure at all.

Note

If you're looking for a better way to create secure channels, Castanet will have the capability to create password-protected channels in the next release.

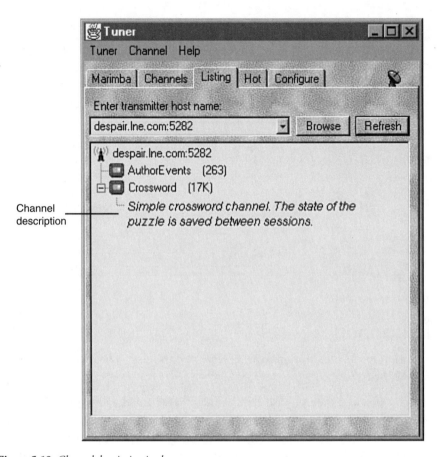

Channel
description

Figure 5.19. *Channel description in the tuner.*

Applet Parameters

The last panel in the properties screen is for channel parameters. These are usually used for applet channels, and they are the key value pairs that would normally appear in <PARAM> tags inside an HTML file. You can also use parameters for options to an application channel; all the parameters specified in this list are passed on to the channel itself for processing.

Channel parameters are indicated by name/value pairs, separated by an equal sign (=), with each pair on its own line. Parameters are case-insensitive, and order is not important.

Figure 5.21 shows some sample parameters for an applet that displays news headlines.

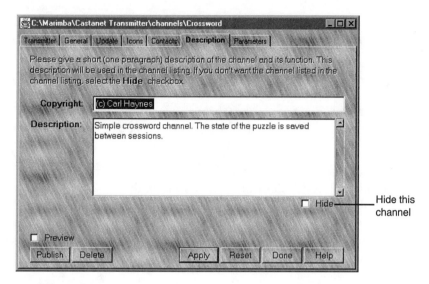

Figure 5.20. *Hide this channel.*

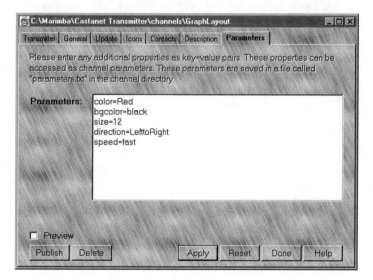

Figure 5.21. *Applet parameter properties.*

Channel parameters, unlike other channel properties, are stored in their own file in your development directory, called parameters.txt (normal properties are stored in properties.txt).

Publishing and Updating Channels

With a channel directory in the Channels Under Development list and a set of properties defined, the moment of truth is when you actually publish the channel to the transmitter and test to see if it's actually there and working.

To publish a channel, choose the channel from the Channels Under Development list and select Edit (or just double-click the channel from the list). Then choose the Publish button. The Publish tool will switch to the Publish window, contact the transmitter's host, create or update the properties.txt and parameters.txt files (if necessary), and then process and store the files on the transmitter. If the publishing process was successful, you'll get a message to that effect. Figure 5.22 shows the publish process for a simple channel.

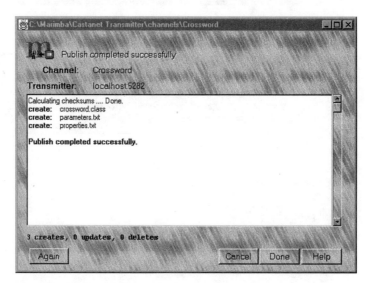

Figure 5.22. *A channel, successfully published.*

To update a channel, all you do is republish it: double-click its directory from the Channels Under Development list and choose Publish. You don't have to add the local development directory to the list or redefine all its properties again; the publish tool saves that information for you.

What if you want to publish a channel to multiple transmitters? You'll need to do this serially, changing the transmitter properties each time to point to a different transmitter.

Previewing Channels

The Publish tool also provides one other publishing feature: a Preview. Previewing a channel checks to make sure you have access to the transmitter, and updates all the channel's properties and parameters, but doesn't actually publish the channel on the transmitter. You can use preview to test the connection to a transmitter, update changes to the properties or parameters for that channel, or find out if the channel needs to be updated, in case you've forgotten.

Password-Protecting Channels

As you learned earlier, in the channel's transmitter properties you can set up a channel password for updating the channel. Use the channel password to prevent other people from publishing your channel.

If the transmitter you are publishing to requires a transmitter password, you'll have to enter both the transmitter and channel passwords the first time you publish the channel. After that first time all you need is the channel password. So, for example, rather than giving out the transmitter password to everyone who publishes to the transmitter, you could set up a channel for a not-very-trustworthy developer such that he or she would be able to publish only their own channels.

Troubleshooting

Sometimes when you try and publish a channel, the publishing process won't work for many different reasons. Usually there will be an error message in the Publish box that will give you some indication of what went wrong and how to fix it. Here are a few of those messages:

- *Publish ignored.* You most likely have the Preview box checked inside the properties for the channel. Choose Done and edit the properties to remove the check from the Preview checkbox.
- *Couldn't connect to* `trans.myserver.com:80`. Make sure that you're running a transmitter on that server and port, that the transmitter is running, and that you have access to that system.

• *Incorrect password for transmitter.* The password you typed in the transmitter properties panel does not match the password the transmitter itself defines for either the transmitter or for the channel. Double-check the passwords to make sure they match.

• *No permission to connect to transmitter.* Your host name is not in the list of trusted hosts defined by the transmitter. You'll need to reconfigure the transmitter to include the host name you want to publish from.

For many other errors, you might be able to get some information about what went wrong from the transmitter's log files. There's a special log file for publishing channels called putback.log, which is updated whenever anyone publishes a channel. You'll learn more about this log file in the next chapter.

Removing Channels

There are actually two meanings to the phrase "removing channels." You can remove a channel from the listing in the Publish tool, which means that you're no longer publishing it from the local system (or no longer updating it), or you can remove it altogether from the transmitter.

To remove a channel from the Channels Under Development list, simply choose its pathname and select Remove. The directory will vanish from the list. Note that this does not delete anything except that channel's entry in this list; it does not remove that channel from the transmitter, nor does it delete any files from the local development directory. In fact, it doesn't even delete the properties and parameters files, so if you added that same directory to the publish tool again, all the old settings would become available again.

Removing a channel from the Channels Under Development list is most useful when you're simply not responsible for publishing that channel any longer—perhaps the channel will receive no more updates, or someone else now has responsibility for that channel.

To delete a channel from a transmitter, select the channel you want to delete and choose the Delete button. The Publish tool will contact the transmitter and remove the channel from that transmitter. The channel will remain listed in the Channels Under Development list and will continue to remain intact on the local system; it just won't be available on the transmitter any more.

If users have subscribed to the channel you've removed, the next time they attempt to update that channel, an error message will appear ("no such channel"). They can then choose to remove that channel or continue with the version they currently have.

Using Publish from the Command Line

Although the vast majority of this chapter has discussed using the publish tool with a graphical user interface (GUI), you can also use Publish from a command line. You can use the command-line version of the Publish tool to automate the publishing process, for example, to update a channel every night at midnight.

On Solaris, the command-line version of the Publish tool is the same as the GUI version (running it with arguments prevents the GUI from executing). On Windows and Windows 95, you'll need to run the version of publish stored in the Command subdirectory of your transmitter installation (typically `C:\Marimba\Castanet Transmitter\Command\putback.exe`). In Windows 95, run the Publish command from inside a DOS shell. Both versions of Publish have the same options and arguments.

To publish a channel on a transmitter using the command-line version of Publish, simply use Publish with the pathname to the directory (which can be an absolute or relative pathname). For example, the Windows version might look like this:

```
Publish C:\Development\Channels\AuthorEvents
```

The equivalent on Solaris might be something like this:

```
publish /home/src/channels/AuthorEvents
```

You can also publish a whole directory of channels using wildcards. For example:

```
publish channels/*
```

Each of these versions of Publish will publish the channel on a transmitter installed on the same machine, running on port 80. To publish a channel on a remote transmitter, use the `-host` option with the name and port number of the host:

```
publish -host trans.myserver.com:5282 channels/*
```

Note

> The port number is optional. If you've installed your transmitter on port 80, you don't need to specify that port number there.

The `-ignore` option enables you to indicate files or groups of files inside your channel development directory that are not to be published—for example, source files, backup files, make files, or files under source code control. Indicate files to ignore using wildcards, separated by commas, inside single quotes:

```
publish -ignore '*.bak,*.java,SCCS/*'
```

This command ignores all files with the extension .bak (saved backup files from a text editor), files with the extension .java (Java source files), and all the files under the subdirectory SCCS (files under source code control). Without an -ignore option, Publish will by default operate as if the ignore option was '*.bak,*~,core,*.java'.

Note

You must include the filenames to ignore inside single-quotes. Using double-quotes or no quotes at all may cause the wildcard expressions to be expanded before publish can see them (resulting in different files being ignored than you expect).

The -n option is used for previewing channels. The -n option lists the operations that the Publish tool will do (creating files, contacting the transmitter, and so on), but it does not actually publish the files on the transmitter. This can be useful for debugging the publishing process before you actually do it.

The -quiet option is useful for automatic updates such as with UNIX cron entries. The -quiet option publishes a channel to a transmitter without printing any debugging or other information to the screen.

And, finally, to remove a channel from a transmitter, use the -delete option. With the delete option you can specify the channel to delete in one of two ways:

- ● The pathname of the channel, in which case the channel is deleted from the last transmitter it was published to.
- ● The name of the channel, in which case you must also indicate the host name and port of the transmitter with the -host option, like this:

```
publish -delete -host trans.myserver.com:5282 ExcellentChannel
```

Table 5.1 shows the options to the publish command and the actions they produce.

Table 5.1. The options and results for the publish command.

Option	Result
-host	Indicates the host name of the transmitter. The host name also can have an optional port number.
-ignore	A set of files to ignore when publishing a channel to a transmitter, surrounded by single quotes. Use wildcards to indicate sets of files, and commas to separate different sets.
-n	Preview the results of a publish, but don't actually store anything on the transmitter.

Option	Result
`-quiet`	Publish the channel without any output to the screen or console.
`-delete`	Delete the channel from a transmitter. With the `-delete` option you can indicate a channel by its local pathname, in which case it's deleted from the transmitter it was last published to, or by channel name, in which case you must also include the `-host` option to indicate which transmitter you want to delete it from.

Summary

At first glance, administering a transmitter seems an awful lot like administering a Web server. You install the software, start it running, and browsers or tuners connect to it and retrieve what they need. The most significant difference is in channel publishing. With Web pages, you just copy the files to the right directory and you're done. With channels, you have to go through this intermediate step: you have to use Castanet Publish to publish the channels so that they're available for that transmitter. Then, when they're published, you use the Publish tool to update them each time there's a change.

In this chapter you learned how to use the Publish tool to administer channels: to add new channels to the channel-management list, to set their properties, and, finally, to publish them to a transmitter and update them after they're there. Installing and configuring the transmitter is easy; for the most part you set it up and you're done. It's the channel configuration that will most likely take up more time and will make up the bulk of transmitter configuration. After reading this chapter, you should have a grasp of just about every aspect of channel management, whether or not you're even responsible for writing the channels themselves.

Transmitter Administration and Performance Tuning

Using the information on installing and configuring the Castanet Transmitter from the previous two chapters, you could go happily on your way publishing and broadcasting channels and never need anything else (except the occasional update to the software). In this chapter, however, you'll learn how to fine-tune the transmitter and its features to better suit your needs and help make sure your transmitter is running smoothly. In this chapter, you'll learn about

- Basic transmitter administration: starting and stopping the transmitter and changing its properties

- Advanced properties to control the resources the transmitter uses

- Transmitter log files

- Performance tuning

Basic Administration

For the most part, the Castanet Transmitter runs itself; it just starts and works (unlike, say, a pet, which you occasionally have to feed and walk and clean up after). However, you should be familiar with the basic administration tasks the transmitter does need, including starting and stopping the transmitter or reconfiguring its properties.

Starting and Stopping the Transmitter

In both Windows and Solaris, starting the transmitter either from the command line or via the Start menu brings up the transmitter configuration GUI, at the end of which is a screen that lets you start and stop the transmitter. (See Figure 6.1.) From this screen, you can temporarily stop the transmitter from accepting connections.

Figure 6.1. *Starting and stopping the transmitter.*

Note

When the transmitter configuration GUI appears, you don't have to change anything in the configuration screens; just keep pressing Next until you can launch the transmitter.

On Windows, you can bring up the transmitter GUI at any time while the transmitter is running by double-clicking on the transmitter icon in the taskbar. (See Figure 6.2.) The transmitter window will then either appear on the screen or as a taskbar entry.

On Solaris, you can iconify and de-iconify the transmitter window to hide or show it.

Transmitter icon

Figure 6.2. *The transmitter icon.*

Using the Command Line to Start the Transmitter

Usually when you start the transmitter, the administration GUI will pop up and you'll have to page through the screens to actually start the transmitter. In both Windows and Solaris, you can start the transmitter with a single argument—the transmitter's channel directory—and avoid the GUI.

In Windows, you can start the transmitter without a GUI by creating a shortcut to the `Transmitter.exe` program in the `Castanet Transmitter` directory, and edit its properties (right-click on the icon and choose Properties from the menu). In the Shortcut panel, add the full directory path to your transmitter's channel directory to the end of the Target field (with quotes around it if there are spaces in that pathname), and choose OK. That shortcut will now launch the transmitter without the GUI.

Note

This solution is less than ideal, because not having a GUI means that you cannot stop or start the transmitter on demand and that the transmitter icon will not appear in the taskbar. To quit the transmitter you'll have to use Ctrl+Alt+Delete. Select the transmitter from that list and choose End Task. The functionality of the transmitter without a GUI will improve in future versions of the transmitter.

On Solaris, you have a couple different command lines you can use. The first is to give the transmitter's channel directory as an argument to the `transmitter` program, like this (here I'm assuming that you're in the `transmitter/bin` directory or that you have that directory in your execution path, and that your transmitter's channel directory is `/usr/local/channels`):

```
transmitter /usr/local/channels/
```

If you installed the transmitter software using the pkgadd version of the install, there is also a script for starting and stopping the transmitter located in `/etc/init.d`. You can use this script to start up the transmitter or, if the transmitter is already running, to start or stop its execution. To start the transmitter, use `start` as an argument to this script:

```
/etc/init.d/transmitter start
```

To stop the transmitter, use `stop` as the argument:

```
/etc/init.d/transmitter stop
```

Reconfiguring Transmitter Properties

When you installed and started the transmitter for the first time, you configured the transmitter with its basic information: its host name and port, its channel directory, and so on. If any of this information changes, you'll need to reconfigure the properties for the transmitter. You can do this in one of two ways:

- Starting the transmitter leads you through the GUI for configuring the transmitter. You can change any of the transmitter's properties at that time.

- Properties specific to the transmitter configuration are stored in a file called properties.txt in the transmitter's channel directory. You can edit this file by hand to change any of the transmitter's properties. Make sure you restart the transmitter after making any changes. See "Transmitter Properties" at the end of this chapter for the list of available properties in the properties.txt file.

Starting the Transmitter at Boot Time

If you installed the transmitter on Windows or if you used the pkgadd version of the installation on Solaris, the transmitter will start automatically each time you boot up your machine. (In Windows you had a choice whether or not to enable this function.)

To disable this feature in Windows, remove the shortcut to the Castanet Transmitter, which is contained in the folder Windows\Start Menu\Programs\StartUp.

If you chose not to have the transmitter start automatically in the installation, you can enable this option by creating a shortcut to the transmitter program in Castanet Transmitter\ Transmitter.exe and putting that shortcut in the folder Windows\Start Menu\Programs\StartUp.

Startup in Solaris is determined by a link in the directory /etc/rc3.d (usually called S19transmitter). That link points to the transmitter script in /etc/init.d. To prevent the transmitter from being launched at boot time, remove the symbolic link (and, by extension, enable startup at boot time by creating a symbolic link from /etc/init.d/transmitter to /etc/ rc3.d/S19transmitter).

Note

Marimba recommends that you start the transmitter at boot time rather than running it through a mechanism such as inetd.

Changing the Transmitter's Channel Directory

If, for any reason, you need to change the transmitter's channel directory (where channels and logs are stored), you can do this in one of two ways:

- The transmitter GUI will enable you to define the transmitter's channel directory. On Windows, this is the only way to change the location of that directory.

● On Solaris, you can edit the file /etc/transmitter.conf. That file contains two properties: server.installdir, whose value is the transmitter's installation directory, and server.datadir, whose value is the channel directory. Change the latter property to the new channel directory, save the file, and restart the server to reflect the changes.

Keep in mind that if you change the transmitter's channel directory, you will have to reset the properties for that transmitter, including its password and trusted hosts, and republish the channels that were available on that transmitter.

Quitting the Transmitter

To quit the transmitter, choose the Exit button from the main transmitter window. Note that in Windows, selecting the close box will only hide the transmitter window; as long as the transmitter icon appears in the right side of the task bar, the transmitter is still running.

Advanced Transmitter Configuration

In addition to the standard set of properties you configured as part of the transmitter installation or configuration, there are several other properties that determine how many resources the transmitter will use on your system.

You can access these properties using the transmitter configuration GUI. After paging through the standard properties, the panel for "Transmitter Setup Complete" will appear. From here, choose the button labeled Advanced (see Figure 6.3) to access the advanced properties. Currently there are two advanced panels for transmitter concurrency and transmitter cache.

Figure 6.3. *Advanced properties.*

Transmitter Processes and Threads

The Transmitter Concurrency properties, as shown in Figure 6.4, are used to determine how many processes and threads the transmitter uses, the combination of which determines how many simultaneous connections the transmitter can process.

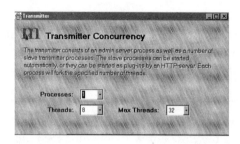

Figure 6.4. *Transmitter concurrency properties.*

The Processes field is the number of processes each transmitter uses on the server. Currently the Castanet Transmitter can have only one process (although you can change the value of this field). Future versions of the transmitter will support multiple processes for better performance.

The Threads and Max Threads fields indicate the number of separate threads per process that will handle incoming connections. The number of threads times the number of processes determines the total number of simultaneous connections that can occur on a transmitter (but, because at the moment you can only have one process, that number is simply equal to the number of threads). Currently, only the value of Max Threads is used. The default value is 32.

Setting the threads to be a larger number will allow the transmitter to handle more connections, but each thread will use some amount of CPU time and memory on the system. Depending on how busy your transmitter is and what else you want to do on that machine, you might want to set this value higher or lower: lower for better performance on the machine itself, higher for better transmitter performance to tuners accessing that machine.

Note

Although changing the number of threads allows your transmitter to process more connections, that value has a cap if you're using a transmitter that only allows in a certain number of users per hour.

Transmitter Memory Cache

On the next panel in the advanced properties is the transmitter memory cache (as shown in Figure 6.5). The memory cache is used to store popular channels in random-access memory, which makes them faster to access by tuners than if they were always read from the disk. The value of this number is megabytes of memory that should be used for the cache.

Figure 6.5. *Transmitter memory cache.*

A higher number for the memory cache means that more channels can be stored in memory, which improves performance for very high-volume transmitters. However, that memory becomes reserved for transmitter use, which means it is not available to other programs running on that server. Depending on the resources you have available for your transmitter and how popular that transmitter is, you may want to set this number higher or lower than the default.

The default value for the memory cache is 4MB.

Setting the Connection Timeout

In any connection between the transmitter and a tuner or a browser, queries and data are exchanged fairly regularly. If, for whatever reason, the tuner or the browser stops responding (due to network lags or system failure), the transmitter will wait for a short time and then free up the thread for another connection. That "short time" is called the *connection timeout*. By default, that value is 120 seconds (two minutes). You can set the connection timeout for your transmitter to wait more or less time, depending on how you want your transmitter to react. (For example, if you're on a not very stable Internet connection, you might want to increase the timeout interval to account for that network stability. If you're on a very busy transmitter, you might want to decrease the timeout to give more tuners a chance to connect.)

To set the connection timeout to something other than 120 seconds, you must add the `server.connection.timeout` property to the transmitter's `properties.txt` file, contained in the transmitter's channel directory. (There isn't a panel for it in the transmitter administration tool.) The value of `server.connection.timeout` is a number representing the number of seconds to wait for the timeout. For example:

```
server.connection.timeout=180
```

This line will set the connection timeout to 180 seconds (three minutes). Remember to restart your transmitter after making any property changes.

Setting the Default HTML Page

In addition to broadcasting channels, transmitters also respond to requests from Web browsers. When you contact a transmitter using a Web browser, either directly from the browser or by using the Browse button from inside the tuner, the transmitter responds with an automatically generated listing of the channels available on that transmitter, including the descriptions of those channels. Figure 6.6 shows a sample page from Marimba's transmitter.

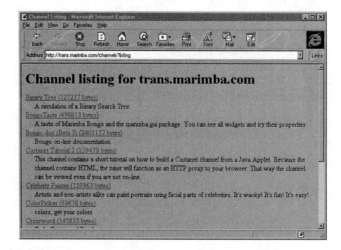

Figure 6.6. *A browser listing of channels.*

If you'd like to customize the page that your transmitter sends back to browsers, you can create your own Web page and then tell the transmitter to send that page to the browser instead. Note that if you do create your own page, that page will not be automatically updated as you add and remove channels from the transmitter (which happens with the automatically generated Web page); you will have to update the HTML page yourself each time there is a change to your transmitter listing.

To change the default HTML page the transmitter sends to a browser, first create that page and store it somewhere on your file system. (The transmitter's channel directory is a good place.) Make sure it has an `.html` or `.htm` extension so it will be recognized by the transmitter as an HTML file.

Then, edit the `properties.txt` file in your transmitter's channel directory and add the property `server.html.listing` to that file with the full pathname to the HTML page, like this:

```
server.html.listing=/usr/local/channels/index.html
```

In this example, my new page is located in `/usr/local/channels` and is called `index.html`.

Don't forget to restart the server to pick up the changes.

A Summary of Transmitter Properties

All the transmitter properties are stored in a file called `properties.txt`, stored in the transmitter's channel directory. You can edit this file by hand, or the transmitter configuration GUI will edit them for you. Note that the transmitter password is encoded and must be set by the GUI.

Table 6.1 shows a list of the available properties you can set in the `properties.txt` file.

Table 6.1. Transmitter properties.

Property	Value
`server.host=hostname`	The fully qualified host name of the transmitter, as defined by DNS.
`server.port=portnum`	The port number on which the transmitter runs, by default port `80`.
`server.password=password`	The password for the transmitter, encoded. You must use the transmitter GUI to change this value.
`server.trustedhosts=host,host,host`	A list of remote hosts that are allowed to publish channels on this transmitter, separated by commas.
`server.threads=number`	The initial number of threads to handle incoming connections. The number of processes times the number of threads determines the total number of simultaneous connections that can occur on the transmitter.

continues

123

Table 6.1. continued

Property	Value
server.maxthreads=*number*	The maximum possible number of threads that can be created on the transmitter. This property is not currently used.
server.processes=*number*	The number of transmitter processes that can handle incoming connections. Currently you can have only one process.
server.memdisk=*number*	The number of megabytes of memory to set aside for the channel cache. A higher number improves transmitter performance.
server.connection.timeout=*number*	The number of seconds to wait before the transmitter times out on a connection. By default the number is 120; a lower number means the transmitter will not wait as long for a response from a tuner.
server.html.listing=*filename*	The absolute path of a page to use for the listing of the channels in a browser. By default, the transmitter generates this page on the fly using the names of the available channels and the channel descriptions. By replacing that default page, you will have to create this information on your own.

Transmitter Logging

Nearly every transaction that occurs with your transmitter—both from the tuner and the publish side—is logged in special files in your transmitter's channel directory. By monitoring these files, you can keep track of how much your transmitter is getting used, what it's being used for, as well as track information for individual channels (if those channels have been defined to set logging information). If you're developing channels, often the logs can help you figure out what's going on and when.

Depending on how often your transmitter is used, you might occasionally want to move these logs elsewhere or delete them altogether to make sure they don't take up too much space on your server. Make sure you restart your transmitter after you do this so the files can be reset.

All the transmitter log files are contained in the folder or directory called logs inside your transmitter's channel directory. There are four kinds of log files that are stored:

- Access logs (in a file called `log`)
- Error logs (in a file called `errorlog`)
- Channel publishing logs (in a file called `publish.log`)
- Logs for individual channels (named for the name of the channel, with a `.log` extension—for example, `MyChannel.log` or `Crossword.log`)

All of these logs are simple text files, with one log entry per line. You can use scripts to process these logs to compile statistics, or simply examine them occasionally with any text editor. The contents of each log are described in the following sections.

Access Log Files

The access log file, called `log`, contains information about basic transmitter actions and requests. The format of the log file is identical to the common log format used by Web servers, so you can use any of the Web server administration tools to compile statistics about your transmitter. More specifically, a log file entry looks something like this (all on one line; I've broken this one up to fit on the page):

```
140.174.94.6 - fz8oy6uhv1xt [16/Dec/1996:18:10:11 -0800]
"POST /Crossword/upd HTTP/1.0" 200 39674 2630 v10 subscribe
```

There are nine parts to this log entry. Those parts are, in order:

- The IP address of the host that made the request.
- A unique tuner identifier. Each individual tuner has its own ID; you can use this to track individual users of a channel that may be connecting from the same host or through a proxy server.
- The date and time of the request.
- The type of operation that occurred, inside brackets. The most important part is between `POST` and `HTTP/1.0`; this contains the name of the channel and the operation (this one is `upd` for an update request). The format will always be `/channelname/ operation`.
- The HTTP result code.
- The number of bytes transferred.
- The number of milliseconds it took from start to finish to transfer the bytes.
- The Castanet protocol version.
- An optional comment, the value of which depends on the command. Updates, for example, have comments of `manual` for manual updates, or `hour`, `minute`, `day`, and so on.

In addition to the standard update-log entries, there are also entries for each listing request (either from a tuner or from a browser) that look like this:

```
140.174.94.6 11/8-00:46:31 HTML index fetched
```

Each time the transmitter starts, you'll also get a log entry to that effect. When compiling statistics on the access logs, you might want to screen out these lines, which look something like this:

```
Transmitter starts: trans.lne.com:5282 Web Dec 25 10:22:26 1996
```

Error Log Files

The error logs are stored in a file called errorlog. The error log contains any errors received by the transmitter, which can include connection timeouts, missing files, or Java stack traces from corrupt channels. Each error includes the IP address of the tuner that caused the error, the date it occurred, and an error message. For example:

```
140.174.94.6 12/25-21:19:45 Connection timed out
```

Publish Log Files

The publish log files keep track of channels that have been published or updated on the transmitter; each time someone uses the publish tool or command to update a channel, it's logged here.

Entries in the publish log file look like this:

```
127.0.0.1 11/23-15:10:19 lemay@despair.lne.com Crossword
```

There are four entries in each line, which represent:

● The IP address of the host using the publish tool. (For example, 127.0.0.1 is localhost, the same system as the transmitter.)
● The date and time.
● The user name and host of the person using the publish tool.
● The name of the channel.

Channel Log Files

The final log files available in the transmitter's channel directory are the log files for individual channels. A channel will keep logs only if it has been written to do so, and the contents of those logs will vary from channel to channel. I won't cover those log files here; you'll learn how to write channels that keep logs in Chapter 12, "Creating Transmitter Plug-Ins."

Improving Transmitter Performance

When you've got a transmitter up and running and people are happily subscribing to your channels, you might discover that your transmitter isn't running quite up to speed—perhaps people are having difficulties connecting, or perhaps updates are slower than they should be. Here are some simple hints for improving the performance of your transmitter:

- Make sure that all the transmitter's files are contained on local disks, as opposed to network-mounted volumes. This includes both the transmitter software itself and the channel directories.

- Increase the threads property for your transmitter, either by using the administration tool (in the advanced properties) or modifying the `server.threads` property in the `properties.txt` file. (You might have to add this property if you're changing it from the default.) More threads means that your transmitter can handle more simultaneous connections.

- Increase the memory cache property using the administration tool or by modifying or adding the `server.memdisk` property to `properties.txt`. This will be particularly useful for very busy transmitters that publish very large channels.

- Consider dedicating a system to the transmitter (as opposed to sharing resources with other Internet services). Add more memory or upgrade the server itself.

- Very large channels that are very frequently updated can severely impact transmitter performance. Consider attempting to make the channel smaller or reducing the update frequency.

- Make sure you're not hitting transmitter limits. The standard transmitter is restricted to 100 unique users (tuners) per hour. (Those users can make as many connections as they want, but only 100 per hour can access the transmitter.) You can add another 100 users per hour by purchasing extra licenses from Marimba or by upgrading to an unlimited transmitter.

In addition to these suggestions, there might be additional Marimba products that can help with very high-load transmitters. In particular, the Castanet Repeater, which was described in Chapter 1, "Castanet Tuner," can distribute the load on a transmitter to multiple mirrors while still providing a single interface for tuners. If most of your transmitter load is coming from a few sites, you can install a Castanet Proxy server to help take some of the load off your transmitter's system, assuming, of course, that you have control over the site where most of the connections are coming from. Otherwise, you'll have to encourage the administrators of that site to install a Castanet Proxy for you.

And, finally, future versions of the transmitter will be available as native executables (the current version is a Java application) or as Web server plug-ins (NSAPI for the Netscape servers and ISAPI for Microsoft's Internet Information Server). These transmitter versions will improve overall transmitter performance as well.

Summary

Running a transmitter involves more than just installing the software and publishing channels. Fortunately, it doesn't involve a whole lot more than that. Other than the occasional tweak to the properties or a check of the logs to make sure not too much is going wrong, there's little you'll need to do to coax a transmitter into running effectively.

Despite that statement, however, in this chapter you learned the few things you will need to know about transmitter administration, whether you're both the channel developer and the administrator or if you just keep the transmitter going so others can use it. Starting and stopping the transmitter, modifying its properties, and understanding the entries in the log files—all of these things can help you manage a transmitter more effectively and help to run smoothly.

This chapter brings to a close Part II and the end of the basic description of how to use the Castanet framework software. In Part III, we'll get into the good stuff—learning how to develop and maintain your own channels.

Developing Channels

seven

How Channels Work

Up until this part of the book, I've been presenting the Castanet technology primarily from the point of view of someone using the tuner or someone responsible for setting up and administering the transmitter. From this point on, we'll be looking at the Castanet technology from the other side of the process, from the point of view of the channel builder or developer. If you're interested in creating your own channels, to publish them on a Castanet Transmitter and have them subscribed to and downloaded via a Castanet Tuner, from this point on you'll get all the information to do just that.

This chapter starts with an overview of how channels work. In this chapter you'll learn more about the process of creating, publishing, and updating a channel, as well as information about the kinds of features you can implement in channels.

Note

> If you've skipped through the first two parts of this book to this section, make sure you have at least a passing understanding of the various pieces of software in the Castanet suite, particularly the tuner and the transmitter.

Channel Distribution: From Developer to Transmitter to Tuner

You've already seen the tools that make up the core of the Castanet technology. You use Castanet Publish to publish a channel on a transmitter. The Castanet Transmitter makes that channel available on a network. And the Castanet Tuner allows users to subscribe to channels on transmitters and to manage updates to those channels. But what's actually going on here?

Castanet automatically "mirrors" the data contained in a channel—be it executable Java classes or text files or HTML—from the developer's original location to the transmitter to each individual tuner's local disk. Each time, then, that the developer makes a change, Castanet keeps track of that change and uses that information to update the data on a client tuner's system (as shown in Figure 7.1). This section explains how it all works.

Developer to Transmitter

As a channel developer or producer, you store your channel data somewhere on your local disk, in its own directory. Inside the channel directory are the files specific to that channel, such as Java class files, images or other media and data.

Note

> For much of this section I'll call the person who creates a channel the *channel developer*. Although the term developer often refers to a programmer, it can also refer to someone creating a Web site or designing a presentation—tasks that don't necessarily involve much programming. To simplify things, however, we'll just call anyone who produces a channel a channel developer.

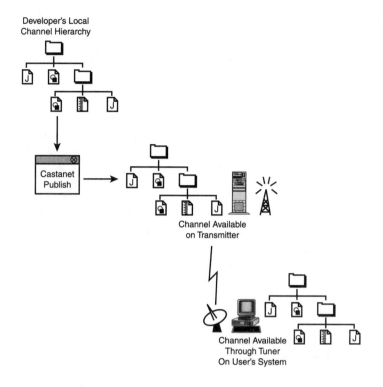

Figure 7.1. *Developer to transmitter to tuner to user.*

When your channel is ready to be published on a transmitter, you run Castanet Publish, set a few basic properties, and publish the channel. The publish tool not only puts the files on the transmitter but also keeps track of the makeup and contents of the channel itself. Part of the publishing process involves calculating checksums for each of the files in the channel and for the channel itself.

Note

A *checksum* is a numeric value that represents the file. Each time you change the file, the checksum changes as well. The checksum provides a fast and simple way to figure out if a file has changed.

With all the checksums calculated, the transmitter stores the channel files in its channel directory, and that channel is ready to be subscribed to by a tuner. Note that the version of your channel in the transmitter's channel directory is not a simple copy of your channel directory; the transmitter stores the files in a special format in its channel directory in order to optimize changes and share identical files between channels. This is one of the reasons why you have to use the publish tool to publish a channel; if you simply copied your files into the transmitter channel directory, the transmitter would not know what to do with them.

To update a channel, you simply make the changes you want to make—to the channel files, to the properties, or to the parameters—and then run Castanet Publish again. This time, the publish tool keeps track of the differences between the first version and the next version so that when a tuner requests an update, the transmitter will sent back only the changes to that channel and not a whole new copy.

Note that as a channel developer you don't have to keep track of the specific changes you've made to your channel. You don't have to create patches or different files or build an updater program. Castanet Publish handles all of that for you. All you need to do is keep working and update each time you have a change that's significant enough to make it available to your users.

So, for example, let's say you've created a Crossword-of-the-day channel, which lets your users play a game of crossword. (There actually is a crossword channel available at `trans.marimba.com`.) You might create the code for that channel and its data file, which contains the hints and the layout for the crossword, and publish that channel to a transmitter. Then, every day, you would change the data file to provide a new crossword and republish the channel. Castanet Publish will move only that data file to the transmitter (since it's the only file that changed), and when a tuner requests and updates, that data file will be the only data that gets sent to the tuner.

Transmitter to Tuner

If you're a channel user, you see the process from the other side: The tuner "mirrors" files contained on the transmitter onto the local disk, and manages updates to those channels.

The first time you download a channel with the tuner, the tuner downloads and installs the channel from the appropriate transmitter in its entirety—with one exception. Files and libraries are shared between channels, and identical files are downloaded only once. So, for example, let's say there's a special Java class library for handling secure network connections called `SSL.zip`. The first time the tuner downloads a channel that requires that library, `SSL.zip` is downloaded and installed with that channel. Then, if there's a second channel that also uses that same library, the tuner checks to make sure it is precisely the same file (using the file's checksum, which the transmitter sends with each file), and the second channel simply uses the first channel's version rather than re-downloading the same library all over again.

As with the storage of channel files on the transmitter, the tuner stores the channel files on your local disk in its special optimized format, to keep track of which files need changing and which files can be shared.

For each update, the tuner contacts the transmitter, and the two negotiate which files the tuner needs to download. The update process starts with what's called an optimized update; the tuner sends a checksum of the entire channel to the transmitter, and if it matches with the checksum the transmitter has, there isn't an update to be made, and the process is done.

Because the channel checksum is small, the tuner and the transmitter can figure this out with barely a dent in the network bandwidth.

If the two channel checksums are different, the tuner and transmitter have to compare each file to see which files the tuner needs to bring the channel up-to-date. This negotiation process means that only the files that have actually changed are downloaded, and even then, often only the actual differences between the two versions of the files are downloaded.

Note

> Keep in mind that for each update, the tuner polls the transmitter for new information. Unlike Internet broadcasting technologies, Castanet is not technically a "push" mechanism. It's more of a repetitive pull. And, because the frequency of updates can be configured on the tuner side, there isn't the problem of too much unwanted data being sent over a network the way there is with Internet broadcasting.

So, for example, let's look at that Crossword channel again. The first time the tuner downloads the Crossword channel, it receives all the files for that channel—all its code plus the current data for the day's game. When it's time for an update, usually the only file that has changed is the data file—and the tuner and transmitter can quickly figure that out by comparing their checksums. Only the data file is sent to the tuner. All the other files are the same, so the tuner doesn't need to download another copy of those files.

With both initial subscriptions and updates, a channel's data is downloaded in one single transaction, with only one network connection, regardless of the number of files in the subscription or the update. This is a significant advantage over the traditional applet model, where each file is downloaded in a separate network connection. Each connection takes a few seconds to start up, and for applets with a large number of files, that can mean significant overhead just for the connections. Channels do not have that overhead.

File negotiation, downloading only the differences in files, and the use of a single network connection minimize the amount of information and the time it takes to successfully update a channel.

Live Updates

Updates can be made at any time, regardless of whether or not the channel is currently running on the user's system. If the channel is indeed running, new data received via the update can be incorporated into the channel on-the-fly. It's up to you, the developer, to decide how to manage an update to a channel. For running channels, for example, you could do the following:

- Incorporate the data quietly into the channel without the user noticing.
- Stop and reload the channel to take advantage of the update.
- Alert the user that an update has occurred and give the user a choice of what she wants to do with it.
- Update the channel on-the-fly to reflect the new data.

If the channel isn't running, the channel developer can choose to start the channel running when new data appears, or otherwise alert the user to the new update (or, of course, just ignore it until the next time the channel starts up). You have a wide range of options as a channel developer for how you want to handle live updates to a channel. You'll learn all about managing live updates to channels in Chapter 11, "Managing Updates and User Information."

Channel Security

The issues behind channel security are similar to that of applet security: If you can instantly download and run programs (applets or channels) from random sites all over the Internet, how can you be certain that those programs will not do malicious things to your system or somehow compromise the security of that system?

The short answer is that you can't be certain. But the system can make it more difficult for the most obvious attacks or compromises to take place.

Castanet uses and builds on Java's applet security model, which has been used by Web browsers all over the world without major incident. This means that Castanet channels are restricted in their behavior in several ways:

- They cannot run programs or libraries on the local system, unless those libraries (DLLs) have been pre-installed by hand in a special tuner directory.
- They can only make network connections to the transmitter where the channel came from.
- They cannot read, write, or delete files on the local system except inside one specific directory for that purpose.

Note

Different browsers might implement different portions of this security model or allow parts of it, but those are the basic rules for how the applet basic security model works.

There are two specific cases where channels differ from applets: the capability to use local libraries and the capability to write files to the local disk.

In the former case, channels can use a local library only if that library has been installed into a special directory on the local system, and the user takes all responsibility for the security and trustworthiness of those local libraries. This mechanism is called tuner extensions, and is described in Appendix C.

The second difference is the ability to save state. Applets cannot read or write to the local system whatsoever. Whereas this is a valuable assumption to make for security reasons (because it prevents an applet from discovering private information or from maliciously changing or deleting files on the user's system), it is also very restrictive for the kinds of features you can include with an applet. Applets, for example, cannot save state on the local system, nor can they save any files that the user may have created inside that applet. The only way to save state inside an applet is to log the information back to the Web server, which uses space and resources on the server. This is not an optimal solution.

With channels, state can be saved and restored to and from the channel's data directory on the client, but only to and from this directory. This allows the channel to save necessary files and information while preventing it from doing damage to other parts of the file system. You'll learn about saving state in channels in Chapter 11.

With permission, channels can also read files from a CD-ROM contained on the local system. So, for example, you could publish a multimedia channel that makes extensive use of really large image files stored on a CD-ROM to prevent having to download those files over the network. To read files from a CD-ROM, the user will have to configure that option in his or her tuner.

Note

The restriction on applets to be able to write to the local file system is one that has been imposed by Web browsers. Both Netscape and Microsoft are planning to ease that restriction in future versions of their browsers (which might be out by the time you read this), allowing the user to decide how much access an applet will have to the client's system—including potentially allowing it to write to the user's hard drive. Despite this easing of restrictions, however, applets may or may not be allowed more freedom depending on how the browser is set up. Channels will always have a data directory, and you can rely on the existence of that directory in the channels you create.

Because executable channels are written in Java, they also inherit Java's built-in security and safety. For example, the lack of explicit pointers in Java means fewer bugs or exploitable security holes in a channel. And, given Java's model for security and consistency checking, it's difficult if not impossible for a malicious individual to try to work around the restrictions in the Java environment.

Future versions of Castanet will include even more sophisticated mechanisms for channel security and access control, including the ability to create password-protected channels (you must have the password to be able to use the channel, not just to publish it), channels that can run over secure network connections, channels that are digitally signed (providing a guarantee that they come from a specific vendor and have not been modified), as well as billing mechanisms for channels and for updates. These mechanisms will also allow channels to be written in other languages, and for Castanet to become a mechanism for the delivery of any kind of software or data, not just Java and HTML-based software and data.

Transmitter Plug-Ins and Channel Feedback

The transfer of a channel's information works, for the most part, in one direction: A channel migrates from the developer through the transmitter and the tuner to the user's system. This does not mean, however, that channel developers can never get data back from the people using their channels. There's a feature of the Castanet technology called the transmitter plug-in, which lets channel developers get data back from their users and handle that data in a variety of ways.

A transmitter plug-in is a bit of software that is part of your channel: You include it in your channel directory, and it gets published to the transmitter just as the normal channel data does each time you run Castanet Publish. Unlike the regular channel, however, the plug-in is not part of the data that is sent to the tuner; instead, it remains on the transmitter and runs when a tuner makes a request for new data from a transmitter.

Note

The term *plug-in* might be confusing if you're used to associating the term with Netscape or Photoshop. Transmitter plug-ins are not installed into a special directory in your transmitter, nor do they simply extend the features of that transmitter. They behave more like filters for channel data. Read on for more information.

Transmitter plug-ins are useful for two purposes: channel logging and channel customization.

Logging

Channel logging is the ability to store information about what the user is doing with the channel and then receive and process that data when the tuner requests an update from a channel. The channel itself can be designed to store data about what the user is up to—sites they might have visited as part of a channel, scores they made on a game, or any other information that the channel might be interested in. Then, when the user makes an update, the transmitter plug-in is run and that logging information can be read and processed by the plug-in. You can do anything with that information that you want; simply write it to a logging file to be processed at some other time, generate statistics on that data, or perhaps update a global list of high scores, which is then downloaded as part of the channel's update.

Note

> You can log data from inside your channel even if you don't use a plug-in. If there's no plug-in to handle log entries, that data is written to the channel log files stored in the transmitter's channel directory.

In many applets, this process is managed by running a program on the Web server where the applet comes from, and then making a network connection from the applet back to that server. Data can then be sent as often as the applet needs to send it. Whereas the transmitter plug-in form of logging accomplishes a similar process, it has several advantages:

● There is no live network connection to hog resources between the tuner and the transmitter. The connection is made to the transmitter as part of a regular update, stored data is uploaded to the plug-in, and the connection is closed.

● Because the transmitter plug-in doesn't require a live connection at all times, this allows channels to be run without a network connection while still collecting and storing information that might be interesting to the channel developer.

● Unlike with applets, the tuner managing a channel can be uniquely identified across updates and sessions. Although personal user information such as a name or an e-mail address isn't available, each tuner has a unique identifier that can be used to track that tuner's behavior across sessions. This is a significant advantage over the Web model where user tracking is extremely difficult.

Channel Customization

Whereas with channel logging the result is to simply keep track of data, channel customization determines which files are sent to the tuner as part of the update, often based on the information the tuner sent in the first place.

For example, the channel could store a set of user preferences as part of the channel's state, in which one of those preferences is language (English, French, German, and so on). The preferences are sent to the transmitter plug-in as part of an update, and the plug-in can process the preferences for the language and then send user interface elements back to the tuner in that appropriate language. Or, for example, in a multilevel game, the channel can keep track of a user's progress through the game and only update the channel to the next level when the user has reached a certain point in the game. With plug-ins this can happen quickly and automatically, to reduce the amount of data sent over the Net at any one time or to provide a custom experience for the user.

You can also use features of channel customizations to dynamically generate files with every update—for example, to extract data from a database and send that data to the tuner automatically.

You'll learn more about transmitter plug-ins in Chapter 12, "Creating Transmitter Plug-Ins."

Types of Channels

As a channel developer, you have several different choices of the channels you can currently create, depending on your situation and how many resources you have to devote to the task. Each different kind of channel provides different features for the user and different capabilities for the developer. You'll learn how to create each of these channels in the chapters further along in this book; this section summarizes the types of channels, their features, and the advantages of using them.

The four kinds of channels you can currently create in Castanet are

- HTML channels
- Applet channels, written in Java
- Presentation channels, written in Castanet's Bongo
- Application channels, written in Java

Note

In the current release of Castanet, you can create executable channels (programs) using the Java language only. Using Java guarantees security and safety for the code that a tuner downloads, as well as providing all the cross-platform features of Java (that is, the ability for a single Java-based channel to run equally well on multiple systems). Future versions of Castanet will allow channels written in other languages and compiled for specific platforms.

HTML Channels

One of the simplest forms of channels you can create for Castanet is the HTML channel, which consists of the usual files you'd find on a Web site: HTML pages, images, media, Java applets. Nearly anything you put on a Web site can be included in an HTML channel.

HTML channels are subscribed to using the tuner in the same way that you subscribe to a regular channel. When you launch an HTML channel, the tuner acts as a proxy between a Web browser and the HTML content. (You'll have to specially configure your browser to work with the HTML channel. Chapter 3, "Using the Tuner," described all this in detail.)

Why bother with an HTML channel? Isn't a Web site just fine the way it is? In many cases, yes, the Web site model works just fine. But publishing a Web site as a channel as well offers several advantages:

- As a channel, a Web site becomes persistent on the reader's disk and is downloaded in the background. This means that each time you visit the Web site, you don't have to wait for each page and image to download. And, because HTML channels update the same way regular channels do—incrementally, in the background—you still get the newest version of the channel each time you visit it.

- You don't need a live Internet connection all the time to browse the Web site. You could, for example, subscribe to a Web site as a channel from a laptop and then take the laptop on a long plane trip. Because the Web site is a channel, you'd still have access to the information on that Web site without needing to be connected to the Web all the time.

Also keep in mind that you can publish the content of an HTML channel both as a regular Web site and as a channel simultaneously, and neither one will interfere with the other. Your readers can browse the site either as a channel or as a regular Web site as they so choose. Set up the publish tool to update the channel side on a regular basis, and you don't even have to worry about it on the development side. You can concentrate on developing and updating the Web site as usual and let the publish tool take care of the rest.

You'll learn how to convert a Web site into an HTML channel in the next chapter, "Building Simple Channels."

Applet Channels

The second-easiest channel to create is an applet channel. Applets are Java programs written specifically to run inside a Web page on a Java-enabled browser. Converting an applet into a channel requires only a few simple steps, and most applets will run as easily as channels as they do embedded in Web pages without any modifications to the Java code.

Applet channels, when run as channels, run in their own windows on the desktop, rather than being constrained inside a Web page and a browser. Other than that, however, they have the same restrictions and limitations as applets inside Web pages do. Applet channels are most useful for porting existing Java code to a Castanet channel quickly and easily.

Because channels can publish applets nearly as-is, you could create a single applet and use the same class both as a channel and as an element of a Web page. Readers visiting the Web page your applet is on would download and run the applet in the usual way; users of Castanet would subscribe to the applet as if it were a channel. If you change the applet, readers of the Web page would get the changes the next time they visit that page; subscribers to the applet channel would get the changes as an update through the tuner.

Applet channels can also be modified to take advantage of tuner functionality and to include advanced channel features such as the capability to save state on the local system, or to log channel data to a transmitter plug-in. However, applets modified in this way usually cannot run outside of the channel mechanism because of their reliance on channel features.

You'll learn more about converting applets into channels in the next chapter.

Presentation Channels

A *presentation* is a special term that refers to user interfaces and simple applications built using Marimba's Bongo program. You can use Bongo to build the user interface or the look of an application or a channel, much in the same way you would use an interface builder for other languages or environments: by creating and arranging various user-interface widgets on a screen using mouse clicks and drags as opposed to writing laborious amounts of user-interface code by hand. Bongo provides a simple interface for creating user interfaces that requires no programming; you can also add actions and interactivity using Bongo's Java-based scripting language.

Presentations created by Bongo can be used as channels. A very simple presentation channel, for example, might have a message of the day or display news headlines. Updates to the channel would be the message or the headline to be displayed.

You can also use presentations as the basis for building full-fledged Java applications. Use Bongo to create the interface, and then add functionality either through Bongo's built-in scripting or just use the presentation file as the front-end for a complete Java application. Bongo's ease of use both in assembling and managing a user interface can make it an excellent alternative to using Java's own AWT.

You'll learn more about creating presentations with Bongo in Chapter 9, "Creating Presentations and Channels with Bongo." For a more complete description of Bongo, you'll want to pick up *Official Marimba Guide to Bongo*, also published by Sams.net.

Application Channels

At the high end of channel development is the application channel. Application channels require the most amount of Java programming in comparison to other channels, but they can also take full advantage of all Castanet's features, including dynamic updates to both active and inactive channels and the ability to save state on the user's local system. Application channels can also use transmitter plug-ins, for the ability to receive data back from a user's system and to customize a channel based on that data.

Applications are essentially regular Java programs. They can be written entirely with standard Sun JDK classes, or they can use presentations created with Bongo as their user interface (or both). What makes an application channel a channel is code to implement the channel interfaces and to react to channel events. You can add this code to existing Java programs (or to applets, for that matter), or you can create a channel entirely from scratch.

Note that application channels are not automatically converted Java applications, as are applet channels. There is no magic wrapper that will allow a regular Java application to run as an application channel. If you want to convert a regular Java application into a channel, you have to add code to implement channel behavior. Also, keep in mind that channels have a similar security model to applets, which means that there are more restrictions on what an application channel can do than there are on regular Java applications.

You'll learn more about creating application channels in Chapter 10, "Creating Application Channels."

Channel Ideas

Even with a basic understanding of how a technology works, sometimes it is difficult to figure out what it's good for—that is, the practical applications you can create with that technology. Here, then, are some ideas for the sorts of things you could create with channels and with the Castanet technology:

- Conventional applications, from browsers to spreadsheets to games. Not a very interesting use of the technology but, nonetheless, very valuable for both the developer and the user because of the lack of an install process and the automatic upgrades. Conventional applications delivered as channels can be distributed faster and in smaller increments, allowing bug fixes and new features to be released and deployed faster. On the user side, channels allow you to avoid the need to keep installing upgrades or to wonder whether the version you have is the latest version.

- News, sports scores, or stock channels. Because channels can be updated at regular intervals, applications that rely on frequently updated data can work exceptionally well as channels. A headlines channel could display current headlines. Stock channels could display running graphs of current stock prices, and sports-score channels would update as the game progresses. And, because of transmitter plug-ins that allow channel feedback, the data that is displayed on the channel can be personalized to reduce download time and to provide a much more interesting application for the user.

- Thing of the Day channels. Similar to the news channels, a Thing of the Day channel could provide a new version of an application every day—for example, a Dilbert Cartoon of the Day or a Crossword of the Day. Thing of the Day channels provide a new experience for as long as you have the inclination to keep updating the data.

● "Disconnected" database clients. Because a channel can store data and send it back to the transmitter as part of an update, channels can be created for client/server applications that would normally require a live connection back to a server. For example, take an order-entry system for, say, furniture. Given a traditional client/server order-entry system, the salesperson would enter the values into a form and then transmit the order to a database via a live network connection. Using the channel version, the salesperson could accumulate multiple forms and then transmit them all as part of an update. This could be useful for field sales where the order-entry system is part of a laptop. Update the channel before leaving on the sales call with the latest form interface and price list (sort of like charging your hard drive, the same way you charge the batteries on the laptop), enter in the orders on the sales call, and then transmit the final orders when the salesperson is back in the office and has a network connection again.

● Media-heavy applications or games. Currently, many games and multimedia presentations on the Web are hampered by the large size of the media. Because channels can incrementally download pieces of data based on user preferences or state, a game or multimedia presentation could be distributed in parts. When you're finished with one level or section in the game, an update would download the next section. And, because the fields are stored on the user's system in-between downloads, you could set the game to update overnight or during an idle period and have it all ready to play when it's time.

● Computer-based training. In a similar scenario to that of the incremental games, a computer-based training course could start out at the first section with the initial subscription, and only allow users to continue to the next section (that is, to retrieve the next update) if they have completed the first section. Because each section is incrementally downloaded, only the sections that users have progressed to are stored on the users' systems, rather than the entire training application.

Summary

In this chapter you got your first peek under the hood of how Castanet and channels work together, and you got a basic overview of the sorts of capabilities available to you as a channel developer. Depending on your background and how technical you want to get, you can create very simple channels that change very little from update to update—or go whole hog and develop very sophisticated channels that rely on frequently changing data, live updates, and feedback data to customize the version of a channel the user sees. From this point on, we'll be working with actual channels and you'll get a feel for the different kinds of channels and capabilities Castanet offers you.

eight

Building Simple Channels

With the overview out of the way, let's get down to the specifics: how, exactly, you construct and publish your own channels. In this chapter, you'll learn about the channel publishing process, from creating the channel on your system to publishing it to testing the result in a tuner. And, as part of that process, you'll create two kinds of simple channels: HTML channels and applet channels.

Creating and Publishing Channels: The Basics

Let's start with a quick review of the basic things you should know to create and publish Castanet channels. They are the things that all channels have in common, and the procedures you'll need to follow when you create any channel, be it a simple HTML channel, an applet channel, or a sophisticated Java channel that can handle live updates and send data back to the transmitter.

The Channel Directory

Each channel you create should have its own directory on your local development system, which I'll call the *channel directory* from now on. That directory can contain all the parts of a channel, complete or not, including class files, HTML files, core files, revision-control directories, or anything else you need for that channel. Don't worry about keeping track of which files are for the finished channel and which are just for development; you'll decide which files are important when you actually publish the channel. Just make sure that each channel has its own directory, and you'll be fine.

In addition to the files you create in that directory, the following files and directories are created by the Castanet publish tool after you publish the file for the first time:

- `properties.txt`, a file that contains the properties of the channel; it is used by Castanet Publish.
- `parameters.txt`, a file used to contain applet parameters (if needed).
- `channel.dir`, a directory for the channel file database and the transmitter properties files.

Castanet Publish uses each of these files to keep track of the channel itself (you could think of them as containing channel meta-information). You'll learn more about these files as you work through the chapter.

Using Castanet Publish

When you're ready to publish a channel, you use Castanet Publish to move the files to the transmitter (even if the transmitter is on the same machine as your local development directory). Because the transmitter keeps track of which files have changed and organizes the files in a special way, you must use Castanet Publish to publish the channel; you cannot simply copy it to the right place and hope it will work.

Castanet Publish is part of the Castanet Transmitter installation. You should have installed the transmitter on your local system so that you have access to the publish tool. Note that if you don't intend to run a transmitter on your local system, you don't actually have to start or run the transmitter itself.

Note

Chapter 5, "Installing and Broadcasting Channels," describes the Castanet Publish tool in detail. Although I provide a quick overview of its use in this section, you might want to refer to that chapter for more detailed information.

You can use Castanet Publish in two ways: as a graphical application, which allows you to step through the process of creating and publishing a channel, or as a command-line application, which allows you to automate the process after the initial properties of a channel have been set up. You can use either method for publishing your channel, although the command-line version of the Publish tool does require that you already have set up the channel properties. You might want to run the graphical version of the Publish tool at least once to create those properties; doing so is easier than creating them by hand.

You start the graphical version of Castanet Publish using the Start menu in Windows (Castanet Publish is located in the Castanet Transmitter group under Programs) or by using the `publish` command in `castanet/transmitter/bin`. The initial screen then appears; choose Channels to move to the main screen. (See Figure 8.1.)

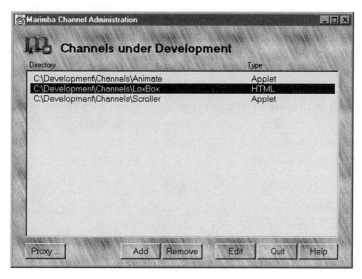

Figure 8.1. *The Main Castanet Publish window.*

This screen shows (or will show) all the channels you're developing on your local system. To publish a channel, you need to add your channel directory to that list. Use the Add button to add your channel directory, indicating its full pathname in the Directory field. (See Figure 8.2.)

If your channel is new, you'll most likely want to use the Create button to convert your development directory into a channel directory. Use Add only if this channel has been published before, perhaps under a different name.

147

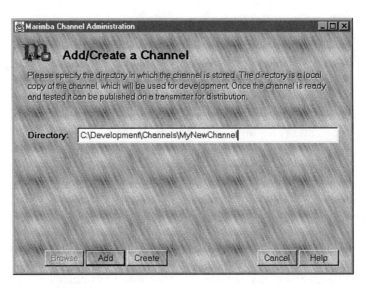

Figure 8.2. *Add a new channel directory.*

Note

Yes, this process is confusing. You would think that you'd use the Create button to actually create a directory that doesn't already exist, but in actuality you also use it to convert an existing directory into an actual channel directory. If you try to use the Add button to add a directory for a channel that has never been published before, you get a `This is not a channel Directory` error. Use Create instead.

Channel Properties

When you first set up a channel to be published by the Castanet Publish tool, you also need to set its properties. After the first time, if you need to change the channel properties, you can either change them inside the graphical version of the Publish tool or edit the `properties.txt` file.

Note

In reality, you don't even need to run the graphical version of the Publish tool the first time, either. You can create the `properties.txt` file by hand, or you can copy it from some other directory and modify it to fit the current channel. I find it easier to set properties with the Publish tool, so that's how I describe it here.

To edit a channel's properties, all you have to do is double-click the name of the channel in the main Castanet Publish screen. The channel properties screen then appears.

Each channel has seven different properties panels: Transmitter, General, Update, Icons, Contacts, Description, and Parameters. I described each of these properties and their values in detail in Chapter 5, so I won't repeat that information here. Here's a quick summary:

● Transmitter properties refer to the transmitter on which this channel will be published, which can be on the local system (localhost) or on a remote system on your network. They indicate which files or directories in your channel directory are development only and should not be part of the final channel—for example, source files or testing files.

● General properties indicate what kind of channel you're using, where your choices are one of the four channel types you learned about in the preceding chapter (HTML, applet, application, and presentation). You'll learn about each of these values as you learn how to create these channels.

● Update properties indicate how often the channel will be updated by the tuner and what to do when the update occurs. These values work in conjunction with the channel itself. You'll learn more about them as you create different kinds of channels.

● Icon properties customize the appearance of the channel both in the tuner and on the desktop. Use these properties to indicate image files in GIF format for the different icons.

● Contacts are names and/or e-mail addresses for the developer or administrator for a channel.

● The Description panel contains the description of the channel as it will appear in the tuner. It also contains copyright information about that channel.

● Parameters are for applet channels and are the same as the parameters you would use in an HTML file for that applet. You can find more information about these parameters in the section "Converting Applets to Channels."

After you choose Apply or Done in any of the properties panels, the channel properties are saved to the channel directory. Most of the properties are stored in the properties.txt file in the main channel directory, with the exception of the transmitter properties, which are stored in the properties.txt file inside the channel.dir directory, and the parameters properties, which are stored in the file parameters.txt.

Publishing and Testing the Channel

With the channel developed in its own channel directory and properties of the channel set, the final step is to actually publish the channel. To do so, you simply click the Publish button inside the graphical Publish tool (you can find it on the properties panels), or you can use the command-line version of the Publish tool. If the publishing process is successful, you can then use a Castanet Tuner to view that channel in a transmitter listing, or you can subscribe to and test that channel to make sure that it's working properly.

In many cases, you might not want to actually publicly publish a channel the first time you publish it, particularly if you're not used to working with channels yet. In this case, publishing a not-quite-finished channel to a publicly accessible transmitter isn't the best of ideas. You can get around this problem in two ways.

The first solution is to publish the channel to a transmitter as a "hidden" channel. Hidden channels are available on a transmitter for testing (use Add Channel from the tuner with the actual name of the channel to subscribe to and test it), but they do not show up in the tuner listing for that transmitter. They therefore are effectively inaccessible to the public unless the public knows the name of that channel. To publish a hidden channel, use the Hide check box in the Description property panel. (See Figure 8.3.) You can "unhide" the channel by deselecting that check box the next time you publish the channel.

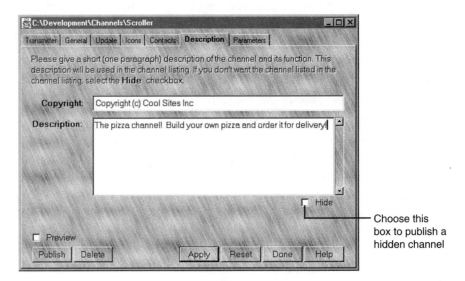

Figure 8.3. *Hiding channels.*

Another solution to the testing problem is to actually install and use two transmitters. The first transmitter is a private transmitter, perhaps installed on your development system itself or on another system available to your internal network (if you have one). This private transmitter acts as a "staging area" for your channels. You can publish your channels to this transmitter and then subscribe to them and test them as long as you like to verify that everything is working correctly. The transmitter that comes on the CD-ROM for this book is good for this purpose, because it is limited to five users an hour.

The second transmitter is the public transmitter, the one that is accessible to other tuners anywhere on the Net. After you've tested your channel and it's ready to be viewed by the outside world, you can modify your channel properties and publish the final version of the channel to the external transmitter. You'll want to purchase and license a real transmitter from Marimba for your public channels so that a reasonable number of users can access them (100 unique users per hour for the basic transmitter).

This mechanism of a staging area for new or untested channels and an external transmitter for finished channels also works for updates. If you're not sure an update will work, or if you want to test the effect of a change, you can publish the updates to the staging area and push the changes outside to the rest of the world only when you're done. And, of course, you're not limited to only one staging area; you could have multiple staging transmitters for local testing, beta testing, and final public versions. This process is similar to how many professional software projects and Web sites are developed; you can use this system for channels as well.

Creating HTML Channels

To take full advantage of the Castanet technology, most Castanet channels are best created as executable programs—as Java applets or applications, or presentations created with Bongo (or some combination of all three). As you learned in the preceding chapter, however, you can also create HTML Web sites that take advantage of many of the features of the Castanet channel technology. For example, HTML channels have these advantages over regular Web sites:

- HTML channels can be downloaded in their entirety, during the system's idle time or overnight, as opposed to a page at a time as with a browser.
- HTML channels are stored permanently on the user's hard drive, so the channel can be read at any time, with or without a live network connection.
- Changes to any of the pages in an HTML channel are downloaded as part of an update and seamlessly integrated into the channel; you don't need to re-download every page each time something has changed.

In this section, you'll learn how to put together an HTML channel: how to create the content, how to publish the channel on a transmitter, and how to test the result.

Create the Web Content

The first step, with an HTML channel or with any channel, is to create a channel directory for that channel and to put the actual content of the channel into that directory.

For an HTML channel, the channel directory you use is the topmost directory for your Web site—for example, the root of all your HTML files or your `public_html` directory if your Web site is stored in your home directory on a UNIX server. You can, in fact, develop your Web site somewhere else and then move it to a channel directory, or you can do all your development in that directory itself. Your channel directory can also double as your final Web directory; Castanet and Web servers are compatible with each other (neither mucks with the other's files), so you don't need to create separate directory structures if doing all your work in one is easier.

You'll find little difference between developing a Web site for use with a Web server and developing one for use as a channel. You can use almost any HTML content (text, images, embedded multimedia, forms, JavaScript, Java applets, and so on) to link between pages or to other URLs on the Web just fine without worrying about the differences between Web and channel distribution.

Note

> Because so few differences exist between developing a Web site for use as a channel and developing a Web site for use with a Web server, I'm going to say very little about HTML or Web design here. If you're interested in looking at developing HTML channels in more detail but don't know a lot about creating Web pages, do pick up a book for that purpose—for example, *Teach Yourself Web Publishing with HTML 3.2 in a Week*, which I also wrote.

You also should watch out for a few differences. The biggest difference between an HTML channel and a normal Web site is that you cannot include CGI programs as part of that channel. CGI programs or scripts, by their very nature, run on a Web server. They cannot be downloaded and run as part of a channel; unlike executable Java programs, they are not designed to run on different systems, and might not even be secure.

The simplest way around this difference is just to make sure that your CGI programs are not part of your HTML channel; that is, make sure that you store your CGI programs outside the channel directory itself. This way, only the HTML files are part of the channel, and they can be downloaded and viewed as a channel. A reader using a browser to browse an HTML channel can access all the HTML content from a local disk as part of the channel, but CGI programs are sent back to the server for execution.

The second gotcha to be careful of when you're developing Web sites for channels is with automatically generated pages such as those created from databases or those that use server-side includes. As with CGI programs, both of these kinds of pages require processing on the server, so they do not work as channels. Only files that are actually stored as files on the Web server can be used in an HTML channel.

The final "gotcha" to mention is not to get too carried away. Unlike normal Web sites, which are downloaded page by page, channels are downloaded in their entirety the first time. If your Web site is especially large and you publish it all as a channel, your readers might balk when confronted with an exceptionally large channel download and not download your channel at all. It's usually a better idea to publish only a small portion of your Web site as a channel instead of the whole thing.

An Example: Lox-in-a-Box

Here's a simple example of an HTML channel (or rather, a small set of pages that you can use as an HTML channel).

The Lox-in-a-Box Web site is for a maker of smoked salmon (lox). The Web site for Lox-in-a-Box contains several pages with information about the Lox-in-a-Box company, its price lists, and a method for ordering lox over the Web (should you be inclined to do so).

Although the actual Lox-in-a-Box Web site might be quite extensive, for the purposes of this example, you can strip it down to the bare minimum files. For this example, the Lox-In-A-Box Web site contains only three files:

● An HTML home page, called index.html, which contains text, a couple images, and a Java applet (for a decorative scrolling marquee). You can see this page in Figure 8.4. Despite the fact that Java applets can be run as channels, in this case the Java applet is a simple media file run as part of the Web page just like it would run outside a channel. Castanet does nothing new to Java applets contained in HTML channels.

● An HTML price list, called prices.html, which contains different prices for different products that Lox-in-A-Box produces. Because the prices on this list may vary as the season progresses, this file will most likely change more frequently than any of the other files on the site.

● An order form, called order.html, which contains a form for ordering Lox-in-a-Box products. Submitting the form calls a CGI script to process the form's input. Note that the CGI script in question is not part of this HTML directory or channel; it's stored elsewhere on the server.

Figure 8.4. *The Lox-in-a-Box home page.*

These three files are in a directory called LoxBox, which you can use as the channel directory. I've included these files on the CD for this book; look in the Examples directory for all the examples from this book.

Create the Properties and Publish the Site

HTML channels are published like any other channels: you start Castanet Publish, add the HTML channel directory to the list of Channels Under Development, set the properties of that channel, and then choose Publish to move the channel to the transmitter.

To publish the Lox-in-a-Box channel, you start up the Publish tool and add the LoxBox directory to the Channels Under Development screen.

Many of the channel properties you learned about earlier in this chapter and in Chapter 5 apply to HTML channels—for example, the transmitter properties and the channel description. The two that apply most specifically to HTML channels, however, are the General and Update properties.

For the General properties panel, you should have the Type of channel set to HTML. The field for Index Page should be set to the topmost home page for your channel—often a file called `index.html` in the channel directory. (It's called just that for the Lox-in-a-Box channel.) This page will be the first one that your readers see when they start up the channel. Ignore the Classpath field; the class path is not used for HTML channels. Figure 8.5 shows the settings for the HTML channel for Lox-in-a-Box.

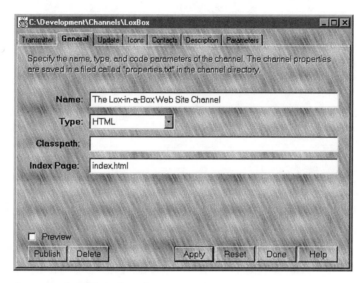

Figure 8.5. *General properties for HTML channels.*

The other property panel you should check is the Update properties panel. Figure 8.6 shows this panel with the settings for the sample channel. Because HTML channels are not real channels per se, the values of the settings in this panel are somewhat superfluous. The only value you definitely need to set is the Inactive Channel Update Frequency; this value should be frequent enough to cover your intended changes to the site. For an HTML channel that changes fairly infrequently (for example, if the Lox-in-a-Box prices change only once a week), setting this value to weekly may be just fine. Set it to a more frequent value if you intend to change your channel more frequently.

All the other settings in this panel refer to executable channels, not to HTML channels. To prevent the tuner from doing more work than it needs to do, you might want to set the Update Frequency of the inactive channel to daily or hourly and the Data Available Action value to ignore.

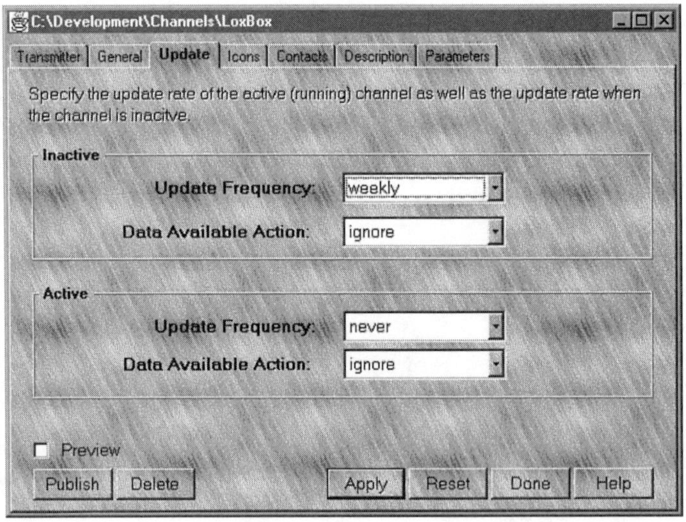

Figure 8.6. *Update settings for the HTML channel.*

Don't forget to set the channel descriptions and contacts. Also, make sure that your transmitter properties are set properly. Then click Publish to store the HTML files on a transmitter in channel form.

With normal Web pages, each time you make a change, that channel is automatically distributed to anyone who visits your site. In contrast, with HTML channels, when you make a change to a Web page (or to any number of pages), you must remember to use the Publish tool again to update the channel. Otherwise, your readers cannot see the changes you've made. As you do with executable channels, always remember to use Castanet Publish to update the channel on the transmitter side after each change or set of changes.

Note

If you're familiar with the process of creating and publishing a Web site, you might think that using Castanet Publish is a clever way of updating a regular Web server—you just make your changes and run Publish to update the server. Unfortunately, because of the way the transmitter stores files and keeps track of the way a channel is organized, the files created by Publish on the transmitter cannot be directly served by a Web server. Publish is suitable only for publishing actual channels, not collections of files.

Test and Use the HTML Site

HTML channels, like all channels, appear in the transmitter listing from a tuner. You can browse and subscribe to them just as you do with other channels. (Figure 8.7 shows the Lox-in-a-Box channel available in a transmitter listing.) As you learned in Chapter 3, "Using the Tuner," however, HTML channels behave slightly differently from "normal" channels: Rather than starting up a window to run the channel, the tuner uses the default Web browser to view the HTML pages in the channel. The catch is that the Web browser must be configured to use the tuner as a proxy so that all Web connections go through the tuner. This way, the tuner can decide whether to load a page from an HTML channel or to visit a Web server over the network to retrieve that page. Configuring the Web browser in this way does not interfere with Web browsing other sites as long as the tuner is running at the time.

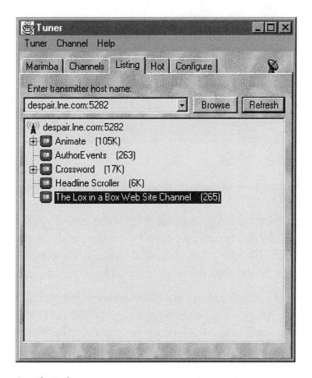

Figure 8.7. *The Lox-in-a-Box channel.*

When you first launch an HTML channel in the browser, the tuner reminds you that you need to configure your browser properly. (See Figure 8.8.) After you configure your browser (or if it's already configured), you can choose Launch to switch control of the browser and view the pages in the channel just as if they were contained on a Web site.

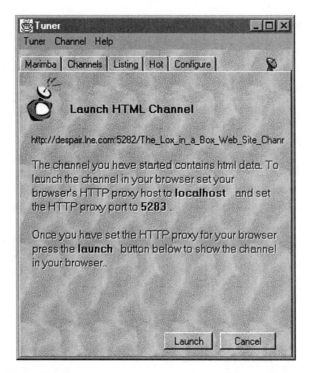

Figure 8.8. Browsing HTML channels.

In the case of the Lox-in-a-Box channel, each page in the channel is browsed from the local copy, although from the URL it appears to come from the Web itself. (The tuner manages whether the page is retrieved from the disk or from the network; it's transparent to the browser itself.) If the reader decides to order a product from the site, he or she can fill out the form and submit it. Because the CGI script to process the form is not part of the actual channel, the tuner knows enough to send the data from the channel back to the server for processing.

When you test an HTML channel of your own creation, you test it in the same way you would any other Web site: follow all the links both on and off the site to make sure that they all work properly. In addition, with HTML channels you should test all your forms and CGI programs to make sure that the data is sent over the network.

What about updates? If Lox-in-a-Box makes any changes to its site—for example, updates the price list or adds content to the Web page—the tuner picks up those changes when the channel is updated, just as it would for a regular channel.

Where to Go from Here

HTML channels simply provide channel-like behavior to a Web site, and as such are interesting only as an alternative way of distributing a set of Web pages. To take full advantage of the Castanet technology for real channels, you actually should develop those channels in Java. If you've worked with applets in Web pages, then read on for an easy way to convert applets into channels.

Converting Applets to Channels

Although you can apply the Castanet technology to HTML channels, Castanet was designed to distribute executable programs written in Java. Much of the Java development that has gone on in the years since the language has become popular is in the realm of applets. Remember that applets are Java programs that run inside Web pages. Most Java applets can be converted into Marimba channels with no modifications; you usually don't even need to recompile the Java code. As you do with the HTML channels, all you essentially need to do is set the channel's properties correctly when you publish the channel, and Castanet handles the rest.

You can also use applets as the basis for creating more sophisticated channels. For example, you can modify an existing applet to take advantage of such channel features as being able to save files to the user's local disk, to send feedback information back to the transmitter, or to handle running updates dynamically. You'll learn about each of these features in Chapters 11, "Managing Updates and User Information," and 12, "Creating Transmitter Plug-Ins."

In this section, you learn how to convert an existing applet (one that is already running successfully inside a Web browser) into a channel. You also learn a few of the differences between applets and channels; you may have to take these differences into account for your applet to work. (You'll find only a few differences; most applets should work just fine as they are.) In Chapters 10, "Creating Application Channels," and 11, you'll look at extending applets to take advantage of tuner and channel features.

Note

> You don't necessarily need to know anything about Java to convert an applet into a channel, because most applets run just fine as channels. If you've been using precompiled applets in your own Web pages and know nothing about the Java language, you should still be able to follow along in most of this section. You should have a basic understanding of how the <APPLET> tag works, however.

Setting Up the Applet

As with HTML channels, the first step in converting an applet into a channel is to create a channel directory that holds the applet and its supporting files. That includes the applet class itself, any other class files the applet uses, and any other images, sounds, or other media. In fact, you need everything you needed to include the applet in the Web page, minus the HTML file that contained it (and having the HTML file along for the ride doesn't hurt).

If the applet source isn't compiled, go ahead and compile it with your favorite Java compiler. Then fire up your Castanet Publish; all you have left to do is set the properties and publish the channel.

Add your applet channel directory to the list of channels under development just as you did for the HTML channel. Double-click that channel directory to set the channel's properties.

As I noted with HTML channels, I won't go over most of the properties you need to set because most of them are common to every channel you publish. You should look at the General, Update, and Parameters property pages, however. In this section, I cover general and update properties; see the next section, "Applet Parameters," for more details about the latter.

For the General properties panel, make sure that the Type of the channel is set to Applet. Figure 8.9 shows the general properties for applets.

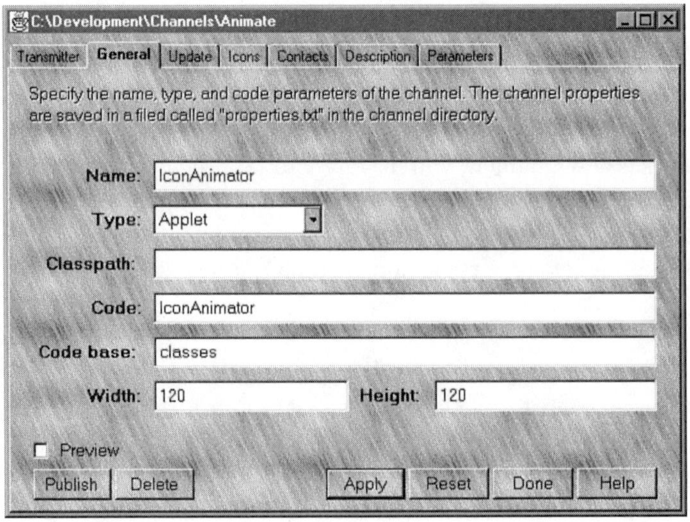

Figure 8.9. General properties for applets.

The most important fields in this page are Code, Width, and Height. The value of the Code field should be the name of the main applet class. This is the same value that you use inside the <APPLET> tag for the value of the CODE attribute; however, here you indicate that value minus the .class extension. So, for example, if your applet class is called IconAnimator.class, the value of the Code field is IconAnimator.

The Width and Height fields set the width and height of the window in which the applet is displayed. These values are the same as the values of WIDTH and HEIGHT inside the <APPLET> tag. By default, the width and height of the applet are both 400 pixels. Make sure that you include the correct width and height in these fields; otherwise, your applet may appear in a window that is too large or too small.

What about the other two fields, Code base and Classpath? The value of Code base is the location of your class files relative to the channel directory, used in the same way the CODEBASE attribute for the <APPLET> tag is used. If your class files are in the channel directory itself, you can leave Code base field blank. If, however, they're stored in a subdirectory—for example, one called classes—enter classes as the value of Code base.

Note

In applets used in Web pages, you commonly see values of the CODEBASE attribute that point to someone else's Web site. For example, the value of Code base might be something like http://www.mycooljavasite.com/applets/. You cannot do this for channels; all the class files must be located in your local channel directory for them to be published as channels.

Classpath is essentially identical to codebase for applets. This field indicates other directories in which to look for Java classes that might be used.

Figure 8.9 shows the sample settings for an applet called IconAnimator. These settings are equivalent to an <APPLET> tag that looks like this:

```
<APPLET CODE="IconAnimator.class" CODEBASE="classes" WIDTH=120 HEIGHT=120>
...
</APPLET>
```

You have slightly more control over the update properties for applets than you do for HTML channels. (See Figure 8.10.) Applets can be active or inactive, so you can update them at different frequencies for each. Set both the Update Frequency menus to have values based on how often you intend to change the applet's code, its properties, or its parameters.

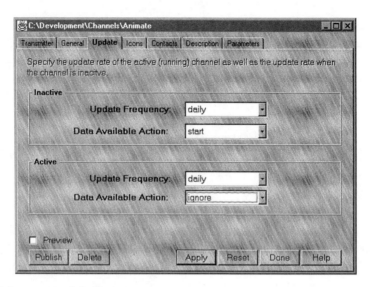

Figure 8.10. *Update properties for applets.*

For the Data Available Action in the Inactive Applet Channels section, you have two choices: ignore or start. For active channels, you also have two choices: ignore or restart. For start or restart, the applet will do just that: launch if its not currently running or restart if it is.

The notify and install options are for channels that can handly dynamic updates. You can convert an applet into a real channel that can handle these kinds of updates; you'll learn about this in Chapter 11.

Applet Parameters

Most applets are written so that they can take different parameters, or options, which determine how the applet behaves when it is run. For example, a scrolling-text applet (one that produces a sort of marquee or LED screen) might have a parameter for the text to print, the color to print it in, and the speed with which to display it. This way, applets can be written generically so that they can be reused over and over again for different purposes.

These parameters to an applet are usually indicated as <PARAM> HTML tags inside the Web page that contains the applet. Because applets running as channels don't have a Web page, you need to specify the parameters to an applet in a different way.

Applet channel parameters are stored in a separate file called parameters.txt in the channel directory. As you do with the properties.txt files, you can either create this file by hand with a text editor, or you can use Castanet Publish to create it. To enter applet parameters, switch to the Parameters property panel in the Publish tool. (See Figure 8.11.)

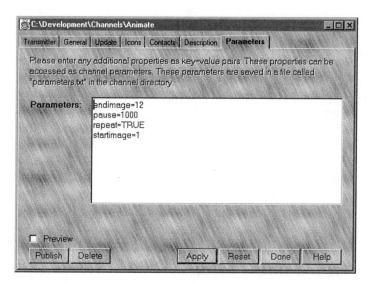

Figure 8.11. Applet channel parameters.

The parameters for an applet channel are key-value pairs that correspond to the NAME and VALUE attributes in the <PARAM> tag. Each key and value is separated by an equal sign, and each pair is on its own line. Say that you have a set of parameters that looks like this as <PARAM> tags:

```
<PARAM NAME=name VALUE="Laura">
<PARAM NAME=age VALUE="29">
<PARAM NAME=value VALUE="priceless">
```

These same parameters look like this as an applet channel:

```
name=Laura
age=29
value=priceless
```

Note that changing the parameters to an applet is considered an update to that applet. If you change the parameters, therefore, don't forget to publish the changes so that tuners can pick them up.

Publishing and Testing

Nothing else is special about applet channels. After you set the properties, you can publish the channel.

Applet channels, when they're run from a tuner, run in their own windows that are the size of the width and height that you give them inside General Properties. (That width and height is fixed just as it is with applets in Web pages.) Applet status and error messages that usually appear in the browser's status line or Java console appear in the tuner's Java console. (You can see the console by choosing Tuner | Show Console.) As with applets in Web pages, iconifying the applet window stops the applet's execution; opening the window again restarts it.

An Example: Scrolling Headlines

Although the process for converting an applet into a channel is rather straightforward, let's work through a simple example.

The applet to use for this example is a small, scrolling-text applet written by Matt Howitt. You can see it in action at `http://www.fas.harvard.edu/~mhowitt/fun/index.html`. Using applet parameters, you can configure not only the text string that scrolls by, but also the font, size, and style, the foreground and background colors, the direction (up and down as well as left to right and vice versa), and the speed. This applet makes a good basis for an updateable headlines applet, but for this example, you can simply convert it as is.

Download the source and class files for this applet into a directory called `Scroller` on your local system. (I've also included this applet as one of the examples on the CD; you can find it in the `Examples` directory.) You actually don't need the source file at all because this applet works as a channel without any modifications. You can bring it along because you'll need it later in the book. The class file is called `ScrollingText.class`.

Inside Castanet Publish, add the `Scroller` directory to the list of channels under development and double-click that name to bring up the channel properties. For the general properties, call the channel `Headline Scroller` and enter `ScrollingText` into the Code field as the name of the class file. For the size, use a width of 500 and a height of 50. See Figure 8.12 for these values.

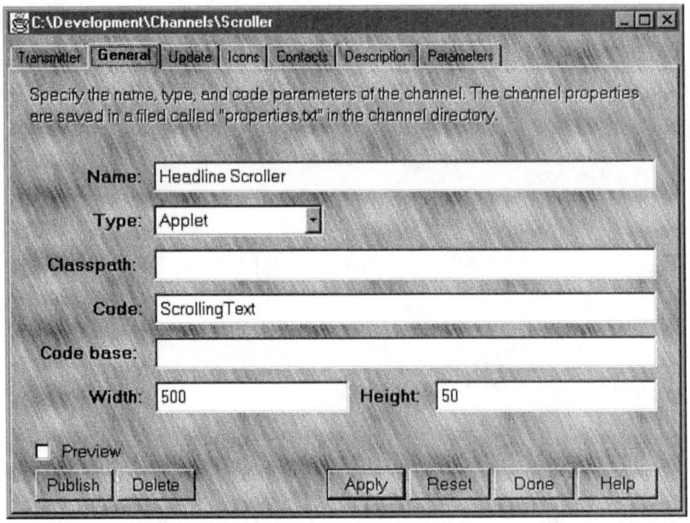

Figure 8.12. *Scrolling headlines general properties.*

For the update properties, you can assume that new headlines will occur fairly frequently, so set both the active and inactive updates to occur once per hour. An applet can't do much with actual actions, so set both to ignore any new data. Starting or restarting the applet displays the new headline.

Finally, you need to set the parameters. The original ScrollingText applet has several parameters. For this example, you can set several parameters: make the background color white (bgcolor=White), the foreground (text) color blue (fgcolor=blue), the font size 24 points (fontSize=24), and the direction of the scroll right to left (direction=RightLeft). Also add the text to scroll: text=New and Improved Headlines Scroller! Now with Argon!. Figure 8.13 shows the parameters as entered into the Parameters properties.

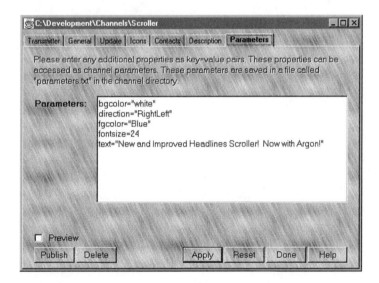

Figure 8.13. Scrolling headlines parameters.

After a quick check back to set the transmitter properties and to fill in the channel description and contact fields, you're effectively done. Click Publish, wait for the tool to generate and publish all the files, and then pull up your tuner. The headlines scroller shows up happily in the tuner listing, and subscribing to it launches the scroller in its own window. (See Figure 8.14.)

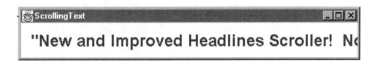

Figure 8.14. The headlines scroller running.

On the transmitter side, you can change the headline or any of the other parameters for the scrolling headlines applet any time you want to, as long as you remember to publish the channel each time.

If you want to try out the ScrollingText applet, Table 8.1 shows a list of the parameters you can use with it.

Table 8.1. ScrollingText applet parameters.

Parameter Name	Possible Values	What It Means
text	Any string	The text to be displayed (default is none).
font	Font name	The font the text will be displayed in (default is Arial).
fontsize	An integer	The size the text will be displayed in (default is 36).
fontstyle	Plain, Bold, Italic, BoldItalic	The style the text will be displayed in (default is bold).
bgcolor	Yellow, Blue, Black, Red, White, Green, Pink, Orange, or an RGB value (0,0,0)	The background color (default is White).
fgcolor	Yellow, Blue, Black, Red, White, Green, Pink, Orange, or an RGB value (0,0,0)	The color of the text (default is Blue).
delay	An integer	The amount of time, in milliseconds, the applet waits in between redraws (default is 50).
dist	An integer	The number of the text moves in between redraws (default is 5). This value and delay determine how fast the scrolling happens.
direction	LeftRight, RightLeft, TopBottom, BottomTop	The direction the text scrolls in (default is RightLeft).
valign	Top, Center, Bottom	The vertical alignment of the text. Ignored if direction is BottomTop or TopBottom (default is Center).
align	Left, Center, Right	The horizontal alignment of the text. Ignored if direction is LeftRight or RightLeft (default is Center).

Gotchas for Converting Applets to Channels

In most cases, you can convert applets to channels without any modifications. Castanet runs the applet inside a "shell" (the `marimba.channel.AppletViewer` class) that fools the applet into believing that it's running happily inside a browser. Some slight differences between applets and applet channels may require you to modify your program, however. Or, you might have to handle behavior differently depending on whether the applet is running as an applet or as a channel. For example:

● Browser features are implemented differently. The `showStatus()` method, used to display a text string in the status line of a browser, exists but displays the text in the status line of the tuner's Java console (which might not be displayed). If you make extensive use of the `showStatus()` method, you might want to implement it so that the status appears inside the applet itself.

   Note that `showDocument()` works just fine; it launches the user's default browser and displays the page there.

● The base URL of the applet is different, which might affect where files are loaded from or connections back to the server where the applet channel came from.

   For applet channels, the base URL of the applet channel is `tuner://host:port/channelname` rather than `http://host:port/directory/`. Files local to that URL (extra media or text files) are loaded from the channel's directory rather than downloaded from a remote server.

   If you're making live connections back to the server from which the applet channel came, you should extract the host and the port from the base URL and use HTTP rather than tuner as the protocol.

● Extra files used by the applet are loaded from the local disk when the applet is used by a channel rather than from over the network when the applet is running in a browser. This makes loading and starting an applet much faster as a channel. If your applet has a "loading" stage in which you display some sort of conciliatory message for the user, you might find that you no longer need that stage with channels.

Note also that applet channels have the same security restrictions that regular applets do. You can modify an applet that, when it runs as a channel, can write state files to the channel's data directory. You'll learn more about how to do so in Chapter 11.

Summary

Congratulations! After only eight chapters, you've created some real channels that you can publish on transmitters and subscribe to on tuners. With HTML channels, you can publish a Web site as a channel so that your readers can download it all at once or read it without a live network connection. With applet channels, you can convert work that you've already done with Java and applets into channels. Later in this book, you'll use applets as the basis for real channels with real channel capabilities.

nine

Creating Presentations and Channels with Bongo

Have you ever tried building a user interface for a Java application using raw Abstract Windowing Toolkit (AWT) code? It's not a lot of fun, is it? Just designing the layout of a window and making sure all the widgets are in the right place can be incredibly time-consuming, particularly with the edit-compile-test cycle of working with Java code. Visual interface builders can help quite a bit, but you still have to deal with a lot of actual code, particularly if you want to create really sophisticated interfaces with dynamic layouts and complicated interactions between different windows and different elements on each window.

That's where Bongo comes in. Using Bongo, you can add and arrange user-interface elements (they're called *widgets* in Bongo-speak) on the screen by dragging them with the mouse, dynamically changing their size and properties, and combining them into different kinds of containers. But Bongo isn't just an interface builder for Java applications, similar to what you would get with a Java development environment. Each Bongo widget can also have a *script*, which is an embedded bit of Java code that can determine the behavior of the object and allows it to interact with other objects in the same presentation. You create the scripts inside Bongo, and you can save and test and run them inside Bongo as well—no compiler needed. In this respect, Bongo is more like HyperCard or Director than it is a simple user-interface builder for Java; it's a tool you can use to create simple applications and presentations without needing to know a lot about actually programming in Java. If you're unfamiliar with Java or with programming, you can most likely do quite a lot with Bongo, or you can even create interfaces to be used by a Java programmer later on. Even if you do know Java, you can use Bongo for quick prototyping or building simple interfaces for your applications.

So what does building interfaces have to do with channels and with Marimba Castanet? Quite a lot, actually. Bongo presentations can be used directly as channels, with or without scripts behind their widgets. You can also create a Java application channel that uses a Bongo presentation as its interface. In fact, creating a channel that uses a Bongo interface is easier than creating one with a more standard AWT interface (as you'll learn in the next chapter). So even if you do intend to create heavy-duty Java-based channels, you might want to learn Bongo anyhow.

In this chapter, then, you'll get a general-purpose overview of how to use Bongo to create simple presentations and how to turn those presentations into channels. In Chapter 10, "Creating Application Channels," you'll learn how to use Bongo presentations in application channels (and finish up covering the four kinds of channels you can create with Castanet).

Note

> A single chapter in this book isn't nearly enough to cover the use of Bongo in all its glory. For that reason, another book with plenty more details is available. *The Official Marimba Guide to Bongo*, by Danny Goodman and published by Sams.net, is the companion book to this one and should be available at the same place you bought this book. Collect both! Win valuable prizes! Impress your friends!

Getting, Installing, and Starting Bongo

Bongo is a separate tool from Castanet itself; you have to acquire and install it separately from the tuner and transmitter software.

An evaluation version of Bongo is available on the CD that comes with this book. You can also download the latest version from Marimba's Web site at http://www.marimba.com/ if you don't have access to a CD-ROM drive, or you can purchase the full version of Bongo. (See Marimba's Web site for details.)

Installing Bongo

If you're using the CD-ROM version, you must install the software onto your hard drive; it will not run directly from the CD. For Windows, you need to be running Windows 95 or Windows NT 4.0, and have at least 8MB of RAM and 4MB of free disk space. For Solaris, you need Solaris 2.4 or higher, 15MB of RAM, and 4MB of free disk space.

Note

Bongo is also available on some other platforms. An alpha version is available from Marimba for the Macintosh/PowerPC but is not stable enough to be included with this book. See also the page at http://www.marimba.com/products/unsupported.html for information about versions of Bongo available for Linux, FreeBSD, and SolarisX86.

For Windows, the transmitter is an executable file called Trans1_0.EXE. On Solaris, it's a compressed tar archive called bongo1_0_tar.Z.

Note

If you're using the transmitter installer from the CD-ROM that came with this book, you can find the transmitter installer in the directory Marimba and then in the subdirectory for your platform (Win95, WinNT, or Solaris)—for example, Marimba\Win95\Bongo1_0.EXE.

To install Bongo for Windows, simply double-click the installer application. You are prompted for an installation location (C:\Marimba is the default), and after you enter it, all the files are installed.

To install Bongo for Solaris, pick a common location (such as home or /usr/local/). Copy the Bongo installer file to that location and decompress it, as follows:

```
cp bongo1_0_tar.Z /usr/local
uncompress bongo1_0_tar.Z
```

Finally, use the following tar command to install the files:

```
tar xvf bongo1_0_tar
```

The Bongo software is installed into a directory called `bongo`. The actual Bongo program is in the `bongo/bin/` directory; you might want to add that directory to your execution path so that you can easily start Bongo later.

After installing Bongo, you can delete the `tar` file:

```
rm bongo1_0_tar
```

Starting Bongo

To start Bongo for Windows, navigate through the Start menu to the Castanet Bongo application. (See Figure 9.1.)

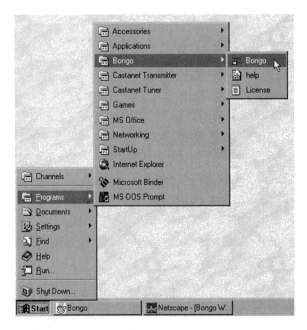

Figure 9.1. *Starting Bongo.*

To start Bongo for Solaris, use the full pathname `bongo` command at a system prompt, like this (substituting the actual location of the Bongo software):

```
/usr/local/bongo/bin/bongo
```

If you put the `bongo/bin` directory into your execution path, you should be able to type `bongo` to start it.

The first Bongo screen, shown in Figure 9.2, then appears on your desktop.

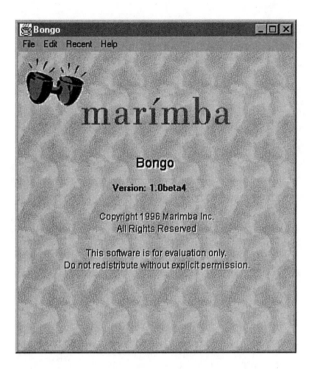

Figure 9.2. Welcome to Bongo.

Quick Start: Creating a Simple Presentation

Although I could sit here and explain to you in detail for a couple pages how Bongo works, you would probably fall asleep on me, and we would never get anything done. So let's jump right in and create a really simple presentation so that you can get a feel for what it's like to work with Bongo.

Choose File | New Presentation. A new, blank, untitled Bongo presentation appears in its own window. (See Figure 9.3.)

When the new presentation appears, the main Bongo screen turns into a window with two panels: one for properties and one for scripts. Click the Properties tab to see the properties of this main presentation; the default properties are shown in Figure 9.4.

The values of the properties in this panel (and the number and type of properties) change depending on the element you have selected in the presentation window. Right now the entire presentation is selected, so its properties appear in the Properties panel.

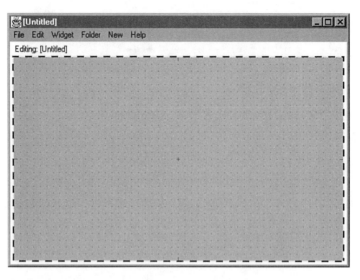

Figure 9.3. *A new, blank presentation.*

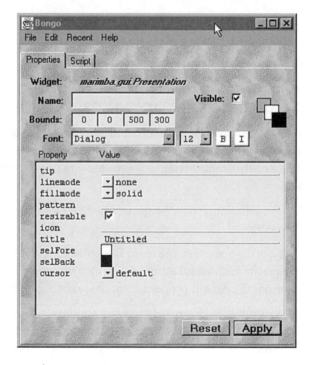

Figure 9.4. *Presentation properties.*

First, change the size of the presentation. The values of the Bounds fields in the Properties page determine the size and position of the presentation (or of any widget inside the presentation). Here, the default size of the presentation is 500 by 300 pixels; if you change these values to 345 and 100 and click Apply, the presentation changes size.

Now, add some widgets to the presentation. A Bongo widget is a user-interface element that you can create, move around, and resize; you also can change its properties and add scripts to it. To create a new widget, select a menu item from the New menu in the presentation window. You can choose from lots of default widgets; for this example, start with a static text box. (See Figure 9.5.)

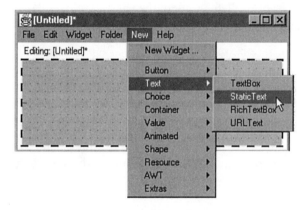

Figure 9.5. *Creating a new static text box.*

A static text box is one in which the text cannot be edited. Static text boxes make great labels for other user-interface elements. Choosing New | Static Text causes a new static text box to appear in the presentation. (See Figure 9.6.)

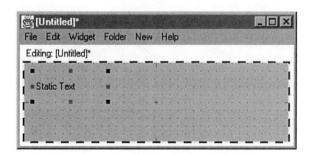

Figure 9.6. *A new static text box.*

The text box is selected, and the properties for that text box appear in the Properties page. Go to the Properties page, and change the font of the text box to Helvetica and the size to 24. Move

175

down to the style property pull-down list box, and choose boxed. Then click Apply to set all the properties. (You must always click Apply for any property changes you make to take effect.) The text box you created then changes in style to reflect your property changes.

The default size, however, is most likely too small to fit the text. You can use the mouse to resize the text box by clicking and dragging the resize boxes. Stretch the text box to fit the full width of the window. Note that the size properties for the text box automatically change to reflect the new size of the text box.

Now, add some more widgets. Choose New | Button | CommandButton in the presentation window. A new button then appears on top of the text box. Using the mouse, drag it just below the text box to the bottom-left corner of the window. Note that you can use the arrow keys to "nudge" it one pixel in any direction to get it placed properly.

You can also move or resize the button using the Properties page. The Bounds field contains values for the x and y position of the widget (with 0,0 in the top-left corner and positive y downward) and for the width and height of the widget. Resize the button to be just a little smaller using these values so that the button is located at an x of 10 and a y of 65, and is 100 by 30 pixels big.

The other property to set for this button is the label, which is an editable field in the properties list. Change it to Some Text and click Apply. Figure 9.7 shows both the properties of the button and its result.

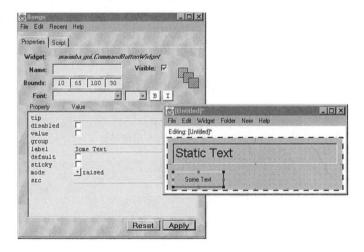

Figure 9.7. The new button widget.

Now, add two more buttons next to this one. Although you could choose more buttons from the New menu and then change their properties to match the first one, it's easier to just copy and paste the button you've got. Select the button, choose Edit | Copy, and then choose Paste.

The new button appears on top of the old one, so drag the new button to the right to make both buttons appear. Choose Paste again, and a third button appears. You can then arrange all three buttons in a row underneath the text box.

Now you have three buttons, all with the same label. Select the middle button and change its label to More Text. (Don't forget to click Apply to make the change.) Choose the third button and change its label to Still More Text.

Got all that? You've now built a simple user-interface presentation, like the one shown in Figure 9.8. At this point, you might want to take a couple minutes and experiment with the various properties you can set in the presentation, such as the styles of the widgets or the background and foreground colors. (You can set the colors using the three squares in the top-right corner of the screen.) Don't forget to save the presentation file so that the inevitable system crash doesn't wipe out all your work. Bongo presentation files should usually have an extension of .gui.

Note

This example is included on the CD-ROM that comes with this book, in the folder Examples and in the folder BongoQuickStart below that. I've saved this presentation file as quickstart.gui.

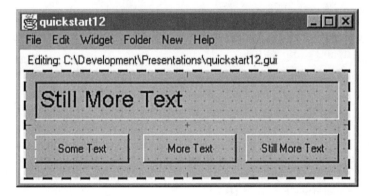

Figure 9.8. *The final presentation.*

When you add new widgets to a presentation and modify their properties, you're in Edit mode for that presentation. To actually make the presentation work, you have to switch to Browse mode. You can choose both of these modes from the File menu in the presentation window. (See Figure 9.9.)

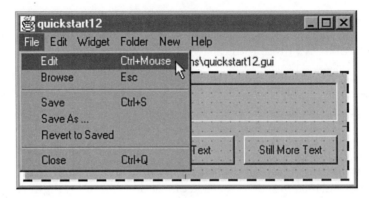

Figure 9.9. *Browse and Edit modes.*

If you switch to Browse mode, you'll find that your buttons are now clickable, although they don't do anything. Later in this chapter, you'll add scripts to make them do things.

Working with Presentations

You use Bongo to create Java presentations. The term *presentation* refers to a window and the user-interface elements, called widgets, that window contains. Presentations can also contain scripts to control the behavior of the widgets. Using scripts, you can create not just a user interface, but also a fully functioning program entirely inside Bongo.

In this section, I'll give you a quick overview of the basic Bongo features for creating presentations and using widgets.

Basics

To create a new presentation, choose File | New Presentation. A new presentation then appears, and the Bongo screen changes to the Properties and Scripts panels. Both of these panels dynamically change to reflect the properties and scripts of the currently selected widget. When you first create a new presentation, the properties of that presentation are shown in the Properties panel. (See Figure 9.10.)

While working with presentations, you can choose from two modes of operation. The default is Edit mode, in which you can add widgets, move or resize them, change their properties, or edit their scripts. The other is Browse mode, in which you can test the behavior of the presentation. When you switch to Browse mode (by choosing File | Browse in the presentation window), the Properties and Scripts panels change to the initial Bongo screen. Switch back to Edit mode by choosing File | Edit.

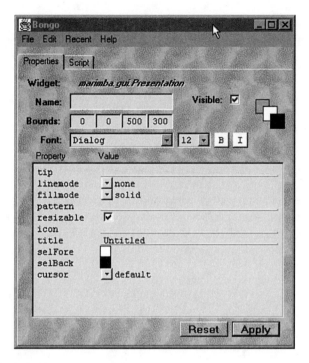

***Figure 9.10.** Presentation properties.*

Choosing and Modifying Widgets

To add a widget to a presentation, choose its type from the New menu in the presentation window. The standard Marimba widgets give you the most basic user-interface elements to choose from, or you can also import custom widgets that you or other Bongo programmers have created. (You'll find a summary of the default widgets in "A Short Overview of Bongo Widgets," later in this chapter.)

The new widget appears in its default state in the top-left corner of the presentation. You can then move or resize it with the mouse, or modify its properties in the Properties panel.

The following are some other features of Bongo relating to widgets:

● You can "nudge" a widget into position using the arrow keys or the Nudge commands from the Widget menu.

● You can arrange multiple widgets into groups by selecting the widgets and choosing Group from the Widget menu. Groups of widgets can then be selected, moved, and resized as if they were one widget.

⬤ You can arrange widgets on top of each other. The To Front and To Back commands in the Widget menu can be helpful in arranging widgets.

⬤ Some widgets can be containers for other widgets, allowing you to nest presentations inside each other. The current presentation, and the outermost container, is indicated by a black and yellow border. To select elements inside a container widget, hold down the Ctrl key and click on that container. The black and yellow border then appears around the subcontainer.

Presentation and Widget Properties

Each widget has a set of properties, including properties common to all widgets and properties for that specific type of widget. For example, text box widgets have different properties from button widgets. When you select a widget in Bongo's Edit mode, its properties appear in the Properties panel. (See Figure 9.11.)

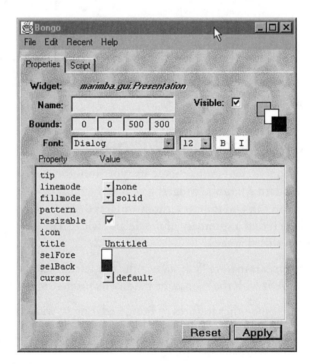

Figure 9.11. *Various widget properties.*

The upper part of the panel contains properties common to all widgets, including the name, bounds, font, and colors. Note also that the Widget field shows the Java class name for the currently selected widget—for example, `marimba.gui.CommandButtonWidget` or `marimba.gui.Presentation`.

The bottom half of the panel contains properties specific to this kind of widget—for example, button labels, check box states, text inside a text box, or the maximum and minimum values of a scrollbar. The properties in this panel change depending on which widget you currently have selected.

Each time you change a widget's properties, you must then click Apply to apply the changes to the widget; you can also press the Return or Enter key to apply the changes. Click Reset to change the properties back to their current values.

For the most part, using Bongo to create simple presentations should be easy if you've ever used a user-interface builder or a drawing tool. After you have the basic presentation in place, you can then add scripts to make the presentation have behaviors.

Adding Scripts to Widgets

Scripts make Bongo different from a standard user-interface builder. By adding scripts to a presentation, you can create simple applications wholly in Bongo. You don't need to drop out of the interface to work in raw Java code (although, as you'll learn in the next chapter, you can also use a Bongo presentation as the interface to a Java application).

Before you get too excited about Bongo scripting, however, you should know that Bongo scripts are written in Java code and require that you have at least a basic understanding of how Java and AWT events work. If you don't have this background, you may find scripting rough going.

In this section, I'll give you a general overview for creating simple Java scripts. For more details, check out *The Official Marimba Guide to Bongo* (by Sams.net Publishing).

The Script Panel

Just as each widget has its own set of properties, it also can have its own script. To edit the script for a widget, select that widget in Edit mode and then choose the Script panel. By default, all scripts are blank. Figure 9.12 shows a blank Script panel.

The Bongo scripts that you create inside these panels are most always reactions to events in the presentation. For example, you can add a script to do something when a button is clicked or when a menu item is selected. Different widgets can respond to different script events.

The actual Bongo scripts, which are written in Java, are based on standard Java event mechanisms such as the `handleEvent()` and `action()` methods. For example, for a button widget, the standard template for a script is the `action()` method, which looks like this:

```
public void action() {
...
}
```

181

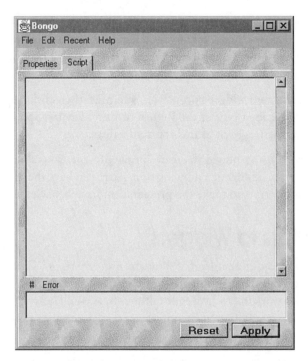

Figure 9.12. *The Script panel.*

Inside that action() method, you can get and set the values of other widgets in the presentations, do calculations, load or play media files, or do anything else to the presentation that you need, using standard Java code. The action() method is called each time the button that contains it is clicked.

Different widgets can take different kinds of scripts. Although it would be nice for Bongo to provide templates for each kind of script a widget can accept, unfortunately, the 1.0 version of Bongo doesn't provide that behavior. You have to look up the possibilities for each kind of widget and add the code yourself. (A future version of Bongo will give you templates for the kinds of scripts you can add.)

After you edit the script for a widget, don't forget to click the Apply button. In addition to saving the script for that widget, Bongo also compiles the script into Java bytecode for you.

Example: Adding a Script to the Text Presentation

Puzzled yet? Bongo scripting can be very confusing, particularly if you haven't seen Java before. An example should help make things at least a little bit clearer.

Let's go back to that presentation you created in the "Quick Start" section of this chapter. Right now, all you have are a few buttons and text fields; no scripts are attached, so the presentation doesn't do anything. You're going to add scripts to each of the buttons so that when you click a button, the text field changes to reflect the label of the button. For example, clicking the Some Text button changes the text field to Some Text, and similarly with the other buttons.

Note that you need to add a script only to the widget that triggers the action. In this case, the three buttons have three separate scripts, but the text field doesn't need a script at all.

Make sure that you're in Edit mode in Bongo, and select the first button (Some Text). The properties then appear in the Properties panel; click the Script tab to switch to the Script panel.

For buttons, the script you usually want to add is the action() script, which is called when the button is clicked and released. The action method looks like this (don't add it yet; I'm just showing it to you here so that you know what it looks like):

```
public void action() {
...
}
```

Inside the action method, you add the code to change the value of the text box. First, however, you need to name the text box so that you can get its values. Choose the text box in the presentation window; then switch to the Properties panel. In the Name field, add a name for the text box widget; for this example, enter theText. Figure 9.13 shows the result.

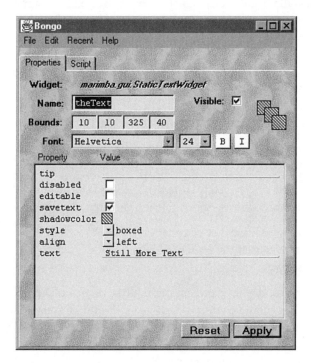

Figure 9.13. *TextBox properties.*

Click Apply. Then go back to the Some Text button and the script for that button. (Make sure that you select the button before turning to the Script panel; otherwise, you'll edit the script for the text box.) Add the `action()` method, as shown previously, to that box.

Inside the script, change the text box's value to be the text inside the button. To do so, you need to get a reference to the text box. You can make this reference in a couple ways. One way is to use the `getWidget()` method with the name of the text box, as follows:

```
StaticTextBox tbox = (StaticTextBox) getWidget("theText");
```

This line actually does three things:

- It calls the `getWidget()` method with the name of the text box (`"theText"`). The `getWidget()` method returns an object of class `Widget`.
- It casts the `Widget` object into an object of `StaticTextBox`, the class of the text box widget you're changing.
- It assigns that `StaticTextBox` widget to a variable called `tbox`.

Make sure that you include the name of the text box exactly as you typed it in that widget's properties, using the same upper- and lowercase.

Now that you have a reference to the text box, you just need to stuff the right text into it. Although you could just duplicate the label of the button here, a most elegant (and reusable) solution is to use the `getText()` method, which returns the label of the button. Use the `setText()` method to change the value of the text box, like this:

```
tbox.setText(getText());
```

Although this script works just fine, it's actually the longer way of changing the text inside a text box. There's actually an easier way: The `setText()` method is defined on all widgets and has a form that lets you specify the name of the widget to change. So you can do precisely the same thing with only one line, like this:

```
setText("theText",getText());
```

With this form, you don't need to store the handle to the text box; this one line works just as well. Figure 9.14 shows the Script panel with the final script (the one-line version) in place.

When you're done editing the script, don't forget to click Apply. Clicking this button compiles the script so that the presentation will work (it also lets you know if you have any errors in your script).

Switch to Browse mode in the presentation. Now when you click the Some Text button, the text of the text box should change to `Some Text`. If it doesn't, make sure that the name of the text box in the properties matches exactly the name of the text box in your script. Make sure also that the Some Text button still has its script. (If you don't click Apply, the button reverts to its previous state—without the script.)

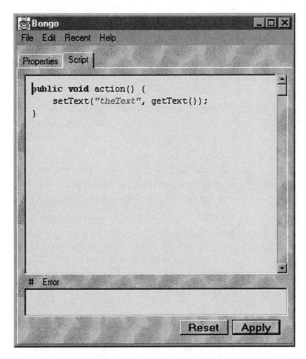

Figure 9.14. *The final button script.*

After you've got the one button working, all you have to do is copy the script to the other two buttons. Because the script is generic enough to work with a button of any label, you don't have to modify the script from button to button. Just copy and paste the contents of the script from one Script panel to another.

Note

> You could also just copy and paste the entire button, and the script will go along with it. In this example, however, because we've already created the buttons, we'll copy the scripts instead.

Despite the fact that this particular script doesn't do anything very exciting, it does give you a basic idea of how scripts work. By adding different methods to the Script panel, you can react to different events for different widgets and have your program act accordingly. Much of scripting is simply understanding the neat things you can do to the different widgets. For more details, check out the documentation that comes with Bongo or pick up the Bongo book I mentioned earlier.

A Short Overview of Bongo Widgets

Bongo comes with a rich set of basic widgets that you can use to create various forms of presentations, and each of these widgets has properties and scriptable values that you can change and modify in the Properties panels or dynamically through scripting. Although I don't have the space to go over all the features of all the Bongo widgets, I can provide a basic overview of the widgets themselves. For further details, you should consult the Widget online documentation or the *Official Marimba Guide to Bongo*.

To get a good visual overview of the kinds of widgets you can use in Bongo, take a look at the demo presentation called `widgets.gui` (contained in the `bongo/demo/examples` folder). It shows many of the default widgets with various properties set. Also, I've included many very simple examples (mostly for the screen shots in this chapter) in the folder called `Presentations` as part of the examples on the CD for this book.

Buttons

Bongo provides five different kinds of button widgets, all of which are subclasses of the class `ButtonWidget`:

- ● `CommandButton` (class `CommandButtonWidget`): A standard clickable button
- ● `MenuButton` (class `MenuButtonWidget`): A pull-down menu
- ● `URLButton` (class `URLButtonWidget`): A button that launches a browser to view a URL
- ● `CheckBox` (class `CheckBoxWidget`): A square box that can be checked or unchecked
- ● `Option` (class `OptionWidget`): A round button that can be selected or unselected

Figure 9.15 shows examples of many of these buttons. (The `URLbutton` is not shown.) The different buttons in each group show different properties including disabled, filled, and boxed.

The first three kinds of buttons provide standard button-like behavior: clicking the button triggers some action. For `MenuButtons`, several options are arranged in a pull-down menu; you can choose different options based on which menu item you select.

Note

MenuButtons are not like combo boxes or selection menus, where you can choose an item and then do something later. `MenuButton` widgets produce actions immediately, just as menus in menu bars might.

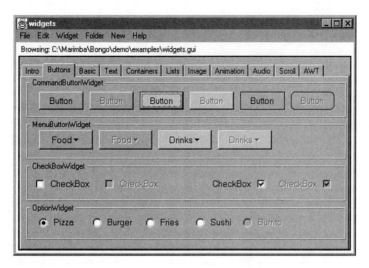

Figure 9.15. *Button widgets.*

URLButtons are similar to regular buttons, except that they have only one action: they switch control to the user's Web browser to load a Web page (the URL for the URLButton is one of its properties).

Finally, CheckBox and Option are special forms of buttons that allow you to set true or false states for options. They do not generally trigger actions themselves; rather their state is tested when some other action occurs. CheckBoxes can be individually checked or unchecked; Options (also called *radio buttons*) are generally arranged in groups so that only one can be selected at any time.

Text Boxes

Text widgets, all of them subclasses of the TextWidget class, allow you to display text either as static labels or as editable text boxes. Bongo has four text widgets:

- TextBox (class TextBoxWidget): A single-line editable text box.
- StaticText (class StaticTextWidget): An uneditable variation of TextBox (and a subclass of TextBoxWidget). It works well for labels.
- RichTextBox (class RichTextBoxWidget): A multiline editable text field.
- URLText (class URLTextWidget): A clickable hypertext link. It displays a URL in the user's default Web browser.

Figure 9.16 shows examples of all these widgets.

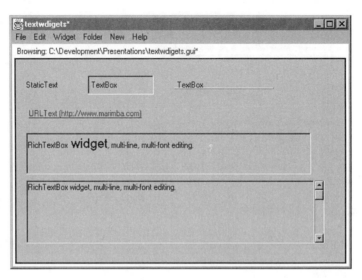

Figure 9.16. *Text field widgets.*

You can script text box widgets to keep track of either mouse or keyboard events, as well as mouse and keyboard focus.

Choices

Choices are widgets for choosing one item out of a list of items. Except where noted, these widgets are subclasses of `ChoiceWidget`:

- `ListBox` (class `ListBoxWidget`): A scrolling list of items. One or more items in the list can be displayed; if the list contains more items than it has space available, the list box includes a scrollbar.
- `DropDownListBox` (class `DropDownListBoxWidget`): A drop-down list of items.
- `DropDownComboBox` (class `DropDownComboBoxWidget`, a subclass of `DropDownListBoxWidget`): A combination of a text field and a drop-down list box; you can either type in a value or select from the list.

Note

At the time of this writing, a `ComboBox` widget is also promised but not yet implemented. Future versions of Bongo will include it.

Figure 9.17 shows some examples of Choice widgets.

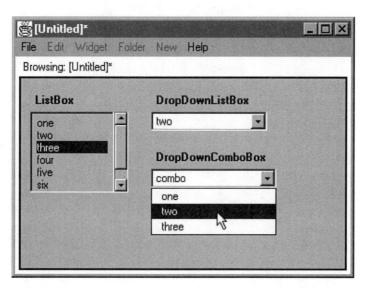

Figure 9.17. *Choice widgets.*

Choice widgets, unlike pull-down menus, generally do not trigger actions. Like check boxes and options, their state is generally tested in response to some other action—for example, a button being clicked.

Containers

Container widgets are simply widgets that can contain other widgets. They include simple widgets to group together other widgets all the way up to very sophisticated layout widgets that include a visual appearance as well as container behavior. Except where noted, all the following container widgets are subclasses of `ContainerWidget`:

- ● `Group` (class `GroupWidget`): A simple group of other widgets.
- ● `GroupBox` (class `GroupBoxWidget`): Similar to a group, except usually drawn with a border and a label. `GroupBoxes` provide a visual appearance as well as grouping behavior. Figure 9.18 shows a `Group` and a `GroupBox` widget.
- ● `Window` (class `WindowWidget`): A floating window with a title bar and a close box. `Window` widgets are not real windows in the sense that they can be moved anywhere on the desktop; they are constrained by the boundaries of the presentation.
- ● `ScrollingContainer` (class `ScrollingContainerWidget`): A scrollable container containing other widgets. You can scroll around inside the "view" of the scrolling container to see all the widgets it contains.

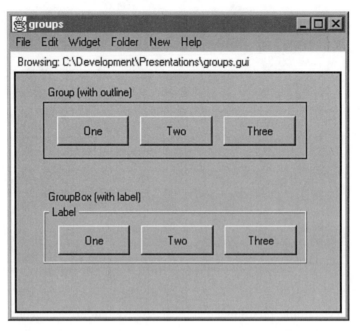

Figure 9.18. Groups *and* GroupBox*es.*

● List (class ListWidget, a subclass of ScrollingContainerWidget): A scrollable list of other widgets, arranged vertically. Figure 9.19 shows a ScrollingContainer and a List widget.

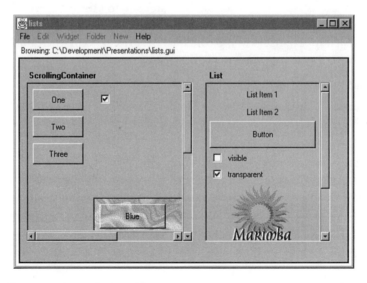

Figure 9.19. ScrollingContainer *and* List *widgets.*

- Table (TableWidget, a subclass of ScrollingContainerWidget) and SparseTable (a subclass of TableWidget): Containers for displaying rows and columns of other widgets or strings. SparseTables are optimized versions of tables that draw only the data that is actually visible; they are more useful for very large tables.

- Tree (class TreeWidget, a subclass of ScrollingContainerWidget) and TreeNode (class TreeNodeWidget, a subclass of GroupWidget): Widgets for implementing Windows Explorer-like trees. The Tree widget itself contains TreeNode widgets, and each TreeNode can contain other TreeNodes. Figure 9.20 shows the Tree widget containing a hierarchy of the widget classes in the marimba.gui package; this tree is an example presentation you can view in bongo/demo/examples/tree.gui.

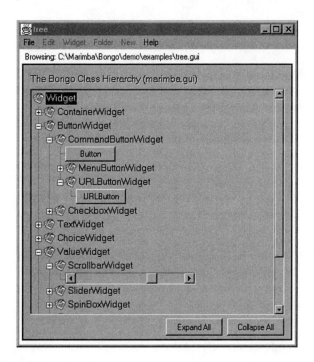

Figure 9.20. Trees *and* TreeNodes.

- Folder (class FolderWidget): This widget allows you to create layered container widgets (each one called a *page*), each with its own *tab* at the top of the folder. Choosing a tab brings that container widget to the front. Figure 9.21 shows a Folder widget with embedded widgets in each page.

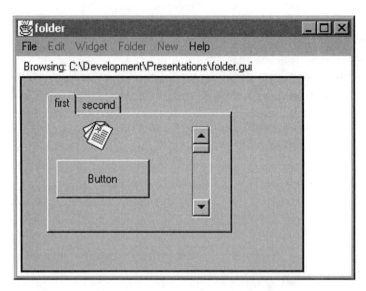

Figure 9.21. *A* Folder *widget.*

Values

You use value widgets to show numeric positions along some scale. Value widgets can either be display only (for example, to show that 50 percent of an operation has occurred), or they can be adjusted by the user (for example, to choose a value between 1 and 10). All the following value widgets are subclasses of the ValueWidget class:

- ● ProgressIndicator (class ProgressIndicatorWidget): A display-only value widget that displays a percentage between 0 and 100 as a set of colored bars (similar to the standard Windows progress indicator).

- ● ScrollBar (class ScrollBarWidget): A scrollbar. Scrollbar widgets can be horizontal or vertical and have variable-sized *thumbs* (boxes).

- ● Slider (class SliderWidget): Slider widgets allow the user to move a box along a scale to select a value. As with scrollbars, sliders can be horizontal or vertical.

- ● SpinBox (class SpinBoxWidget): Spin boxes allow you to type in a number in a text field or to use up and down arrows to increment that value.

Figure 9.22 shows the various Value widgets.

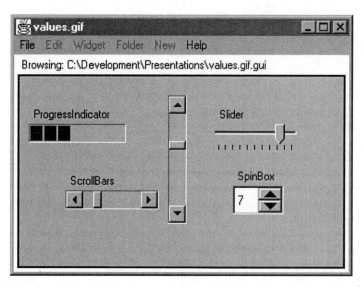

Figure 9.22. *Value widgets.*

Animation

Bongo provides two widgets for creating simple animation inside your presentation. Both of them are subclasses of the class `AnimatedWidget`:

● `AnimatedText` (class `AnimatedTextWidget`): Creates a scrolling text marquee.

● `AnimatedImage` (class `AnimatedImageWidget`): Creates a simple animation. You must give the widget the source for each individual image frame in the animation, and the frames must be named `T1.gif`, `T2.gif`, `T3.gif`, and so on.

Shapes

The shape widgets provide simple decorative elements for presentations; no actions are associated with these elements. All the following are subclasses of the class `ShapeWidget`:

● `Line` (class `LineWidget`)

● `Rectangle` (class `RectangleWidget`)

● `Oval` (class `OvalWidget`)

Media (Resources)

Media or resource widgets allow you to import external image, audio, and other presentation files into the current presentation and play them. The following media widgets are generally subclasses of `ResourceWidget`:

- `Image` (class `ImageWidget`): Displays an image. You can display it at various positions within the presentation or scale it to fit.
- `Audio` (class `AudioWidget`, a subclass of `ImageWidget`): Imports and plays an audio file. (The audio file has an icon associated with it, which is why it's a form of `ImageWidget`.) Audio widgets can be triggered via a variety of actions.
- `Presentation` (class `PresentationWidget`): Allows you to import another presentation file by reference.

Figure 9.23 shows some sample resources.

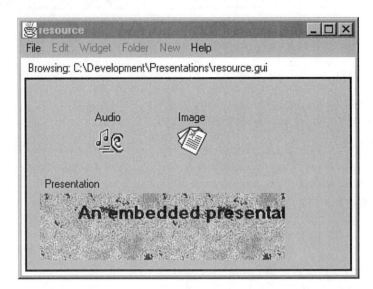

Figure 9.23. *Resource widgets.*

AWT

Finally, AWT widgets (subclasses of `AWTWidget`) are the last group of widgets I'll cover in this chapter. They allow you to mix AWT components and user interface elements, as well as entire applets, into your Bongo presentation.

● Component (class ComponentWidget): Allows you to incorporate AWT widget classes (or subclasses of those classes you've created in Java) into a Bongo presentation. You cannot use the Bongo property editor to set the properties of these objects; all your work must be done in raw Java and compiled into a class file. Switch to Browse mode to see the AWT component in all its glory.

● Applet (class AppletWidget): With this widget you can include an entire Java applet in a presentation and interact with that applet as if it were contained in a Web page.

Figure 9.24 shows both some basic AWT elements (note that they appear very much like widgets) and an embedded applet.

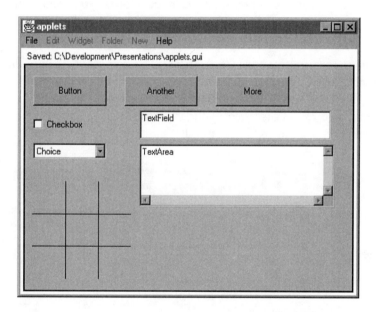

Figure 9.24. AWT widgets.

Converting Bongo Presentations to Channels

Just when you thought you were reading the wrong book, at the end of this chapter, I finally get back to the original point: creating Castanet channels. Bongo presentations can be used as channels almost as easily as HTML Web sites and applets can. If you do all your development scripting inside Bongo, and your presentation works happily inside Bongo, then you're all set. All you need to do is to publish the presentation with the right set of channel properties.

To publish a presentation as a channel, first collect your `.gui` files and any other media (images, audio, Java classes, or other files) that the presentation uses into a single channel directory. In addition to your own channel files, there's one other file you'll need: `bongo.zip`. This is the Marimba library that contains all the classes that make Bongo work; you'll need to include it with each channel you create that uses Bongo presentations. But don't panic; keep in mind that because the tuner can share files between channels, often the users of your presentation channel will already have the `bongo.zip` library. If that's the case, the tuner won't bother downloading your copy. But, because you cannot guarantee that your users will have it, you should include it just to make sure.

You can get the `bongo.zip` library from the lib directory in your Bongo installation. Copy it to your channel directory, fire up Castanet Publish and add that directory to the list of Channels Under Development.

The properties for presentations are identical to all other channels, with the exception of the General properties. In the General Properties panel, you should make sure that the type of channel is Presentation, that you've included the name of the presentation file in the GUI File field, and that `bongo.zip` is listed in the class path field. Figure 9.25 shows the General properties for the sample presentation (called `quickstart.gui`) created earlier in this chapter.

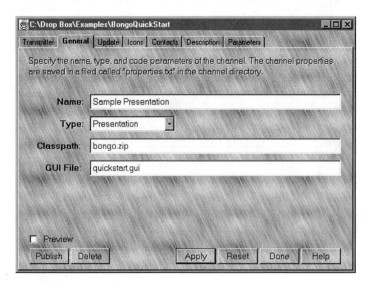

Figure 9.25. *General properties for presentations.*

Other than making sure that the general properties are correct and that you've included `bongo.zip` with every presentation, you don't need to do anything else to get a channel to work as a presentation. After you publish the presentation channel, you're done. You can subscribe to and run that presentation from a tuner just as if you were running it inside Bongo itself.

Summary

Marimba's Bongo is a terrific tool for creating presentations—graphical user interface-based applications with any number of elements (widgets) and scripts to control their behavior. In this chapter, you learned the basics of how to use Bongo to create these kinds of presentations and how to convert these presentations into Castanet channels.

If you haven't had enough of Bongo from this chapter, you should definitely check out *The Official Marimba Guide to Bongo* (published by Sams.net), the companion volume to this book, which contains just about everything you could ever want to know about Bongo.

Three down and one to go! In the next chapter, we'll dive into the last kinds of channels we have left to discuss: application channels.

ten

Creating Application Channels

Although it is entirely possible to create a Marimba Castanet channel with an HTML Web site, a precompiled applet, or an already-built Bongo presentation, true channels are written and compiled in Java and implement several interfaces and events that allow them to coexist with the transmitter and the tuner. There's no other way to allow a channel to accept dynamic updates, to save local files to the user's channel directory, or to send feedback data to the transmitter. To take full advantage of the features Castanet gives you in channel development, you have to use an application channel.

In this chapter, you'll take the first step toward creating real Castanet channels. The channels you create in this chapter will have all the earmarks of a channel, including using the important interfaces and classes in the marimba package and implementing the correct methods and events in your Java code. In the following chapters, you'll build on what you learn in this chapter to add updating and other features.

Working with Java

For this chapter, and for the remainder of this book, you'll be working almost exclusively with the Java language to create full-featured Castanet channels. Beyond this point, things are going to get fairly technical. So before you get in too deep, make sure that you already have the following tools and skills:

● You should have access to a Java development tool such as Sun's JDK or a tool such as Symantec's Café or Microsoft's Visual J++, and know how to use it.

Note

If you use a Java development environment other than Sun's JDK, Marimba recommends you recompile your files with the JDK before publishing them. There have been instances of channels that have thrown Class Not Found exceptions when compiled with third-party development environments that vanished once the code was recompiled.

● You should understand the Java language, including class and interface inheritance, and how to construct classes and implement interfaces.

● You should have a passing understanding of Sun's AWT, including event management.

If you're missing any of this background, you definitely should become familiar with Java before going on.

Note

A great place to start learning Java is the book *Teach Yourself Java in 21 Days*, which I also wrote, and is published by Sams.net Publishing. The text of this book in HTML form is contained on the CD that came with this book.

Note

The 1.0 version of Castanet works only with Sun's 1.02 JDK, not with the newer JDK 1.1. Although future versions of Castanet will support the JDK 1.1 features, for the purposes of this book, you should make sure that you're running a 1.02-compatible compiler and bytecode interpreter.

The `marimba.zip` and `bongo.zip` Libraries

The classes and interfaces you'll be working with in the next couple of chapters are part of the Marimba class libraries. They were installed when you installed the Castanet Transmitter and Bongo. After you start writing applications in Java that use any of the features of Castanet channels, you must make sure that your Java development environment knows about these libraries, usually by editing your CLASSPATH variable or setting the preferences to include these libraries.

The two Marimba class libraries are stored in the files `marimba.zip` and `bongo.zip`. Whether you need one or both depends on the sorts of channels you plan to create:

- ⬤ If you plan to use any of the presentation capabilities of Bongo, you need both `marimba.zip` and `bongo.zip` in your CLASSPATH. They're both in the `lib` directory of your Bongo installation.

- ⬤ If you plan to create channels without presentations (that is, adapt a standard AWT application or applet into a channel), the only library you need is `marimba.zip`. You can find it in the `lib` directory of your Castanet Transmitter installation.

Add the directory paths to each of these files to your CLASSPATH, or configure your development environment to find these files.

Warning

Be careful which `marimba.zip` you use; the `marimba.zip` file in the transmitter installation is different from the `marimba.zip` file in the Bongo installation. (It's a superset of the transmitter's version that includes the classes that let you use presentations in channels.) If you start out not using Bongo for your channel and then switch, you'll also need to switch `marimba.zip` files. Or, avoid the problem altogther, install Bongo, and use the Bongo version all the time.

The `marimba.zip` and `bongo.zip` files provide several packages for general and utility classes you can use while developing your own channels. A full description of these packages is contained in Chapter 14, "An Overview of the Marimba Classes." You'll use the following packages most often:

- ⬤ `marimba.channel`: Classes and interfaces for creating and using channels, including the special wrapper classes for playing applets as channels. This package is contained in `marimba.zip` (although the Bongo-specific classes are missing from the transmitter's version of that library).

- ⬤ `marimba.gui`: Classes particular to Bongo presentations and to using those presentations inside channels. This package includes all the Bongo widget classes. These classes are contained in the `bongo.zip` libraries.

- `marimba.plugin`: Classes for creating transmitter plug-ins. You'll learn about these in Chapter 12, "Creating Transmitter Plug-Ins." These classes are in `marimba.zip`.
- `marimba.io`: Extensions to the standard Java input and output classes to handle channel-specific I/O; they are contained in `marimba.zip`.

Note

In addition to the class libraries, the Bongo and transmitter distributions come with source code for many of these classes. Exploring the source can often help you figure out what's going on in a class or help you figure out what you want to do. Feel free to examine those source files as you create your own channels.

In addition, the API documentation for these classes is available on Marimba's Web site (`http://www.marimba.com/doc/`) or as channels from `trans.marimba.com`. (They're called Bongo doc and Transmitter doc, respectively.)

Anatomy of an Application Channel

Creating application channels in Java is quite similar to creating applets with Java's AWT. If you have any experience with the former, then channels aren't going to seem all that different. Many of the basic methods are the same, and the event and security models are nearly the same as with applets as well. Some basic differences do exist, however.

The heart of all application channels is the Application interface in the `marimba.channel` package. The Application interface provides four important methods for channels:

- `start()`
- `stop()`
- `setContext()`
- `handleEvent()`

I'll cover the first three methods in this chapter in some detail and touch on `handleEvent()` as it's used to interact with presentation widgets. In Chapter 11, "Managing Updates and User Information," you'll learn in detail about update events you can process inside `handleEvent()`.

To create a channel, your main channel class can inherit from any class (usually from a standard Java class like `Frame`), but must implement the Application interface. A basic class template for a channel, then, might look something like the one shown in Listing 10.1. (You'll learn more about the various parts of this template as the section progresses.)

Listing 10.1. A channel template.

```
import marimba.channel.*;

public class MyChannel extends Frame implements Application {

ApplicationContext context;

public void start() {
    // ... initialize the channel
}

public void stop();
    // ... clean up after the channel
}

setContext(ApplicationContext context) {
    this.context = context;
}

public boolean handleEvent(Event evt) {
    return super.handleEvent(evt);
}

}
```

The `start()` and `stop()` Methods

The two methods that drive a channel's life cycle are the `start()` and `stop()` methods.

The `start()` method is called when the channel first starts running. Unlike the `start()` method inside an applet, the channel's `start()` method is called only once, to initialize the channel. It's therefore more analogous to an applet's `init()` method or an application's `main()`. Here's the basic template for the `start()` method:

```
public void start() {
    // ... initialize the channel
}
```

The `stop()` method, analogously, is called once when the channel is about to be destroyed. Inside `stop()`, you add any code to clean up after your channel, including closing windows, killing threads, and releasing any other objects for garbage collection. You might also want to save any state for the channel or reset global values.

```
public void stop();
    // ... clean up after the channel
}
```

The `setContext()` Method and the Application Context

If the Application interface is the heart of the channel, the Application context is its brain. The Application context is, most simply, an object that implements the ApplicationContext interface, also part of the `marimba.channel` package. What the Application context actually provides, however, is a set of methods for interacting with the tuner, finding out information about the channel and its properties (for example, its parameters or how often it's been configured to do updates), and to write log and property files for use by transmitter plug-ins. Chances are good that, at some point in the lifetime of your channel, you'll want to get access to this information.

When your channel is first executed by the Castanet tuner, the `setContext()` method is called just before the `start()` method is called. The `setContext()` method is called with an existing `ApplicationContext` object that contains the channel's Application context. In the body of your `setContext()` method, you should store that context somewhere so that you can use it later. A typical template for `setContext()` inside your channel might look something like this:

```
setContext(ApplicationContext context) {
    this.context = context;
}
```

With the application context stored in the context instance variable, you can then call its methods by referring to that variable.

The `handleEvent()` Method

Worth mentioning at this point is the `handleEvent()` method, which is the fourth method the Application interface provides. `handleEvent()`, like the standard AWT `handleEvent()` in `java.awt.Component`, is used to manage user events that occur inside the application. Inside `handleEvent()`, you should trap any typical events (mouse clicks, key presses), but also manage update events (which you'll learn about in the next chapter).

With normal Java applications, you would test for the `WINDOW_DESTROY` event and then call `System.exit()`. For channels, you should call the `stop()` method on the application context, which manages the existing process (including calling the `stop()` method for the channel). Here, then, is a basic template for `handleEvent()`:

```
public boolean handleEvent(Event evt) {
    switch (evt.id) {
        // ... trap different events

        case WINDOW_DESTROY:
            context.stop();
            return true;
    }
    return super.handleEvent(evt);
}
```

Useful Classes for Creating Channels

Implementing a basic framework for an application channel—or converting a Java application to a channel—doesn't require a whole lot of work. The simple steps you learned in the preceding section are really all you need to follow to get your Java application to work in the channel mechanism. But before you actually start mucking with code, you should know about several classes in the `marimba.channel` package that make this job even easier.

The `ApplicationFrame` and `ApplicationPlayerFrame` classes contain a basic implementation of everything you need to run a basic channel, including basic implementations of `start()`, `stop()`, `setContext()`, and `handleEvent()`.

`ApplicationFrame` is a subclass of the AWT class `Frame`, which implements simple default behavior for all the basic methods, and contains a context variable to hold the context. In fact, the framework in Listing 10.1 is similar to the one provided by the `ApplicationFrame`. If your Java application normally subclasses from `Frame` (to put up a window and use AWT components), subclassing from `ApplicationFrame` instead gives you all the additional channel behavior you need.

`ApplicationPlayerFrame` is a special class for incorporating a Bongo presentation into a Java application that is also a channel. This latter case is one of the easier ways to construct channels by tying together Bongo for the presentation, the Application interface and Application context for the channel behavior, and your own Java code for the meat of the channel. `ApplicationPlayerFrame` inherits from the Bongo class `PlayerFrame`—a special class that the tuner uses to play presentations as channels. `PlayerFrame`, in turn, inherits from `jav.awt.Frame`. So with `ApplicationPlayerFrame`, you have access to the full AWT hierarchy as well as Bongo widgets.

If you subclass either of these classes for your own channels, don't forget to call your superclass's `start()`, `stop()`, and `setContext()` methods, if you override them.

You can find more information about `ApplicationPlayerFrame` in the section "Creating Channels That Use Bongo Presentations."

Using the Application Context

In the `setContext()` method for your application channel, the current application context is usually assigned to an instance variable called `context`. With that context object in hand, you can call various methods that let you get information about the channel and perform tuner operations such as requesting a channel update or a restart. You'll learn about many of the context methods as we proceed through this chapter and the next, but Table 10.1 contains a quick summary of many of the more important methods so you know the sorts of things you can do from inside your own channel.

Table 10.1. `ApplicationContext` methods.

Method name	What it does
`channelFileExists(String)`	Returns `true` if the given relative path exists in the channel.
`getChannelName()`	Returns the full name of the channel.
`getChannelStatus(String)`	Returns the current channel status (one of `unsubscribed`, `subscribed`, or `running`).
`getParameter(String)`	Returns the value of an application parameter, as stored in the `properties.txt` or `parameters.txt` file for the channel (and set in the Castanet Publish).
`getServerName()`	Returns the name of the server (transmitter) for this channel. The transmitter name is of the form `hostname:port`.
`listChannelDirectory(String)`	Returns an array of strings representing the names of files in the given directory. To list the entire channel, use . as the argument. Returns null if the path does not exist.
`listChannels()`	Returns an array of strings representing all the subscribed channels.
`removeChannel(String)`	Remove this channel.
`restart()`	Restart the channel.
`startChannel(String, String)`	Start some other channel. The first argument is the same of the transmitter; the second is the name of the channel.
`stop()`	Stop the channel.
`subscribeChannel(String, String)`	Subscribe to a channel (don't start it). The arguments are the name of a transmitter and the name of the channel.
`unsubscribeChannel(String)`	Unsubscribe from the named channel.
`update()`	Update the channel.

Notes on the Channel Security Model

The security model for application channels is similar to that of applets. Application channels have their own security manager, which restricts the kinds of operations you can perform inside your channel. If you're used to working with applets, the security model is actually more relaxed; you now can save state to the user's local disk in specific directories. If you've been working primarily with stand-alone applications, however, be aware of the channel security restrictions:

- Channels cannot make network connections to any systems other than the original transmitter from which they came.

- Channels cannot read or write files except to a specific directory for that purpose.

- Channels cannot automatically execute local programs or native libraries on the local system. (Installing native code into the tuner is possible, but that requires a conscious effort by the user of that tuner. You'll find more details on this subject in Appendix C, "Tuner Extensions.")

- Channels cannot create threads in ThreadGroups other than the one in which they were created.

Creating Channels That Use Bongo Presentations

Probably the easiest way to construct a channel from scratch is to create its interface in Bongo and then build the channel around that interface. Castanet provides both a class to do this, `ApplicationPlayerFrame`, and the infrastructure in the tuner to make linking together an interface and a Java channel program extremely easy—almost magically so, particularly if you're used to doing a lot of hand-coding in the AWT.

Even if you're used to working in the AWT, using a combination of Bongo and Java has several significant advantages over using AWT alone:

- Bongo's visual tools make creating user interfaces easy. Bongo is also extensible, so you can create and integrate your own widgets into the Bongo model.

- Bongo UI files are stored separately from the rest of the Java code—and can be modified independently of that code without your needing to recompile anything. For larger projects, this capability allows UI designers to work independently of programmers, and the UI designers don't need to know extensive details about Java itself.

- Bongo uses its own graphics and updating model, which means that you no longer have to keep track of painting and repainting. Bongo's model also uses double-buffering, which makes for faster and more efficient screen updates.

- You can write all the event management code for your Bongo widgets in Java, or you can combine Bongo's built-in scripting with external event management. The two interact seamlessly, allowing you to create basic operations entirely in Bongo and shift the more complicated operations to Java itself.

The disadvantage, of course, is that by using Bongo you must also include all the Bongo classes with your channel when you publish it, as you do with Bongo presentations. As with the presentations, however, the zip files are only downloaded once and shared between channels that use them.

Combining Java and Presentations

The following are the four steps to creating a channel that uses a Bongo presentation:

● Create the interface using Bongo, and make sure that you name all the widgets you plan to modify or change. You can use scripting inside Bongo for some basic operations; scripting does not interfere with your Java code.

● Create a main Java application class that is a subclass of `ApplicationPlayerFrame`.

● Inside the Java class, use special methods to interact with the UI widgets in the presentation.

● Publish the channel with references in the channel's properties to both the main Java application class and the presentation file.

These steps are easier than they sound. Much of the linkage between the Java code and the presentation is automatic and managed by the tuner infrastructure and the application context. Let me go over the steps in more detail, and then I'll walk you through a simple application so that you can see the results.

Using the `ApplicationPlayerFrame`

As you learned earlier in this chapter, the `ApplicationPlayerFrame` class provides the basic channel structure you need to make your Java code interoperate with Castanet as a channel, including implementing the Application interface and storing the default application context in an instance variable called `context`.

In addition, the `ApplicationPlayerFrame` class also gives you access to the methods and utilities in a class called `PlayerUtil`. `PlayerUtil` is a Bongo-related class (from the `marimba.gui` package) with which you can gain access to various widgets inside the presentation. The `ApplicationPlayerFrame` class keeps track of the `PlayerUtil` object for the current presentation in the instance variable called `util`.

To use `ApplicationPlayerFrame`, simply create a Java class that extends it. Note that you need to import `marimba.channel` (for the application channel-related classes), `marimba.gui` (for the Bongo-related classes), and typically `java.awt` as well. Listing 10.2 shows a simple template.

Listing 10.2. A template for an `ApplicationPlayerFrame` class.

```
import java.awt.*;
import marimba.channel.*;
import marimba.gui.*;

public class MyChannelPresentation extends ApplicationPlayerFrame {
...
}
```

Note that you don't have to implement the Application interface; the `ApplicationPlayerFrame` class does this job for you. In fact, `ApplicationPlayerFrame` also includes basic versions of each of the four channel methods. You need to override them only if you need to do special things to initialize the application—for example, to read in saved state, to set up a network connection to the transmitter, or to create other windows that the application might use. In many simple cases, the only method you ever need to override is `handleEvent()` to process input from the users of your channel.

Linking Java and the Presentation Together

Note that nowhere in the preceding section did I mention opening the Bongo presentation file or otherwise creating an instance of a class to hold it, or using any methods to display the presentation onscreen. This was not an oversight. If you use `ApplicationPlayerFrame`, you don't have to do any of that work by hand in your channel class. Castanet and the `ApplicationPlayerFrame` class manage that process through the channel properties when you publish the channel. Figure 10.1 shows the general properties for an application channel that uses a presentation.

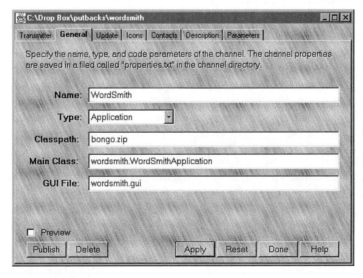

Figure 10.1. *Application channel properties.*

Note

The `bongo.zip` library is in the class path field for the reasons you learned in Chapter 9. You must include the Bongo libraries with every channel that uses Bongo features. See the section titled "Putting It All Together: Publishing and Testing" for more.

If you simply include the name of the presentation in these properties, the `ApplicationPlayerFrame` class and the tuner open and display the presentation for you. Bongo also manages the display and updating of the screen. The only thing you have to concentrate on in your Java code is processing input from your users and interacting with the widgets in the presentation to produce a result. (I told you this process was easy.)

To interact with the widgets in the presentation, you intercept events from the presentation in your `handleEvent()` method. Bongo gets first crack at any events, so if built-in scripts are included in the presentation, these scripts can handle a lot of the simple events. But no scripts are included in the presentation, or if a particular event isn't covered by a script, you can intercept and handle that event in your Java code.

In addition to handling simple events, however, you also need a way to get values out of and put values back into the widgets in the presentation. You do so using that `PlayerUtil` object I mentioned earlier; it's stored in the `util` instance variable.

The `PlayerUtil` object provides a set of useful methods that you can use to get and set values and properties of various widgets. For example, if you have a text box widget named `Password` in your presentation, you can use the following line of Java code to extract the text from that text box widget:

```
String passwd = util.getText("Password");
```

To get ahold of a widget object to call more specific widget methods, you can use the `getWidget()` method and cast that widget object to the appropriate class:

```
SliderWidget slider = (SliderWidget)util.getWidget("volume");
slider.setValue(0); // mute the volume
```

Keep in mind that widget names are case sensitive. Make sure that the name you use in your Java code matches that in your presentation; otherwise, the connection between the two does not work.

In your Java code, you might also find the `getName()` method useful; it's defined on all widgets. In events in particular, you may have a reference to a widget (the target of an event) where you don't know the actual name of the widget. Using the `getName()` method and the `equals()` test, you can test to see whether the widget you have is indeed the one you want:

```
if ( ((Widget)evt.target).getName.equals("volume")) {
   // ... the event is coming from the widget named "volume."
}
```

Table 10.2 shows a few of the `PlayerUtil` methods that you may find useful in your Java code. You can call them via the `util` instance variable (for example, `util.getValue()`). Keep in mind that by getting a reference to the widget itself via `getWidget()`, you can call any method that any widget supports.

Note

Which methods do the widgets support? I don't have the space to go into all of them. The online API documentation for Bongo and *The Official Marimba Guide to Bongo* (Sams.net Publishing) have lots of information about these methods, as well as the complete set of methods defined in `PlayerUtil`.

Table 10.2. `PlayerUtil` methods.

Method name	What it does
`getText(String)`	Gets the text from the text box widget named in the argument. Returns a `String` object.
`setText(String, String)`	Sets the text in the text box widget (named in the first argument) to the text in the second argument. Returns void.
`clearText(String)`	Clears the text box named in the argument.
`getValue(String)`	Gets the value of the widget named in the argument. Returns an object. (Different widgets have different values; you usually need to covert the return value to something useful.)
`setValue(String, Object)`	Sets the value of the widget named in the first argument to the object in the second argument (usually a `String` or a `Number` object). Returns void.
`getBoolean(String)`	Gets the value of the Checkbox or Option widget named in the argument. Returns true or false.
`setBoolean(String, boolean)`	Sets the value of the Checkbox or Option widget named in the argument to the value of the second argument (true or false). Returns void.
`getChoice(String)`	Gets the value of the Choice widget named in the argument. Returns a string.
`setChoice(String,String)`	Sets the value of the Choice widget named in the first argument to the string in the second argument. Returns void.

continues

Table 10.2. continued

Method name	What it does
show(String)	Shows the widget named in the argument.
show(String, boolean)	Shows or hides the argument named in the first argument. If the second argument is true, shows the widget; if false, hides the widget.
getWidget(String)	Gets the Widget object named by the argument. Returns a Widget object (which you most likely need to cast to a more specific widget class).

An Example: The Thermometer Channel

Let me show you a simple example to demonstrate how easy it is to create a channel that uses both a Bongo presentation and the ApplicationPlayerFrame class. This example is fairly simple. It doesn't do anything you couldn't do in Bongo alone, but it serves to demonstrate just how easy it is to put together a channel with ApplicationPlayerFrame.

The example in this section is a simple temperature converter to convert between Fahrenheit and Celsius temperatures and vice versa. The interface contains two spin box widgets for typing in the temperature directly (or incrementing it by one) and a slider for choosing the temperature via more direct means.

The Presentation

Figure 10.2 shows the presentation I created in Bongo for this example. Three widgets here are of note:

- The slider on the left has a range of 32 to 212 (it's a Fahrenheit slider); it's named slider.
- The spin box widget in the top right has a minimum of 32, a maximum of 212, and is named fahr.
- The spin box widget in the lower right has a minimum of 0, a maximum of 100, and is named cels.

I saved this presentation as Thermometer.gui and stored it in my channel directory (which I called Thermometer as well).

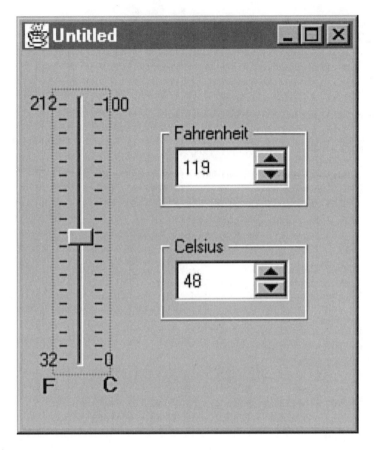

Figure 10.2. *Thermometer presentation.*

The Java Code

Also inside my channel directory, I created a Java file called `ThermometerApplication.java`. The code for that application is shown in Listing 10.3.

Note

The code for this example, and for most of the examples in this book, is available on the CD-ROM that comes with the book. You don't have to retype it all in from here.

Listing 10.3. The `ThermometerApplication` code.

```
 1: import java.awt.*;
 2: import marimba.channel.*;
 3: import marimba.gui.*;
 4:
 5: public class ThermometerApplication extends ApplicationPlayerFrame {
 6:
 7:  public boolean handleEvent(Event evt) {
 8:
 9:     if ((evt.id == Event.ACTION_EVENT) && (evt.target instanceof Widget)) {
10:       Widget targ = (Widget)evt.target;
11:
12:       // redirect target to spinbox if user has changed text
13:       if (targ instanceof SpinBoxTextWidget)
14:         targ = ((SpinBoxTextWidget)targ).getOwner();
15:
16:       if (targ instanceof ValueWidget) {
17:          int temp = ((ValueWidget)targ).value;
18:         int newtemp = 0;
19:
20:         // user has changed value of fahrenheit spinbox
21:          if (targ.getName().equals("fahr")) {
22:           newtemp = (temp - 32) * 5 / 9;
23:           SpinBoxWidget dest = (SpinBoxWidget)util.getWidget("cels");
24:           dest.setValue(newtemp);
25:           util.setValue("slider",String.valueOf(temp));
26:           return true;
27:
28:         // user has changed value of celsius spinbox
29:          } else if (targ.getName().equals("cels")) {
30:           newtemp = temp * 9 / 5 + 32;
31:           util.setValue("fahr", String.valueOf(newtemp));
32:           util.setValue("slider",String.valueOf(newtemp));
33:           return true;
34:
35:         // user has changed  slider
36:          } else if (targ.getName().equals("slider")) {
37:           newtemp = (temp - 32) * 5 / 9;
38:           util.setValue("fahr",String.valueOf(temp));
39:           util.setValue("cels",String.valueOf(newtemp));
40:           return true;
41:       }
42:     }
43:   }
44:   return super.handleEvent(evt);
45:}
46:
47:}
```

Note the following about this example:

● Inside the class, I didn't need to override start(), stop(), or setContext(). Because I don't need to change their behavior, I can rely on the default definitions from the ApplicationPlayerFrame class. The only method I've overridden in this class is handleEvent().

● The `handleEvent()` method tests for events of type `ACTION_EVENT` (line 9), and then only if those actions are triggered by widgets. These actions are triggered by the various widgets; most of the time that's what you're interested in when you're interacting with a Bongo presentation. This `handleEvent()` method could be easily extended to catch other events or even other action events that are not generated by widgets.

● The `handleEvent()` method manages three specific events: when the users change the value of the Fahrenheit spin box, when they change the value of the Celsius spin box, or when they adjust the slider. You can test for each different widget by name (lines 21, 29, and 36) and then act accordingly.

● In the first set of tests (lines 20 through 26), I showed two different ways of accessing the values in the widgets. The first way uses the `getWidget()` method to get the actual spin box widget called `cels` and then sets the value using the `setValue()` method for that spin box (lines 23 and 24). The second method, in line 25 and throughout the rest of the method, is somewhat easier. Here all you have to do is use `util.setValue()` with the name of the widget and the value (converted to a String object).

● As with all `handleEvent()` methods, if you actually process the event, you should return true from the method. If you don't, you should pass the method up to the parent to make sure that the event has a chance to percolate through the entire hierarchy. Note the line in 44 where I pass the event on.

● The lines in 12 through 14 are there to work around a widget bug. The spin box widget is made up of both a slider-like widget and a text box, and the text box events do not percolate unless the event target is reset to the spin box that contains that text box. This will be fixed in a later version of Bongo (and might be fixed by the time you read this).

With the Java code written, all you have to do is compile it. Make sure that you have the `bongo.zip` and `marimba.zip` libraries from the Bongo installation available to your Java compiler or to your development environment.

Putting It All Together: Publishing and Testing

The final step is simply to publish the channel. The channel properties determine the link between the Java code and the presentation, so you cannot simply run the Java class and have it work. You have to run it from inside the Castanet framework.

Fire up Castanet Publish and add the development directory (called Thermometer) to the list of Channels Under Development. Then edit the properties for that channel. Next, switch to the `General` properties. Figure 10.3 shows the properties for the Temperature Converter channel.

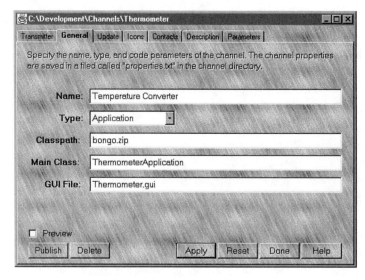

Figure 10.3. *Properties for the Temperature Converter channel.*

The type of channel is Application; this is true whether or not your channel uses a presentation. As long as it implements the application interface, it's an application channel. The main class for the application is the one just created and the one that has the start() and stop() methods in it; here it's called ThermometerApplication (don't include the .class extension in the properties). And, finally, the presentation file that goes along with this channel is the Thermometer.gui file.

One other entry is important to note here: the file bongo.zip, which is included in the classpath field of the properties. This library should also be copied to your channel directory and published along with the channel. Whereas your users always have access to the channel classes through the tuner (the classes in marimba.zip), they might not have access to the bongo classes. If your channel uses any of the classes for Bongo presentations, including ApplicationPlayerFrame, you must publish the bongo.zip file along with your channel and include it here in the properties. This way, you can guarantee that your channel will work on your users' machines.

Note

Although you need to compile your files against the marimba.zip library, you don't need to include it with your channel. marimba.zip comes with every tuner; bongo.zip does not.

After you publish the channel, you can subscribe to it via a tuner and launch it just as you would any other channel. The tuner controls start up your main class, run the start() and setContext() methods, and open and display the presentation. If you've set up the properties correctly, you should now be able to interact with your channel.

If your channel runs into difficulties, you have to go back to your original code, make changes, republish the channel, and then update and relaunch it from the tuner to make sure that your changes work. See "Debugging Hints" for ideas on how to help with the debugging process for presentation-based or any kind of channel.

Using Multiple Presentations in a Channel

Setting up an application to use one presentation works exceptionally well when you have only one presentation. But what if your application uses multiple presentations, with different presentations appearing at a time?

The PlayerUtil class, which is available in the util instance variable, can help with this situation. The setPresentation() method allows you to open and set the current presentation for your application. However, inside a channel, you have to indicate the presentation file you want to open as a URL from the current channel directory. Here's a snippet of code to do just that:

```
try {
   util.setPresentation(new URL(context.getBase(), "mynewspresentation.gui"));
catch (MalformedURLException e) {
   e.printStacTrace();
}
```

Each time you work with URLs, you have to enclose your statements inside a try and catch block to catch any URL exceptions that might occur. The line here that contains the call to setPresentation() gets the current URL from the application context (using the getBase() method) and then appends the name of the presentation file to the end of that. (This example assumes that your GUI file is in the top level of the channel directory.)

If you want to pop up a new window with its own presentation and its own event management inside your application, then you have to worry about subclassing the class PlayerFrame. You use PlayerFrame to present Bongo presentations inside a channel window. It's the same class that allows the tuner to run a Bongo presentation as a channel without any other code. When you subclass the PlayerFrame class, be sure to create a constructor that takes an application context as an argument. And when you create the new PlayerFrame instance, pass in the current application context to that window so that you have access to it from that class. Also in that constructor, use the setPresentation() method to open the presentation you want to use for that window. Here's a simple example that opens a window for the presentation present.gui:

217

```
import java.awt.*;
import java.net.*;
import marimba.gui.*;
import marimba.channel.*;

public class NewFrame  extends PlayerFrame {
MainFrame parent;

public NewFrame (MainFrame parent, ApplicationContext context) {
    super();

    this.parent = parent;

    try {
      util.setPresentation(new URL(context.getBase(), "present.gui"));
    catch (MalformedURLException e) {
      e.printStackTrace();
    }
}

public boolean handleEvent(Event evt) {
    // deal with events from this presentation
}

{
```

Official Marimba Guide to Bongo, also published by Sams.net, contains examples of how to create subclasses of `PlayerFrame` and use them for your own presentations.

Converting Stand-alone Java Applications to Channels

If you do decide to stick with pure Java for your channels, you've already learned most of what you need to do to convert your existing framework to a channel-compatible framework. The following are the specific operations you need to do:

- Implement the `marimba.channel.Application` interface.

- Instead of a `main()` method or a constructor that initializes the application, do all your initialization inside the `start()` method and all your cleaning up inside `stop()`. The tuner uses these methods to start and stop your channel.

- Implement a `setContext()` method to store the `ApplicationContext` object that is passed to you from the tuner. An instance variable called `context` is good for this example.

- To shut down the application (either via a menu item or a `WINDOW_DESTROY` event), instead of calling `System.exit()`, call `context.stop()`. Calling this method shuts down things in the tuner cleanly. Make sure that in your `stop()` method you close all your windows, kill all your threads, and release any other objects you're using. The same runtime is used for all channels, so if you're messy, you can have an impact on someone else's channel.

● Parameters to the application should be passed to the channel via the `parameters.txt` file in the channel. You can use the `context.getParameter()` method to read and process those parameters, instead of using `System.getProperty()`.

● Access all other channel files by URL using the `context.getBase()` method. All data and media files should be relative to this URL.

You'll learn about adding update and file-saving features to channels in the next chapter.

Converting Applets to Applications

Because of the special class that the tuner uses to run applets as applications (`marimba.channel.AppletViewer`), there's little you need to do to convert an applet to a channel, unless you want to go whole hog and port your applet code altogether (in which case, many of the same rules as for applications apply. Here are some things to keep in mind:

● You can gain access to the methods in the channel's application context through the use of the `getAppletContext()` method (a standard `java.applet.Applet class method`), by casting that result to `marimba.channel.AppletContext` and then by calling `getApplicationContext()` on that object, like this:

```
ApplicationContext context =
    ((AppletContext)getAppletContext()).getApplicationContext();
```

You can then use that context and call its methods just as if the applet was a real channel. More about this in the next chapter.

● If you do decide to port your applet code to a channel, keep in mind that the definitions for the `start()` and `stop()` methods are slightly different, because channels do not start and stop running repeatedly the way an applet does. The `start()` in channels is closer in definition to `init()` in applets; `stop()` is more like `destroy()`.

● Be careful of the methods such as `showStatus()` that take advantage of browser features. These methods operate differently when the applet is run as a channel. (`showStatus()` messages, for example, show up in the status line of the tuner's Java console, not in the tuner or channel's windows.)

Debugging Hints

Because the process of writing-compiling-publishing-updating-testing channels can be really slow, debugging becomes particularly important. It can keep you from spending all your time in the process and not enough in actual code. Unfortunately, few tools are currently available for debugging a channel before it's published. Until better tools are available, here are some suggestions for debugging channels:

- Scripting can be done inside Bongo and tested much faster than the same operation in a Java application. For simple operations, consider using a combination of scripting and Java event handling.
- Both Bongo and the tuner have a Java console, which can display error messages and print output such as that produced by System.out.println().
- All Bongo widgets have a list() method, which prints all the values and properties for a widget to help with debugging.

Summary

Congratulations! After only 10 chapters, you've finally created your first real Castanet channel. In this chapter, you learned all about creating application channels, which are Java programs that are run from inside the tuner and can respond to updates and other tuner features.

The marimba.channel package contains the classes and interfaces you'll most likely use as you create your own channels: the Application interface; the ApplicationPlayerFrame class, which you can use to create application channels that use Bongo presentations; and the ApplicationFrame class for converting pure Java applications to channels. In addition, marimba.channel contains the definition of the Application context (the ApplicationContext interface), which is used to interact with the tuner and the local channel directory.

With the basic framework for the channel in place, the next step is to add features specific to channels to that application. Read on to the next chapter for details!

CHAPTER eleven

Managing Updates and User Information

With the basic framework in place for your Castanet channel, the next step is to add the features that make channels interesting: the capabilities to handle live updates from the transmitter and to save state on the user's local disk. The Castanet framework provides several events and methods to accomplish both of these capabilities.

This chapter is divided into two main parts: the first will teach you all about handling updates to application channels whether or not those channels are running; the second will fill you in on how to save state in both application channels and applets running as channels.

The Castanet Update Mechanism

As I've mentioned throughout this book, Castanet channels can be automatically updated at regular intervals so that the version of a channel that is running on a tuner is essentially guaranteed to be the most up to date at all times. This capability is useful for simple executable channels, in which new bug fixes and new features can be downloaded and incorporated into the new channels so that the next time you start them the new version is available. But Castanet's update mechanism also allows you to create channels with live updates—channels that rely on the frequent updating mechanism to incorporate new data and new information into the channel even as it's running. The mechanism Castanet uses to update channels—both live, running channels and inactive channels—involves a sophisticated conversation between the tuner and the channel, with the help of the channel properties, the application context, and a special set of events specifically for updates.

As a channel programmer, you have a wide variety of choices for how to manage updates, from the very simple (ignore the new data until the next time the channel is restarted, as you might for a basic executable program) to the very complex (incorporate the new data into a running channel, or, if the channel isn't running, make a decision whether to launch the channel).

How Updates Work

When an update occurs, the tuner and the channel negotiate how to handle the new information that has arrived as part of the update. Different things happen depending on whether or not the channel is running. If your channel is indeed running, the conversation between the tuner and the channel goes something like this:

⬤ When the tuner is about to make an update (either because the update interval is up, or because the channel specifically requested an update), it sends a "data update" event to the channel. This event gives the channel a chance to save any profile or log data to be sent back to the transmitter. (This case usually happens only when the channel includes a plug-in. You'll learn more about it in Chapter 12, "Creating Transmitter Plug-Ins.")

⬤ The tuner makes an update request from the transmitter. The tuner and transmitter negotiate any new files for the channel, and those files are downloaded to the local machine. The tuner stores those files in a holding area—not in the channel directory.

⬤ The tuner sends a "data available" event to the running channel. This event says "Data is here; what should I do?" The channel can respond by restarting (which also tells the tuner to install the data) or by telling the tuner to go ahead and install the data while the channel is still running.

● The tuner installs the data and sends a "data installed" event to the channel (if it's still running). The channel can then do whatever it needs to do to update itself—change the values of widgets or reset any counters, for example.

If the channel isn't running, the process works slightly differently. For inactive channels, when the tuner makes an update, the channel properties determine what to do. There are three values for the Data Available Action event for inactive channels:

● `ignore`: Ignores the update and installs the data. The next time the channel starts it is updated and ready to go.

● `start`: Starts the channel with the new data installed and available.

● `notify`: Sends a "data notify" event to the channel. The channel can then decide whether to start based on the data. You'll learn more details about this value in the section "Updates to Non-Running Channels."

Update Events and Helper Methods

Channel update events are part of the standard Application interface in the marimba.channel package. In your channel application, you need to test for and handle these events in your `handleEvent()` method, just as you would test for and manage any other events in your application. The four channel update events and the reactions you're expected to have to these events are as follows:

● `DATA_UPDATE_EVENT`: The update is about to happen; save any profiles or log information.

● `DATA_AVAILABLE_EVENT`: The update has happened, and the data is waiting in the holder area, ready to be installed. Usually, you either call `context.restart()` or `context.installData()` in response to this event. The former stops the channel, installs the data, and restarts the channel. The latter installs the data quietly while the channel is still running. (Note that you, the programmer, don't install any of the data yourself; you just tell the tuner to install it.)

● `DATA_INSTALLED_EVENT`: You get this event when `installData()` has been successful; the channel has been updated with new data. In response to this event, you incorporate the new data into your running channel.

● `DATA_NOTIFY_EVENT`: You get this event only when the channel isn't running—or rather, the tuner starts up just enough of your channel for you to be able to handle this event. See "Updates to Non-Running Channels" for more information on this case.

If you're using either the `ApplicationFrame` or `ApplicationPlayerFrame` classes for your channel, a default version of `handleEvent()` manages the `DATA_AVAILABLE_EVENT` and `DATA_INSTALLED_EVENT` events in a sensible way. (These two are typically the events you use.) To make this default implementation easier to use, `ApplicationFrame` and `ApplicationPlayerFrame` define two event handler methods: `notifyAvailable()` to handle `DATA_AVAILABLE_EVENT` events, and `notifyInstall()` to handle `DATA_INSTALLED_EVENT` events.

The `notifyAvailable()` Method

The `nofifyAvailable()` method from either `ApplicationFrame` or `ApplicationPlayerFrame` looks like this:

```
public void notifyAvailable(String dir) {
    if ("restart".equals(context.getParameter("update.action")))
        context.restart();
    else if ("install".equals(context.getParameter("update.action")))
        context.installData("");
}
```

In this default implementation, the channel checks its properties (available from the application context using the `getParameter()` method) to determine what to do next. You set these properties in the publish tool. For active channels, three possible values are available for the Data Available Action under Active channels: `ignore`, `restart`, or `install`. (See Figure 11.1.)

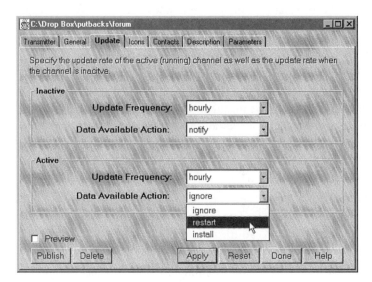

Figure 11.1. *Update properties for active channels.*

If the update property (update.action) is set to restart(), the notifyAvailable() method calls context.restart(), which tells the tuner to stop the channel (call stop()), install the data, and start the channel (call setContext() and start()).

If the properties for the Data Available Action have been set to install, then this method calls context.InstallData(). The null string argument to installData() says to install all the new data; you can also choose to install only some of the data by indicating a filename as the argument to installData().

Finally, if the update property is set to ignore, this method does nothing. The new data will not be installed until the next time the user starts the channel.

If you want different behavior for managing updates, you can override this method in your own subclass of ApplicationFrame, as long as you use the same signature:

```
public void notifyAvailable(String dir) {
...
}
```

The notifyInstall() Method

The second event handler method that ApplicationFrame and ApplicationPlayerFrame provides is notifyInstall(), in response to DATA_INSTALLED_EVENT events. This method is called in response to the context.installData() method to let your channel know that the new data has been installed and is ready for you to process it.

The default implementation of notifyInstall() looks like this:

```
public void notifyInstall(String dir) {
}
```

Not very useful, is it? That's because generally you want to do your own thing here—call a method to load a data file or to update the values of your widgets, for example. This empty template for notifyInstall() is available in the ApplicationFrame and ApplicationPlayerFrame classes so that you can remember to override it in your own subclasses.

Finding Out Which Files Will Be Updated

Both the notifyInstall() and notifyAvailable() methods take one argument: the string argument of the event, which is always null (""). The original intent of this argument was to provide the path to the topmost directory that contained files that would change, so you could figure out which files to actually install as part of the update, if any. Unfortunately, this didn't work, as the properties.txt file that comes with the channel always changes, and the argument is always a null string ("").

Instead, you can use `context.getPendingUpdates()` inside the body of your `notifyInstall()` or `notifyAvailable()` methods to find out which files will be created, changed, or deleted as part of the updates. The `getPendingUpdates()` method returns an object of type `Updates`. `Updates` is a class in `marimba.channel`, whose methods will allow you to check for which files are going to be changed as part of the update. There are three methods to choose from: `getDeletes()`, `getCreates()`, and `getUpdates()`, all of which return an Enumeration object. The `Enumeration`, in turn, contains strings representing paths to the files which will be deleted, created, or changed as part of the update, respectively. You can use this information to pick which files to install, should you so choose.

Updates to Non-Running Channels

Previously in this chapter, I mentioned `DATA_NOTIFY_EVENT`, which is sent only to channels that aren't running. This may seem kind of silly—if the channel isn't running, how can it possibly handle the event? In reality, the process is more complicated than that. Managing updates to channels that aren't running is a special case that allows the channel to decide, on the fly, if an update is worth starting up the channel. You could think of this process as the tuner nudging your channel awake and saying, "I have this data. What do you want to do?" Your channel then either decides that the data isn't important and goes back to sleep, or it becomes fully awake and launches to handle that new data. Here's how it works:

● The tuner receives an update, and the channel properties for inactive channels are set to `notify`. It installs the new data into the channel directory.

● The tuner instantiates the channel class, calls `setContext()`, and then posts the `DATA_NOTIFY_EVENT` event.

● At this point, enough of the channel is running for the channel to be able to react to the event. The channel can then decide what to do next. If the event handler returns false, the tuner shuts down the channel. If the handler returns true, the tuner calls `start()` to fully launch the channel with the new data installed and available.

So what sort of situation would the channel need in order whether to decide to start? Perhaps the channel has preferences that allow the user to decide whether to launch the channel when new data is available. In response to the `DATA_NOTIFY_EVENT`, the channel could check those preferences and respond in kind. Or, perhaps, the channel should start itself only during business hours while someone is potentially there to pay attention, in which case the channel could check the current time on the system. Or your channel might have some other reason for deciding whether to launch based on new information. With this mechanism in place, you have that choice.

If you do want to process events of this type, you have to add a test for the `DATA_NOTIFY_ACTION` event in your `handleEvent()` method. No helper methods are defined by default, so you don't have to override them. Return false to ignore the new data or true to start the channel, something like this:

```
public boolean handleEvent(Event evt) {
   switch (evt.id) {
      case DATA_NOTIFY_EVENT:
         boolean start = test_to_see_if_you_need_to_start();
         if (start)
            return true;
         else return false;
   }
}
```

Keep in mind also that, when you handle this event (say, in the method I've called test_to_see_if_you_need_to_start() in the example), the start() method for your channel has not yet been called. You therefore may have to initialize some values before you have enough information to work with.

After you modify your channel to take advantage of these kinds of events, don't forget to set the properties for that channel when you publish it so that the Data Available Action for the Inactive channel is notify. (See Figure 11.2.)

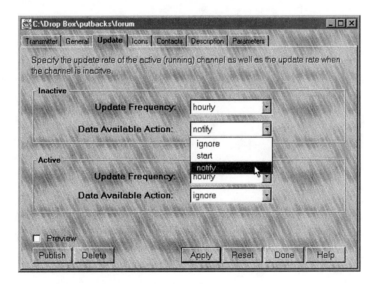

Figure 11.2. Set the Data Available Action to notify.

Updating Applications and Applets

If you create a channel from scratch from the ApplicationFrame or ApplicationPlayerFrame classes, templates for event management are there for you. If you convert an existing application or applet to a channel, however, you'll have to manage updates differently.

If you convert a pure Java application to a channel by implementing the Application interface, neither `notifyInstall()` or `notifyAvailable()` will be available to you. You'll have to implement those methods yourself, or handle all the update events in your own `handleEvent()` methods, just as you manage other events. You can use the source to `ApplicationFrame` and `ApplicationPlayerFrame` (or the examples shown in the preceding section) as a template to manage your own events.

If you're using an applet as a channel, unfortunately with the current version of Castanet, events are not passed to your applet class, so you cannot intercept or handle live update data. However, you can set up your applet such that if new data arrives as part of an update, you can tell the applet to restart itself. The tuner stops the applet and then reloads all the applet's code and data—effectively updating the running applet.

To take this step, you don't need to modify the applet code at all. Simply change the Update properties for that channel in Castanet Publish so that the value of the Data Available Action menu is `restart` and then republish the channel. (See Figure 11.3.)

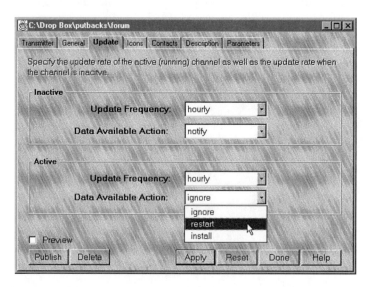

Figure 11.3. *Set the Data Available Action to* `restart`.

Having this value for your applet channel causes the tuner (actually, the applet context in which your applet is running) to restart the applet if any data is available for that update.

An Example: The Weather Channel

Background is all well and good, but an example can really help make it all clear. For this example, I'll walk you through building a channel that relies on frequently updated data and incorporates updates to that data into the channel even if it's running.

The channel created here, called the Weather Channel, is shown in Figure 11.4. It provides basic weather information about three cities: San Francisco, New York, and London, including the conditions (sunny, cloudy, raining), the temperature, and the humidity. The data that the weather channel displays is updated on a regular basis (say, every 15 minutes), and is updated on the fly even if the channel is running. So if you run the weather channel, you can be sure of having the latest up-to-date weather information for these three cities.

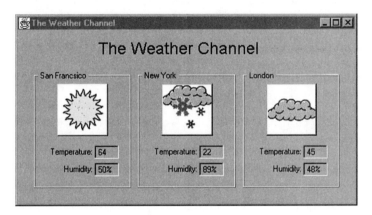

Figure 11.4. *The Weather Channel.*

Note

The source for this channel is available on the CD-ROM for this book, in the directory `Examples` and the subdirectory `Weather`.

This channel is made up of four files:

- The interface, created in Bongo, which includes a set of images for each of the different conditions (sunny, partly cloudy, cloudy, rainy, snowing).
- A text file, called `data.txt`, which stores the raw weather data for the cities.
- A main Java class to manage the channel, including loading in the data and handling update events.
- A utility Java class called `WeatherData`.

The Presentation

I created the interface for this presentation in Bongo, with essentially nine parts: three image widgets for each of the condition images (with the names `SFimg`, `NYimg` and `Limg`), three static text widgets for the temperature (`SFtemp`, `Nytemp`, and `Ltemp`), and three for the humidity (`SFhum`, `NYhum`, and `Lhum`).

Note

My implementation of this channel is terribly inefficient, as will become more apparent later when you see the Java code. This interface might make a lot more sense if I had written a custom Bongo widget for each of the cities. The widgets would make the channel easier to update and allow the creation of a menu of cities in which the user is interested. However, because I haven't covered creating bongo widgets in this book, explaining it this way is easier. If you're interested in learning more about custom widgets, check out *The Official Marimba Guide to Bongo* (by Sams.net Publishing).

Five condition images are also included; they're stored in a directory called images. Figure 11.5 shows these images:

Figure 11.5. The five condition images.

The Framework

The main framework for this channel is contained in a file called WeatherChannel.java. You can start by creating the basic framework for this channel and then add the methods for loading the data and for managing the updates later.

This channel uses several classes from other packages, including input classes from marimba.io, URL classes from java.net, and the StringTokenizer class from java.util to parse the data file. The first part of the class, then, is this prodigious set of import statements:

```
import java.awt.*;
import java.net.*;
import java.util.*;
import java.io.IOException;
import marimba.gui.*;
import marimba.channel.*;
import marimba.persist.*;
import marimba.io.*;
```

Next is the definition of the channel class, called WeatherChannel, which inherits from ApplicationPlayerFrame. Inside that class is an instance variable to store the name of the data file ("data.txt"), a set of constants for the kind of weather condition (they will be important later in the class), and a basic start() method. The start() method here does two things: it sets the value of the title bar (a nice UI feature), and it calls the loadData(), method (defined in the next section), which opens, reads, and parses the data file. Here's the basic class framework:

```
public class WeatherChannel extends ApplicationPlayerFrame {

/* data file */
String src = "data.txt";

/* conditions */
static final int SUNNY = 0;
static final int PARTLY_CLOUDY = 1;
static final int CLOUDY = 2;
static final int RAINY = 3;
static final int SNOWY = 4;

/* override start to read in the initial data */
public void start() {
  super.start();
  setTitle("The Weather Channel");
  loadData();
}

}
```

Load the Data

All the actual weather data for this application channel is stored in a separate file. This way, the data can be updated independently, without having to update the entire channel each time. But what this also means is that as part of the start-up process for the channel, you have to open and read that data from the file. To do so, you can define a method called loadData(), which goes into the class file just below the start() method.

loadData() has several important features. The first is the input class it uses: the class FastInputStream. This class is part of the marimba.io package, and is an optimized buffered input stream. It's much more efficient than the standard Java IO classes, so you can use it here. (Because the Bongo classes are already included as part of this channel, there's no penalty in taking advantage of other classes as well.)

The second important feature is the use of a utility class called WeatherData, which is a simple class that collects the weather data into a single structure. The WeatherData class looks like this:

```
public class WeatherData {
String city;
int conditions;
String temp;
String humidity;
}
```

Each of the instance variables in the WeatherData class corresponds to an entry in the data.txt file. The data.txt file itself stores the weather information, one city per line, with the different bits of data separated by spaces. Comments are lines that start with a hash sign (#). A sample data.txt file might look like this:

```
# weather channel data file
# city conditions temperature humidity
#
SF 0 0 50%
NY 1 0 89%
L  0 0 20%
```

If you keep these features and the format of the data file in mind, the rest of the loadData() method should be straightforward. First, you open the FastInputStream using a URL. (You can get the base URL from the application context; you'll learn more about that in the section on saving state.) Next, use the standard Java StringTokenizer class to read each bit of the data file into an instance of the WeatherData class, and then call the fillWidgets() method. This method is used to actually update the widgets in the presentation with the data you've read from the file. And, finally, you wrap all the stuff in loadData() in a try/catch block to make sure that you catch any URL or I/O errors.

Here's the complete loadData() method:

```
public void loadData() {
    try {
        URL base = new URL(context.getBase(), src);
        String str;
        WeatherData data;
        FastInputStream in = new FastInputStream(base.openStream());

        while ((str = in.readLine()) != null) {
            str.trim();
            data = new WeatherData();
            if ((str.length() > 0) && !str.startsWith("#")) {
                StringTokenizer st = new StringTokenizer(str);
                data.city = st.nextToken();
                data.conditions = Integer.parseInt(st.nextToken());
                data.temp = st.nextToken();
                data.humidity = st.nextToken();

                fillWidgets(data);
            }
        }
        in.close();
    }
    catch (MalformedURLException e) {
        e.printStackTrace();
    }
    catch (IOException e) {
        e.printStackTrace();
    }
}
```

You can now move on to the fillWidgets() method, which simply uses the PlayerUtil object stored in util and the setValue() method to put the data into the right spot in each widget in the presentation.

Note

With this method, it should become all too apparent that my design could be much better implemented. With a better interface, this code could probably be shrunk down to only a few lines.

Because all of fillWidget() is straightforward (using the same widget methods you've learned about before), I'll simply print it here. Note that when you use the setValue() method on image objects, you're setting the path to that image (unlike other widgets that have real displayable values.) Keep in mind as well that because the interface was created in Bongo, Bongo manages updating the screen for the new images automatically; you don't have to deal with paint() or repaint() at all as you do when you use the AWT.

```
public void fillWidgets(WeatherData data) {
    String cityimg  ="";
    String citytemp = "";
    String cityhum  = "";

    if (data.city.equals("SF")) {
        cityimg = "SFimg";
        citytemp = "SFtemp";
        cityhum = "SFhum";
    } else if (data.city.equals("NY")) {
        cityimg = "NYimg";
        citytemp = "NYtemp";
        cityhum = "NYhum";
    } else if (data.city.equals("L")) {
        cityimg = "Limg";
        citytemp = "Ltemp";
        cityhum = "Lhum";
    }

    switch (data.conditions) {
        case SUNNY:
            util.setValue(cityimg, "images/sunny.gif");
            break;
        case PARTLY_CLOUDY:
            util.setValue(cityimg, "images/pcloud.gif");
            break;
        case CLOUDY:
            util.setValue(cityimg, "images/cloudy.gif");
            break;
        case RAINY:
            util.setValue(cityimg, "images/rainy.gif");
            break;
        case SNOWY:
            util.setValue(cityimg, "images/snow.gif");
            break;
    }
    util.setValue(citytemp, data.temp);
    util.setValue(cityhum, data.humidity);
}
```

Add Update Management

At this point, you can compile, publish, subscribe to, and run the weather channel, and it would work just fine. But to get new weather data through updates, you would need to quit and restart the channel each time. That's no fun at all.

Instead you can add methods to deal with updating the channel as it runs. This way, no matter how frequently the weather data gets updated, the running channel always displays the latest information. To do this, you can override with the `notifyAvailable()` and `notifyInstall()` methods that the `ApplicationPlayerFrame` class gives you.

The default `notifyAvailable()` checks to see if the properties for the channel indicate whether the channel is to restart or the channel is to be notified. I know how the channel will be published, and that the properties will indicate that the data is to be installed, so my version of `notifyAvailable()` is much smaller. The only data I'm interested in is the data.txt file. If there's anything else to update, it can be installed the next time the channel is restarted.

My new version of `nofityAvailable()` does only one thing: it installs the data.txt file in the channel directory. Note that if you call the `installData()` method with a null argument (`""`),all the new data is installed. Here I've called it explicitly with the data file to speed up the process:

```
public void notifyAvailable(String dir) {
context.installData(src);
}
```

After the data has been installed, the tuner sends the `DATA_INSTALL_EVENT`, which is then passed to `notifyInstall()`. Inside `notifyInstall()`, you need to do whatever you need to do to process that new data file (remember, the default implementation of `notifyInstall()` is empty). Fortunately, because the data loading is factored into its own method, this is easy. All you need to do is to call `loadData()` again, and the new data is loaded and displayed in the existing presentation. Easy!

```
public void notifyInstall(String dir) {
    loadData();
}
```

And that, believe it or not, is it. These two small methods are all you need to make automatic updates to live channels. Of course, if your channel is more complicated than the simple channel created here, then your update methods could very well be much more complex than these, but that's the basic idea.

Publish the Channel

Just as a reminder, let me go over organizing your files into a channel directory and publishing the channel so that all the settings are right.

You can put all the channel files into a directory called Weather, which includes the following files:

● `weather.gui`, the Bongo presentation for the user interface to the weather channel.

● `WeatherApplication.class` and `WeatherData.class`, the compiled Java files for the channel.

● `data.txt`, the weather data file.

● The images directory, which contains the five weather images (all of them GIF files).

● The `bongo.zip` library. Don't forget this one! You can't guarantee that your users won't have it. (Chances are, they will, but better safe than sorry.)

To publish the channel, you set the General properties to refer to the `WeatherApplication` as the main class, `weather.gui` as the presentation, and `bongo.zip` as the classpath. Figure 11.6 shows these settings.

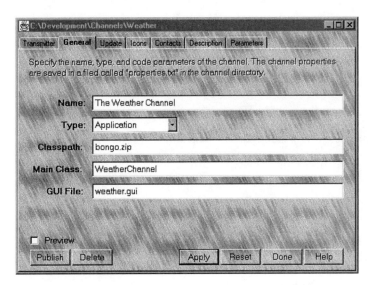

Figure 11.6. General properties for The Weather Channel.

You also should check the update properties of the channel. Inactive channels can update only once a day, and you can ignore new data (it is installed when the user decides to start the channel). For active channels, however, set the frequency to something reasonable. (I don't think anyone needs to know about changes in the weather more than once an hour, so I set the interval to an hour.) Also, set the Data Available Action to `install`. (This setting triggers the update events in your channel.) Figure 11.7 shows the update properties for this channel.

235

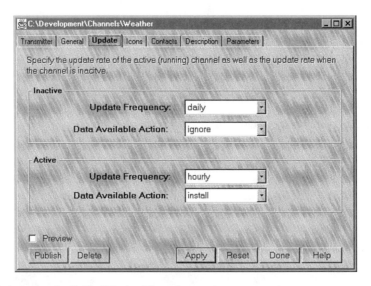

Figure 11.7. *Update properties for The Weather Channel.*

Note

If you set the Data Available Action to restart, what happens? Remember that when you overrode the original version of notifyAvailable(), you took out the check for the restart property. Therefore, context.restart() never gets called. The data is installed regardless of the update properties, but restart doesn't work unless you explicitly call context.restart() in your event handler methods.

The Complete Code

Listing 11.1 shows the full code for the WeatherApplication.java file, built in the preceding sections. You can also view this code on the CD-ROM that came with this book.

Listing 11.1. Complete code for the Weather Channel.

```java
import java.awt.*;
import java.net.*;
import java.util.*;
import java.io.IOException;
import marimba.gui.*;
import marimba.channel.*;
import marimba.persist.*;
import marimba.io.*;

public class WeatherChannel extends ApplicationPlayerFrame {

/* data file */
String src = "data.txt";
```

```
/* conditions */
static final int SUNNY = 0;
static final int PARTLY_CLOUDY = 1;
static final int CLOUDY = 2;
static final int RAINY = 3;
static final int SNOWY = 4;

/* override start to read in the initial data */
public void start() {
  super.start();
  setTitle("The Weather Channel");
  loadData();
}

/* notifyAvailable is called just before the data is
actually installed. It's like the tuner is asking
permission. installData() says OK, go ahead.
Here we'll restrict the install to the data file
because that's all we care about. All other new data
will get installed when the channel restarts */
public void notifyAvailable(String dir) {
    context.installData(src);
}

/* notifyInstall is called after the data has been installed.
Here's where we process the new stuff. */
public void notifyInstall(String dir) {
    loadData();
}

/* read in the data.txt file, which has the current weather values
we'll display. Format is
city condition temperature humidity
*/
public void loadData() {
    try {
        URL base = new URL(context.getBase(), src);
        String str;
        WeatherData data;
        FastInputStream in = new FastInputStream(base.openStream());

        while ((str = in.readLine()) != null) {
            str.trim();
            data = new WeatherData();
            if ((str.length() > 0) && !str.startsWith("#")) {
                StringTokenizer st = new StringTokenizer(str);
                data.city = st.nextToken();
                data.conditions = Integer.parseInt(st.nextToken());
                data.temp = st.nextToken();
                data.humidity = st.nextToken();

                fillWidgets(data);
            }
        }
        in.close();
    }
```

continues

237

Listing 11.1. continued

```java
        catch (MalformedURLException e) {
            e.printStackTrace();
        }
        catch (IOException e) {
            e.printStackTrace();
        }
    }

    /* fill in widget data. This is so not efficient (kludge!  kludge!)
    This app would be much better implemented with
    each city as a custom bongo widget; that'd let them get
    reused here as well as dynamically built. */
    public void fillWidgets(WeatherData data) {
        String cityimg ="";
        String citytemp = "";
        String cityhum   = "";

        if (data.city.equals("SF")) {
            cityimg = "SFimg";
            citytemp = "SFtemp";
            cityhum = "SFhum";
        } else if (data.city.equals("NY")) {
            cityimg = "NYimg";
            citytemp = "NYtemp";
            cityhum = "NYhum";
        } else if (data.city.equals("L")) {
            cityimg = "Limg";
            citytemp = "Ltemp";
            cityhum = "Lhum";
        }

        switch (data.conditions) {
            case SUNNY:
                util.setValue(cityimg, "images/sunny.gif");
                break;
            case PARTLY_CLOUDY:
                util.setValue(cityimg, "images/pcloud.gif");
                break;
            case CLOUDY:
                util.setValue(cityimg, "images/cloudy.gif");
                break;
            case RAINY:
                util.setValue(cityimg, "images/rainy.gif");
                break;
            case SNOWY:
                util.setValue(cityimg, "images/snow.gif");
                break;
        }
        util.setValue(citytemp, data.temp);
        util.setValue(cityhum, data.humidity);
    }

    }
```

Saving State

Now that you've grasped updates, let me cover "saving state" in your channel. Saving state is the ability to store information about the current state of the application on the users' machines—for example, their current position in a game, or files they've created using your channel. You can also save state for things like user preferences for the channel.

The ability to save state in channels on the users' machines is a significant advantage to using channels over applets. To save state in an applet, applet developers usually have to save the state back to the Web server where the applet came from. This process requires an application running on the server to process that data, file space on the server to store it, and an extra network connection to take up bandwidth and time for the applet to run. Being able to save local state is a much better idea.

Note

> If saving state to the local system is that great an idea, why can't applets do it? When applets first arrived on the Web, the security concerns were so great that browser developers decided not to let the applets have any access to the local file systems whatsoever. Although this was good for security and for encouraging warm, fuzzy feelings among nervous Java users, it has restricted the kinds of applications that can be developed with Java.
>
> Browser developers have also come to the conclusion that perhaps denying access to the file systems altogether is a bit extreme. Both Microsoft and Netscape are planning to loosen security in future versions of their browsers, configurable by the user, for saving local state in applets. But in the meantime, you can save state in channels right now.

Channels are given access to one directory on the local file system: the channel's data directory. Most other local file accesses are restricted or forbidden. I say "most" because there's one other exception: If the user allows it by setting an option in the tuner, channels can also read files from a CD-ROM.

In this section, you'll learn about the channel's data directory and the classes and methods you can use to help read and write local files from that data directory.

A Note on Accessing Channel Data

Before you dive into the meat of this section, I need to make an important distinction here between accessing files that are part of the channel itself and reading or writing files that are part of the local data for that channel.

You'll commonly want to read or process files that are part of the actual channel itself—for example, the data file in the Weather Channel example. These files are created on the transmitter side and sent to the tuner as part of a channel subscription or an update. These files are stored as part of the channel and are not to be modified by the user running that channel.

You can read any of these kinds of files in your channel code from any location in your channel directory, with one restriction: you must use a URL to access them. You can get the base URL of the channel itself by using the `context.getBase()` method. That URL will be of the form `tuner://hostname:port/channel`, where the `hostname` and `port` are the hostname and port of the transmitter from which the channel came, and the `channel` is the local directory path to that channel. You can then append the pathname of the file you want to access to that URL (the standard `java.net.URL` methods let you do this) and use the `openStream()` method to attach an input stream to that file. Here's an example template of how to do this using the `FastInputStream` class from `marimba.io`:

```
URL base = new URL(context.getBase(), "myfile.txt");
FastInputStream in = new FastInputStream(base.openStream());
```

Accessing Local Data

Accessing channel data using `getBase()` is different from accessing local channel data. The former is data used by every instance of the channel, regardless of who has downloaded it. The latter is for saving files and data specific to an individual instance of a channel—for example, preferences files, scores a user has made in a game, local state files, and so on. With channels, you can read and write any number of local state files using standard file access methods—with the one restriction that those files can be contained only in a special data directory intended for just that purpose.

The data directory is located on a user's local disk, in the `.marimba` directory used for storing channel files (the default directories are `C:\Windows\.marimba` or `C:\WinNT\.marimba` on Windows systems, `$HOME/.marimba` on UNIX systems). Inside the `.marimba` directory is a subdirectory for each transmitter, and inside these directories are the channel and data directories. The channel directory stores the channel data for each channel; the data directory contains the data.

You don't really need to know this specific information to access the data directory for your channel; the application context provides methods for just that purpose. Two methods, `context.getDataDirectory()` and `context.getDataBase()`, give you the pathname to the local data directory. The former returns a string; the latter returns a URL object.

To open a file called `preferences.txt` in the local data directory, then, you can use the following two lines (which use `java.io.File` and `marimba.io.FastInputStream` classes):

```
File f = new File(context.getDataDirectory(), "preferences.txt");
FastInputStream fs = new FastInputStream(f);
```

After the input stream is open and attached to a file, you can read it using standard input methods just as you would read any other file. The same process applies to writing files; just use the `getDataDirectory()` method to get the pathname to that file.

Note

Earlier versions of the Castanet software used `getChannelDirectory()` for this same purpose. This method is obsolete and will be removed from a later version of Castanet. If you're working with code that uses this method, you should switch over to `getDataDirectory()`.

In addition to the basic files you can read and write into the data directory for your channel, Castanet also defines two special kinds of files: *channel log* files and *channel profiles*. These files are used to generate feedback data to the transmitter and are part of the transmitter plug-in mechanism. You'll learn more about these files in Chapter 12.

Accessing the CD-ROM

The Castanet Tuner has an option in its configuration screens that allows a channel further access to the user's local disk: It allows channels to read files from a CD-ROM. You can use this feature to create a hybrid channel and CD-ROM product; you could store extremely large files on the CD, and then have the bulk of the channel as a regular updateable program.

To read files from the CD-ROM, you open and read the files using I/O streams, just as you would with a regular Java application. (The `java.awt.FileDialog` class may be useful so that the user can point you to the CD-ROM.) However, because the option to allow the channel might or might not be turned on, trying to open a file from the CD may result in a security exception. If you catch that security exception in your channel code, you can tell the user to enable this option in the tuner and try again.

See Marimba's Web site (`http://www.marimba.com/developer/`) for examples of how to read files from a CD-ROM.

An Example: An Estimated Tax Calculator

To demonstrate the use of saving state in the channel's transmitter directory, I created a simple channel that calculates estimated income taxes based on income and deductions. If I had written this channel so that it didn't save state, the users of the channel would have to reenter the data each time they started the channel. It's much more usable if I save the data when the channel quits and then reload it when the channel starts up again.

Figure 11.8 shows the channel interface which, like most of the channels in this section, is created in Bongo.

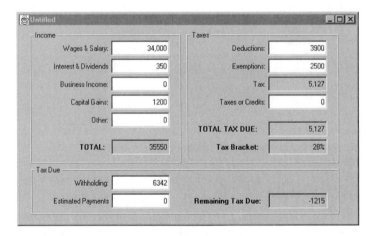

Figure 11.8. *The Tax Calculator channel.*

Note

> To keep things simple, this channel calculates taxes only for single people. Apologies to all those married folk; you'll need to write your own income tax calculator.

The Java code for this example is a subclass of `ApplicationPlayerFrame` called `TaxesApplication`. A single instance variable called `src` is included. This variable contains the name of the file to which you save the current channel state. Here's the basic framework for the channel:

```
import java.awt.*;
import java.net.*;
import java.io.*;
import marimba.channel.*;
import marimba.gui.*;
import marimba.io.*;

public class TaxesApplication extends ApplicationPlayerFrame {

String src = "values.txt";

}
```

When the channel starts up, the first step is to read any local data that might have been saved. When the channel shuts down, you have to save the local data to a file so that it can be restored when the channel starts up again. To do both these things, you can override the start() and stop() methods to call functions called readValues() and writeValues()for reading and writing the local data. The following shows both start() and stop() methods for this class:

```
public void start() {
    super.start();
    readValues();
}

public void stop() {
    super.stop();
    writeValues();
}
```

Now, working backward, start with the definition of writeValues(), which takes the values the user has entered into the application and saves that data to a file on the local machine. Listing 11.2 shows the code for the writeValues() method.

Listing 11.2. The writeValues() method for the Tax Calculator.

```
 1: public void writeValues() {
 2:     File vfile = new File(context.getDataDirectory(), src);
 3:     try {
 4:       FastOutputStream fs = new FastOutputStream(vfile);
 5:
 6:       fs.println(util.getValue("wages"));      // wages & salary
 7:        fs.println(util.getValue("int"));            // interest & dividends
 8:        fs.println(util.getValue("business")); // business income
 9:        fs.println(util.getValue("capgains")); // capital gains
10:       fs.println(util.getValue("otherinc")); // other income
11:       fs.println(util.getValue("deduct"));    // deductions
12:       fs.println(util.getValue("exempt"));     // exemptions
13:       fs.println(util.getValue("credits"));   // credits
14:       fs.println(util.getValue("withhold")); // withholding
15:       fs.println(util.getValue("estpayment")); // estimated payments
16:
17:       fs.close();
18:     }
19:     catch (IOException e) {
20:       e.printStackTrace();
21:     }
22:}
```

Here's a line-by-line description of what's going on, in case you're lost:

● Line 2 creates a new File object (File is a standard java.io class) with the pathname returned from the getDataDirectory() method and the name of the file contained in src. The result is the full local pathname to the values file.

243

- Line 4 opens the file and attaches an output stream (an instance of FastOutputStream) to that file.

- Lines 6 through 15 extract the values from the important widgets in the tax calcula-tor and write those values to the file, one per line. Note that you only write the widgets that have user input; widgets such as Total Income and Total Tax are automatically calculated and don't need to be saved.

- Line 17 closes the output stream.

- All the output code is wrapped in a try/catch block to catch any I/O errors that might occur.

After the data is saved, the next step is to read it back in when the application starts up again. The readValues() method, which is analogous to the writeValues() method, is shown in Listing 11.3.

Listing 11.3. The readValues() method for the Tax Calculator.

```
 1: public void readValues() {
 2:     File vfile = new File(context.getDataDirectory(), src);
 3:     if (vfile.exists(src)) {
 4:         try {
 5:             FastInputStream fs = new FastInputStream(vfile);
 6:
 7:             util.setValue("wages", fs.readLine());      // wages & salary
 8:             util.setValue("int", fs.readLine());         // interest & dividends
 9:             util.setValue("business", fs.readLine()); // business income
10:         util.setValue("capgains", fs.readLine()); // capital gains
11:         util.setValue("otherinc", fs.readLine()); // other income
12:         util.setValue("deduct", fs.readLine());   // deductions
13:         util.setValue("exempt", fs.readLine());    // exemptions
14:         util.setValue("credits", fs.readLine());  // credits
15:         util.setValue("withhold", fs.readLine()); // withholding
16:         util.setValue("estpayment", fs.readLine()); // estimated payments
17:
18:             fs.close();
19:         }
20:         catch (IOException e) {
21:             e.printStackTrace();
22:         }
23:     }
24:}
```

If you figured out writeValues(), readValues() shouldn't be too much of a stretch, although you should note one interesting line. Line 3 has a test to make sure whether the values file actually exists. The first time the calculator runs, it doesn't have any saved values. If you try to open the values file, it doesn't exist, and that would lead to errors. This one if statement makes sure that the file is actually there before going on.

Saving State in Applets and the Applet Context

Because applets can run as channels, you can modify an applet to take advantage of the state-saving capabilities of channels. And, if you trap your exceptions right, you can create code that works equally well if the applet is run as an applet in a Web page or as a channel.

When applets run as channels, they run inside a channel "shell" called AppletViewer (part of the marimba.channel package). Most of the time you don't need to know anything about the AppletViewer class; simply setting the properties of the applet channel causes everything to run seamlessly. However, an applet running inside an AppletViewer can gain access to an application context for the channel, and use many of the methods that application context provides, through the use of an AppletContext object.

To get ahold of the application context from inside your applet code, use the standard getAppletContext() method (from java.applet.Applet). Cast that object to an instance of AppletContext, and call getApplicationContext() on that object, like this:

```
ApplicationContext context =
((AppletContext)getAppletContext()).getApplicationContext();
```

With the channel's application context in hand, you can then use any of the common application context methods with that context, including getDataDirectory() to get the directory for saving local files. Here's a bit of sample code that saves state between invocations of an applet channel:

```
import marimba.channel.*;

public class MyApplet extends java.applet.Applet {
    ...

void init() {
    String dir = (((AppletContext)getAppletContext()).getApplicationContext()).
            getDataDirectory();
    try {
        FileInputStream in =
            new FileInputStream(dir + File.separator + "state.bin");
        // load the state
        ...
    } catch (IOException e) {
        // applet; can't read state from local disk
    } catch (FileNotFoundException e) {
        // there was no state
    }
}

void destroy() {
    String dir = (((AppletContext)getAppletContext()).getApplicationContext()).
            getDataDirectory();
    try {
        FileOutputStream out =
            new FileOutputStream(dir + File.separator + "state.bin");
        ...
```

```
    } catch (IOException e) {
        // applet; can't save state to local disk
    }
}
}
```

Note that if you do create combination applets that are intended to be run both as regular applets and channels, watch for the IOException and make sure you handle it in some way (remember, applets cannot write to local files). In addition to trapping the exceptions, you'll also have to distribute the marimba.zip library with those applets so that they can run properly.

Summary

In this chapter, you learned about updates and saving state, two of the features that make channels interesting.

Updates are handled through the use of four events, part of the standard Application interface for channels: DATA_AVAILABLE_EVENT, DATA_INSTALL_EVENT, DATA_UPDATE_EVENT, and DATA_NOTIFY_EVENT. The first two are the most common and allow you to decide on the fly whether to accept a live update and, if so, to process the new data when it arrives. DATA_NOTIFY_EVENT is particularly interesting, as it allows your channel to decide whether to start based on the new data.

Saving state in channels is essentially identical to saving state in applications, with one exception: you have to use the getDataDirectory() method to get the location of the channel's data directory, and you can read or write from only that one directory.

After this chapter, you should have all the basics for creating channels that seamlessly interact with the Castanet technology. In the next chapter, however, you'll learn how to add the features provided by transmitter plug-ins, which allow your channels to send feedback data when they're updates, and which allow you to customize the data that is sent to the tuner during an update.

twelve

Creating Transmitter Plug-Ins

A lot of the attention concerning Castanet channels involves the ability to do automatic updates—the ability to get the most recent data of a channel from the transmitter down to the individual tuners without a lot of effort on the part of the user. There is so much focus on updates, in fact, that one might think that all the data in Castanet flows in one direction: from the transmitter to the tuner.

Castanet also provides a mechanism for sending data back from each individual tuner—in a method somewhat analogous to submitting a form on a Web page. That channel data is sent to the transmitter as part of an update, and a special program on the transmitter site can then process that data and react dynamically—changing the results a channel gets from an update or otherwise processing the information in some useful way.

That special program on the transmitter is called a transmitter plug-in. In this chapter, you'll learn how to create and use transmitter plug-ins for your own channels.

What Plug-Ins Are and How They Work

If you've used Adobe Photoshop or Netscape Navigator, you're already familiar with the general concept of the plug-in: a plug-in is a program that, when installed in the right place inside your main program, extends the larger program or gives you extra functionality in a manner that's integrated with that larger program. Transmitter plug-ins work in a similar way: You create a plug-in as part of your channel, and that plug-in is installed on the transmitter when you publish that channel. When your channel is updated, special channel information is sent back to the transmitter from the tuner, and the plug-in has an opportunity to process that data.

Creating a plug-in isn't all that difficult, but it does require that you understand the process of how a channel stores feedback data, how that data is sent back to the transmitter, and how the tuner and transmitter negotiate an update.

Channel Feedback Data

In Chapter 11, "Managing Updates and User Information," you learned about how to write local data files to the channel's local data directory. I made a mention in that chapter of two special kinds of data files: channel logging and profile files. The data in these two files is the data that is sent back to the transmitter (and the plug-in) when your channel is updated.

Logging information is simply that—information you may be interested in keeping track of as your channel runs. For example, this could be the choices your readers make for what they see in your channel, the URLs of documents they visit, how often they start and run your channel, or anything else that you might find interesting. Each time the user does something that interests you, you log that event using a special method. When the channel is updated, all the log entries are packaged and sent as a unit to the plug-in.

Profile data is intended to change less often than logging data. Profile data is data about the preferences of your user; for example, you can create a preferences panel for your channel that asks your user for his or her preferred language, and stores that information in the profile. Generally the user only sets the profile information once, or very infrequently. Along with the logging information, the profile file is also uploaded to the transmitter plug-in when the channel is updated.

Processing the Feedback Data

When the channel is updated, the tuner packages the log and profile files and sends them up to the transmitter. The transmitter then runs your plug-in if it exists. Now what? You can use the plug-in to take the logging file and process it, storing the statistics in a special file or in a database. That's one use of the plug-in. But the really interesting thing you can do with a plug-in in response to logging or profile information is to customize the contents of the channel update.

When the tuner negotiates an update to a channel with the transmitter, the tuner tests the checksums of the files and directories it has in the channel with the checksums of the files and directories the transmitter has for that channel. Based on the differences between those checksums, the tuner can construct a list of the files it needs in order to update that channel. From inside your plug-in, you can access that list of files and add or remove files from the list. Those files are sent back to the tuner, which installs them just as the tuner would install any other channel files.

So, for example, your channel could have a preferences window that lets the user choose her preferred language (English, French, German, and so on). Those preferences would be saved as profile data, which would be sent up to the channel as part of the update. In your plug-in, you can read that language preference and then modify the list of channel files so that the user interface that is downloaded to the tuner is the right one for the right language. It is entirely transparent to the user of that channel; the user sets her preferences and magically gets the interface in the right language. But the plug-in allows you to customize the channel on the fly so that the tuner doesn't have to download UI files for all the languages, just the files the user actually needs.

You could use logging information to customize a channel as well—for example, to track the sorts of topics that your reader shows an interest in, and to provide channel data that is focused to that specific information. Using channel plug-ins and the information the channel sends, there's no limit to the sorts of interesting customizations you can make to a single channel.

Creating Plug-Ins

Plug-ins are Java files, just like channels are. In fact, they're developed and stored as part of your channel, and require modifying your channel files as well. There are three steps involved to creating plug-ins:

● Setting up your channel directory correctly
● Modifying your channel files to process logging and profile information correctly
● Developing the plug-in itself

The Channel Directory

Transmitter plug-in files are stored in the same channel directory as your channel files, but they're not downloaded to the tuner the way most of your channel data is. In order for the transmitter to be able to tell the difference between normal channel data and plug-in data, you've got to put the plug-in data in a special place. That place is a directory called `plugin` inside your channel directory. The `plugin` directory contains any files that your plug-in needs, and it also has its own `properties.txt` file.

The plug-in's `properties.txt` file is *not* created by Castanet Publish when you publish your channel; you have to create it yourself. It's a simple text file with only one line in it:

```
main=yourchannelplugin
```

The value of `yourchannelplugin`, in this case, is the name of your main plug-in class, minus the `.class` extension. The transmitter needs this file so that it knows which class to instantiate when your plug-in starts up.

Note that your plug-in's `CLASSPATH`—that is, where it locates other Java classes—includes both the `plugin` directory and the enclosing Java directory. This allows you to share utility class files between the channel and the plug-in, without having to copy them to both places.

With your channel directory set up, the next step is to start modifying the actual channel code.

Developing the Channel

To take advantage of a plug-in's features, you need to modify your class file to use special methods and features (or create your channels with these features in mind). The logging and profile information that the channel sends to the plug-in are not normal data files; they must be read and written in special ways, using methods in the application context. Also, you might want to trap the event `DATA_UPDATE_EVENT`, which is posted just before the tuner makes an update. You can use that opportunity to save the profile or do special logging just before the update occurs.

Channel Logs

To create an entry in the channel log, use the `context.appendLog()` method. The `appendLog()` method takes one argument, which can either be a `String` object or an array of bytes. Whatever you log is up to you, based on the goals of your channel and the information you're interested in tracking. When the log information is processed by your plug-in, that plug-in will get the information you logged plus a time stamp and the ID of the tuner where the information came from. So, for example, if you had a channel for a dynamic Web bookmarks list, you could keep track of the URLs your users actually visited by logging the URL something like this:

```
context.appendLog("URL: " + target.getValue("URL"));
```

Then the log entry for that call to `appendLog()` would look something like this:

```
fx8oy6uhvlxt 21/12 20.59.56 URL: http://www.marimba.com
```

Channel Profiles

Profile information isn't quite as easy. Because a profile file is supposed to store preferences in much the same way a local data file saves state, you'll need to read the existing preferences before writing any new preferences. You'll also need to write any user interfaces for setting those preferences yourself; all the channel gives you are two methods: `getProfile()` and `setProfile()`.

Both `getProfile()` and `setProfile()` are application context methods. The `context.getProfile()` method returns an array of bytes with the profile data in it (empty if the profile hasn't been created yet). You'll need to then somehow process that array of bytes into a form you can use in your channel.

The `context.setProfile()` method takes one argument: an array of bytes representing the profile data to be saved and sent to the plug-in on update. It returns a Boolean: true if the profile was saved, false if there was an error while writing the profile. The contents of the byte array overwrite any existing profile data, so be sure to read the old values before writing new ones.

Preparing for Updates

In Chapter 11, when I discussed channel update events, I briefly mentioned the `DATA_UPDATE_EVENT`. This event occurs just before the tuner actually makes an update back to the transmitter; it is a warning that the logging and profile data is about to be sent for processing. By trapping this event in your `handleEvent()` method, you have a chance to save the profile or log any last-minute data just before the update occurs.

There's no specific method for the `DATA_UPDATE_EVENT` defined in any of the standard channel classes because this event is not as frequently used as the `DATA_NOTIFY_EVENT` or `DATA_INSTALL_EVENT` events. To trap it, you must use `handleEvent()`, like this:

```
public boolean handlEvent(Event evt) {
   switch (evt.id) {
      case Event.ACTION_EVENT: // process widget actions.
         ...
      case DATA_UPDATE_EVENT:
         // ... save logs and profiles
   }
}
```

Developing the Plug-In

With everything is set up in your channel to send feedback data to the plug-in, the last step is to develop the plug-in itself. Inside that plug-in you'll process the data sent back from the channel, and customize the channel contents, if necessary. In this section you'll learn about all three of these things.

The `Plugin` Class File

All plug-ins must be subclasses of the `Plugin` class, part of the `marimba.plugin` package. The basic template for a plug-in file, then, looks like this:

```
import marimba.plugin.*;

public class MyPlugin extends Plugin {
...
}
```

The default version of the `Plugin` class defines a number of methods, but the three most important (and the three you will most likely need to override) are these:

- ● `init()` is called once when the plug-in is started in response to the first channel update. Use `init()` to initialize the plug-in.
- ● `processRequest()` is called once each time the channel is updated and new data is available. Do the bulk of the plug-in processing from this method.
- ● `destroy()` is called once just before the plug-in is halted. Use this method to clean up or save local files.

The `init()` and `destroy()` method signatures look like this:

```
public void init() {
...
}

public void destroy() {
...
}
```

By default, `init()` has no definition, but `destroy()` closes the files that were opened at other points in the plug-in's lifetime. You should call `super.destroy()` if you override `destroy()` in your own plug-in class.

The `processRequest()` method looks like this:

```
public void processReqeust(ReqeustContext context) throws IOException {
...
}
```

The `RequestContext` argument is the special context object for this call to your plug-in; the request context for the plug-in is analogous to the application context for the channel in that the context provides the way to access not only the information from the update, but also information about that update itself including the tuner ID and the channel and server name. By default, processRequest logs the channel's log data to a central location; you should call super.processRequest() either at the beginning or end of your version. (The default implementation of processRequest()simply logs the channel feedback information to the server, and that can happen at any time.)

Processing the Data

Inside the processRequest() method is where most of the plug-in's work takes place. This is where you'll read the logging data, write any local state files, and customize the channel.

The first step is usually to read the log or profile data. On this side of the process, the profile is easier to read. Just use the getProfileData() method, defined on the request context:

```
byte[] theData = context.getProfileData();
```

The data you get back from this method is a simple array of bytes; it's up to you to process that data into a form you can use.

Processing the log entries is more difficult, because multiple log entries can be packaged as one update request. To get the log entries, you have two choices. The first choice is the getLoggingData() method, defined on the request context and called like this:

```
byte[] theLogs = context.getLoggingData();
```

As with getProfileData(), the getLoggingData() method returns the log entries as a simple array of bytes. You have to process out the information yourself. The second choice is usually the easier way to proceed: Call the Plugin class's getLoggingEntries()method, using the context as the argument. The getLoggingEntries() method returns a Vector object:

```
Vector theLogs = getLoggingEntries(context);
```

The Vector object contains instances of the LogEntry class (also part of the marimba.plugin package), one for each log entry that was passed to the transmitter. The LogEntry class has two instance variables: timestamp and data. Use the data instance variable to get the original information that you logged in the channel in appendLog().

You can use an Enumeration and a loop to work through the various LogEntry objects in the vector, like this:

```
for (Enumeration e = theLogs.elements; e.hasMoreElements() ; {
    LogEntry le = (LogEntry)e.nextElement();
    String s = new String(le.data, 0);
    // .. the log is in the string s; process it as you will.
}
```

253

Working with Local Files

Because the plug-in runs on your transmitter, it's generally assumed to be a trusted bit of code. Your plug-in has access to any part of the transmitter's file system; you can read and write local files at will as you need them to process the data you get from the logs or the profile or to store local state between requests.

However, for reasons of consistency between plug-ins, local data files are generally stored in a central location: the data directory, contained inside the transmitter's channel directory. Each channel has its own directory inside data in which it can store any files it needs.

The easy way to get ahold of this special channel directory is to use the Plugin method getDataFile() with the name of the file you want to read from or write to. This method returns a File object, which you can use to open the data file. The first time you write to it, you should make sure your channel directory exists and create it if it doesn't. Here's some simple code to do that:

```
try {
    File theFile = getDataFile("theoutputfile.txt");
    if (theFile.exists() == false) {
      File dir = new File(theFile.getParent());
      if (dir.exists() == false)
          dir.mkdirs();
    }
    FastOutputStream rf = new FastOutputStream(theFile);
    //write to the stream
    rf.close();
}
catch (IOException e) {
    e.printStackTrace();
}
```

Customizing Channel Lists

With the logs and profiles processed, the last task of the plug-in is to customize the list of files that is sent back to the tuner, if necessary. (You don't have to customize the channel if you don't want to; there's nothing wrong with, say, simply taking logging information and storing statistics about it.)

To customize the channel, you modify the channel's index. This is the list of files and checksums that the transmitter sends to the tuner as part of an update request; the tuner then uses this list to figure out which files it needs in order to bring its version of the channel up to date. By modifying the channel index as part of the plug-in's operation, you can dynamically change the files the transmitter appears to have.

There are three operations you can do to the channel index: You can delete a file, rename a file, or add a file. The first two are the easiest, so I'll cover them first.

For each of these operations, modifying the channel's index is a temporary measure for this specific request; the next time the tuner requests an update, you will have to modify that index all over again.

Deleting and Renaming Files

To delete a file from the index, use `context.deleteFile()` with a single string argument, representing the path and name of the file to delete, from the top of the channel directory. The argument for a file stored at the top level of the channel directory, then, would be just the name of the file. For a file stored in a subdirectory, the path would be the name of that directory plus the name of the file (watch out for separator characters):

```
context.deleteFile("updatedata.txt");
```

Deleting a file from the index means that this file will be deleted altogether from the tuner's version of the channel.

To rename a file, use `renameFile()` with two string arguments: the path to the original file and the path to the new file:

```
context.renameFile("updatedata.txt", "updatedata.old");
```

Adding Files

Much of the time in your plug-in you'll want to add a new file or add data to the channel's list. To add files to the list of updates, use `context.addFile()`. Unlike `deleteFile()` and `renameFile()`, for `addFile()` you have four different versions to choose from.

The simplest version takes two arguments: a `String` path name and a `File` object. The path name is the path to the file as it should appear in the channel, minus the channel name. So, for example, if you're sticking a file called `results.txt` at the top level of the channel directory, the path would be simply `"results.txt"`.

The second argument is a `File` object pointing to the location of the file on the transmitter's local disk. This version of `addFile()` is useful when you want to take different versions of the same file and choose among them for one main channel file, as in this example:

```
context.addFile("main.gui", (new File(getDataFile("mainfrench.gui"))));
```

In response to this call, the new file's checksum is calculated and that file is dynamically added to the channel's index. Note that this has an effect on optimized updates, because the checksum of the transmitter's (unmodified) channel index is now different from the tuner's checksum (which includes your new file). Each update runs through your plug-in, and you have to re-add the file each time.

The second version of addFile() is similar to the first; it also takes a String for the channel's path to the file and a File object for the local path, but it also takes a third argument: the checksum of that file as a Checksum object. (Checksum is part of the marimba.util package.) If you just add the file to the list, the checksum will be calculated for you, so you don't have to worry about it if you don't want to. However, for files that are frequently added or used repeatedly, you can calculate the checksum yourself, ahead of time, and then just submit it here to speed up the update.

You can use the Plugin method calculateChecksum() to calculate the checksum of the file; calculateChecksum takes either a string argument (the path to the file from the plugin directory) or an array of bytes, and returns a Checksum object:

```
Checksum cs = calculateChecksum("mainfrench.gui");
context.addFile("main.gui", guiFile, cs);
```

The last two versions of addFile() are more complex, but they provide extra functionality for handling the data your plug-in inserts into the channel index for updates and for proxies. Both of these versions of addFile don't actually add a physical file; instead they add an array of bytes as the contents of that file. Both also have an extra argument for the file's "disposition." This argument determines how the file data is processed in the channel index and by proxies for later channel update requests. I'll cover the dispositions in the next section.

The third version of addFile() takes three arguments: a String for the path name to the file as it will appear on the channel, an array of bytes for the data in that channel, and an integer representing the file's disposition:

```
context.addFile("highscores.txt", hiscoredata, IF_NEEDED);
```

The fourth and final version of addFile() is similar, except that it adds the checksum for the data as an argument to speed up processing that file. To get a checksum for an array of bytes, you can use the calculateChecksum() method with a byte array argument:

```
Checksum csb = calculateChecksum(dataarray);
context.addFile("data.txt". dataarray, cs, IF_NEEDED);
```

File Dispositions

If you use either of the addFile() methods that take a file disposition as an argument, you have four different dispositions to choose from (all are defined in the Plugin class):

●   IF_NEEDED: This is the best choice for data that will be sent to tuner on a semiregular basis. The IF_NEEDED disposition adds this file and its checksum to the channel's index, so the file's data is only sent to the tuner if the tuner doesn't already have that file (or if it has a different version). Because this disposition dynamically changes the overall index checksum, optimized updates will no longer work for this channel; each update will go through the plug-in and you'll have to modify the list of files each time. This is the default disposition for adding files using the addFile() methods without dispositions.

● ALWAYS: Use ALWAYS if the data you're sending back to the tuner changes extremely frequently. An ALWAYS disposition always sends the data for the file for every single update request, regardless of whether or not that data has changed. For ALWAYS the filename and checksum are not added to the channel's index, so optimized updates continue to work as usual. Files with ALWAYS dispositions are also never cached by a Castanet proxy.

● PERSISTENT: Use this disposition for data that changes only semifrequently but for which there are frequent update requests. File dispositions marked PERSISTENT are treated as if they are a file for a small amount of time after the plug-in adds them to the index (at least five minutes); this allows them to be cached by the proxy or by the tuner such that subsequent updates soon after the first don't have to go through the plug-in each and every time.

● ASK_ME: The most complicated of the file dispositions, the ASK_ME disposition means that the plug-in itself will handle every request for this specific file—for example, to extract the file from a database or to generate it based on other data. The idea here is that the plug-in can keep a local copy of the data cached and send it back if the data hasn't changed. If you use a file disposition of ASK_ME, you also need to override the methods getData() and getDataLength() from the Plugin class.

In practical use, the IF_NEEDED disposition is often the most commonly used. Use ALWAYS or PERSISTENT for frequently updated or frequently requested data to optimize the speed of the update through the plug-in; use ASK_ME for dynamically generated data that requires more sophisticated processing than the standard index and file mechanism.

An Example: The Survey of the Week

For the last half of this chapter, let's create a channel that relies heavily on the ability to send data back to the transmitter from the channel itself. This is a channel that gives you a chance to vote on different questions, one a week. Figure 12.1 shows the initial survey screen when it comes up (with a sample question that applies especially well to this chapter).

Choosing an option and selecting the Submit button triggers a live update. The tuner sends your vote up to the transmitter, where a plug-in intercepts that data and stores it in a results file. The plug-in then sends that results file back to the channel, which updates the results bars at the bottom of the page to reflect all the current results. (See Figure 12.2.) This includes not only the user's current votes, but also the votes of everyone else who's running the channel.

The channel itself automatically updates every half an hour, and the plug-in intercepts those updates as well. For automatic updates, no data is sent to the plug-in from the channel, but the plug-in continues to send down a new version of the results file, so the channel continues to reflect the current vote count even after the user has cast her own vote.

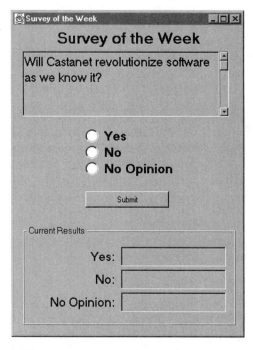

Figure 12.1. *The initial survey screen.*

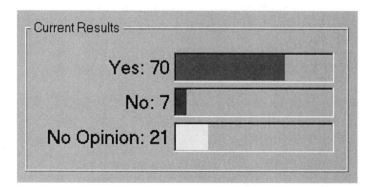

Figure 12.2. *The updated results.*

Once a week the question changes, the results are set back to zero, and the survey starts all over again.

You know the routine by now. To create a channel like this one, you start with the Bongo presentation and add the code. I won't go into the details of the presentation itself; let's jump right into the code for the channel, which is also on the CD-ROM in the Survey subdirectory of the Examples directory.

Create the Channel

Like most channels, the Survey channel uses a Java class, SurveyApplication.java, to initialize the interface and to process the actions that occur with that interface. The basic framework is the same: You'll subclass the ApplicationPlayerFrame class and override the appropriate methods to manage three major events in the channel's lifetime:

- For initializing the channel, override the start() method to read and display the current question for the survey.
- For handling the vote submission, override handleEvent() to process the mouse click on the Submit button.
- For automatic updates, override notifyInstall() to update the interface when new data arrives (either new results or a new question).

Let's look at the pieces separately. I've printed the code in its entirety later on in this section so that you can see it in one place. I'll start with the start() method:

```
public void start() {
   super.start();
   setTitle("Survey of the Week");

   loadQuestion();
}
```

The start() method does only two things: It sets the title bar for the channel and calls a subroutine called loadQuestion(). The latter method is shown in Listing 12.1.

Listing 12.1. The `loadQuestion()` method.

```
public void loadQuestion() {
    try {
        URL base = new URL(context.getBase(), question);
        FastInputStream fs = new FastInputStream(base.openStream());
        util.setValue("question", fs.readLine());
        fs.close();
    }
    catch (MalformedURLException e) {
        e.printStackTrace();
    }
    catch (IOException e) {
        e.printStackTrace();
    }
}
```

You saw a method similar to this one for The Weather Channel; this method simply opens the channel file `question.txt` and reads its contents into the question widget (the big scrolling text box at the top of the screen). Storing the question separate from the interface means that question can be changed frequently without having to change the whole interface each time. As with The Weather Channel, it makes updates faster and easier for both the transmitter and tuner side of the process.

The second step for the channel (and the most important one) is to override `handleEvent()` to submit the vote when the user clicks on the Submit button. Listing 12.2 shows the `handleEvent()` method for this class.

Listing 12.2. The `handleEvent()` method.

```
 1: public boolean handleEvent(Event evt) {
 2:     if ((evt.id == Event.ACTION_EVENT) &&
 3:         (evt.target instanceof CommandButtonWidget)) {
 4:             if (util.getBoolean("yes")) context.appendLog("yes");
 5:             else if (util.getBoolean("no")) context.appendLog("no");
 6:             else if (util.getBoolean("noop")) context.appendLog("noop");
 7:             context.update();
 8:
 9:             return true;
10:     }
11:     return super.handleEvent(evt);
12: }
```

This is probably the most important method in the class from the point of view of understanding plug-ins, and the heart of it are the three tests in lines 4 through 7, which test the value widgets and call the `context.appendLog()` method. The `getBoolean()` tests are standard widget calls; `getBoolean` tells you which of the choices have been selected. (They're grouped together, so only one can be selected at a time.) And `context. appendLog()` creates a log entry for that action. The log entry you create with `appendLog` can look any way you want it to; for this example, the log entry simply has a string that tells the plug-in which option the user voted for (`"yes"`, `"no"`, or `"noop"` for a Yes, No, or No Opinion vote, respectively).

The `appendLog()` method does not in itself trigger an update. Each time you call `appendLog` the tuner stores up each log entry on the local disk until the next update occurs; then it packages all the log entries and sends them as a group to the transmitter. In this case, however, we'll force the issue; in line 7, we call `context.update()`, which tells the tuner to request an update for this channel and send the log data to the transmitter.

Note

Be careful about calling `update()` from your own channels. The idea of a channel is that it shouldn't need to spend a lot of time contacting the server; it should be able to call updates in a more leisurely fashion—for example, late at night. Also, forcing an update inside your channel bypasses the ability for the user to turn off updates altogether in the tuner. For this example, I've used `update()` so that we get instant gratification from the plug-in.

Clicking the Submit vote triggers an update, but updates can also occur automatically. Let's move onto the methods for updating the channel, then, which allows us to process the new data from an update whether it arrives in response to a vote or automatically.

For The Weather Channel, we overrode both the `notifyAvailable()` and `notifyInstall()` methods. The first of these methods is used to decide which data to install when new data arrives. In this example, we'll rely on the default definition of `notifyAvailable()`, which, if the properties for the channel have been set to "install," simply installs all the new data. This is precisely what we want to do, so there's no reason to override that method. Instead we'll move on to `notifyInstall()`, which is called after that new data has been installed:

```
public void notifyInstall(String dir) {
    loadQuestion();
    loadData();
}
```

Here we'll do two things to process the new data. The first is to call the `loadQuestion()` method again. If a new question arrives, we'll want to update the survey to reflect that. The second is to call a method called `loadData()`. Part of the update to the channel is a file called `results.txt`, which contains the current vote count for the question. The `loadData()` method is responsible for opening and reading that file and updating the results information. Because that method simply calculates the new values for all the widgets in the interface, I won't show it here; you can see it in Listing 12.3 if you're interested.

Note that for the most part, the only difference between this channel and the weather channel is the use of the appendLog() method. For channels that use plug-ins, that is usually the only change you'll need to make. Listing 12.3 shows the complete code for this channel so that you can see how it all fits together.

Listing 12.3. The code for SurveyApplication.java.

```java
import java.awt.*;
import java.net.*;
import java.io.*;
import marimba.channel.*;
import marimba.gui.*;
import marimba.io.*;

public class SurveyApplication extends ApplicationPlayerFrame {

String question = "question.txt";
String results = "results.txt";

public void start() {
    super.start();
    setTitle("Survey of the Week");

    loadQuestion();
}

public void loadQuestion() {
    try {
        URL base = new URL(context.getBase(), question);
        FastInputStream fs = new FastInputStream(base.openStream());
        util.setValue("question", fs.readLine());
         fs.close();
    }
    catch (MalformedURLException e) {
        e.printStackTrace();
    }
    catch (IOException e) {
        e.printStackTrace();
    }
}

public void loadData() {
    try {
        if (context.channelFileExists(results)) {
            URL base = new URL(context.getBase(), results);
            FastInputStream fs = new FastInputStream(base.openStream());
            int yt = Integer.parseInt(fs.readLine());
            int nt = Integer.parseInt(fs.readLine());
            int not = Integer.parseInt(fs.readLine());

            float votes = yt + nt + not;
            yt = (int)((yt / votes) * 100);
```

```
            nt = (int)((nt / votes) * 100);
            not = (int)((not / votes) * 100);
            util.setValue("yestot", "Yes: " + yt);
            util.setValue("yesbar", String.valueOf(yt));
            util.setValue("notot", "No: " + nt);
            util.setValue("nobar", String.valueOf(nt));
            util.setValue("nooptot", "No Opinion: " + not);
            util.setValue("noopbar", String.valueOf(not));

            fs.close();
        }
    }
    catch (MalformedURLException e) {
        e.printStackTrace();
    }
    catch (IOException e) {
        e.printStackTrace();
    }
}

public void notifyInstall(String dir) {
    loadQuestion();
    loadData();
}

public boolean handleEvent(Event evt) {
    if ((evt.id == Event.ACTION_EVENT) &&
        (evt.target instanceof CommandButtonWidget)) {
            if (util.getBoolean("yes")) context.appendLog("yes");
            else if (util.getBoolean("no")) context.appendLog("no");
            else if (util.getBoolean("noop")) context.appendLog("noop");
            context.update();

            return true;
    }
    return super.handleEvent(evt);
}

}
```

Create the Plug-In

Right now you could compile that channel file and run it, and it would work just fine. The transmitter doesn't get confused when it gets log or profile data intended for a plug-in; if there isn't a plug-in available to process it, the transmitter simply logs the data it gets from the tuner and goes about its merry way. You'll find that log data in a file named after your channel in the transmitter's channel directory, inside the logs. Those log entries have three parts: the tuner ID (a unique identifier for each tuner), a time stamp, and the data you sent in the appendLog() method. More about this when we actually write the code to process those entries.

But this is a chapter about plug-ins, so let's create one here to handle the data that comes back to the logs. As you learned earlier in this chapter, plug-ins inherit from the class `marimba.plugin.Plugin`. They also must be contained in their own directory inside your channel directory, called `plugin`. Don't forget to create that directory and store your plug-in files inside that directory.

Note

The `marimba.plugin` package is contained in the library `transmitter.zip`, part of the transmitter distribution in the `lib` directory. You need to add this library to the `CLASSPATH` of your development environment to be able to compile your Java plug-in files.

Let's build this file from scratch, because much of it will be new. We'll start with the basic class framework—a whole lot of imports plus the basic class definition:

```
import java.io.*;
import java.util.*;
import marimba.plugin.*;
import marimba.io.*;
import marimba.util.*;

public class SurveyPlugin extends Plugin {

}
```

We'll need a few instance variables for this class to refer to the results file the plug-in stores and to the results data. To help with the latter, I've created a helper class called `Results`, which simply has fields for the various result values. We'll create an instance variable to hold an instance of that class here (`rdata`), along with a variable for the name of the requests file (`requests`) and for a `File` object (`rfile`) that will refer to that requests file:

```
String results = "results.txt";
Results rdata;
File rFile;
```

The `Results.java` class looks like this:

```
public class Results {
int yestotal = 0;
int nototal = 0;
int nooptotal = 0;
}
```

The fields in that `Results` object will be important later on in the class.

When you subclass the `Plugin` class, the three methods you will potentially override are `init()`, `processRequest()`, and `destroy()`, for starting up, processing data, and stopping. Keep in mind, as you decide which ones to override, *when* each method is called during the plug-in's life cycle. When the plug-in is first launched, `init()` is called, `processRequest()` is called for each update, and `destroy()` is called when the transmitter is brought down. Both `init()` and `destroy()` are called only once during the plug-in's lifetime; `processRequest()` is called as many times as there are updates from tuners.

For this example, we'll override `init()` and `processRequest()`. The `init()` method is used to initialize the plug-in, and we'll take this opportunity to read in the transmitter's local copy of the results so that we have it in memory to change when a tuner makes an update.

To get a local data file for the plug-in, use the `getDataFile()` method with the name of the file you want to create. This method returns a `File` object with the full path name to the file; you can then open and read or write to that file at will.

Note

Actually, you can read or write any files on the transmitter from your plug-in—no security restrictions—but it's considered good form to put your data files into the standard place where they belong.

The results file, if it exists, consists of three lines, representing the total Yes votes, the total No votes, and the total No Opinion votes. In our `init()` method, shown in Listing 12.4, we'll read those values from the file into an instance of the `Results` class, stored in the `rdata` instance variable:

Listing 12.4. The `init()` method for the plug-in.

```
public void init() {
   super.init();
   /* plug-in's copy of the results file */
   rdata = new Results();
   rFile = getDataFile(results);
   if (rFile.exists()) {
   try {
       FastInputStream fs = new FastInputStream(rFile);
       rdata.yestotal = Integer.parseInt(fs.readLine());
       rdata.nototal = Integer.parseInt(fs.readLine());
       rdata.nooptotal = Integer.parseInt(fs.readLine());
       fs.close();
   }
   catch(IOException e) {
       e.printStackTrace();
   }
   }
}
```

After `init()` is called, the plug-in is ready to start processing update requests. In order to do anything with those requests, you'll need to override the `processRequest()` method in your plug-in. (This will usually be the case.) The order of business inside `processRequest()` usually goes something like this:

● Read the log or profile entries the tuner has sent.

● Process them in whatever way you need to.

● Modify the list of files being sent back to the tuner to add or remove files based on the log or profile data.

● Clean up, saving any local files or clearing any values that need to be reset before the next request comes in.

Listing 12.5 shows the processRequest() method for this Plugin class. I'll go over it line by line so that you know what's going on.

Listing 12.5. The processRequest() method in the plug-in.

```
 1:public void processRequest(RequestContext context) throws IOException {
 2:        /* grab log entries */
 3:        Vector logs = getLogEntries(context);
 4:
 5:        /* update results */
 6:        for (Enumeration e = logs.elements() ; e.hasMoreElements() ; ) {
 7:            LogEntry le = (LogEntry)e.nextElement();
 8:            String s = new String(le.data, 0);
 9:            if (s.equals("yes")) rdata.yestotal++;
10:            else if (s.equals("no")) rdata.nototal++;
11:            else if (s.equals("noop")) rdata.nooptotal++;
12:        }
13:
14:        /* ship results back to tuner */
15:        String s = rdata.yestotal + "\n" + rdata.nototal + "\n" +
16:            rdata.nooptotal + "\n";
17:        int len = s.length();
18:        byte[] b = new byte[len];
19:        s.getBytes(0,len,b,0);
20:        context.addFile(results,b,IF_NEEDED);
21:
22:    try {
23:        /* write the new data back to the local file */
24:        if (rFile.exists() == false) {
25:            File dir = new File(rFile.getParent());
26:            if (dir.exists() == false)
27:                dir.mkdirs();
28:        }
29:        FastOutputStream rf = new FastOutputStream(rFile);
30:        rf.println(rdata.yestotal);
31:        rf.println(rdata.nototal);
32:        rf.println(rdata.nooptotal);
33:        rf.close();
34:    }
35:    catch (IOException e)
36:    { e.printStackTrace();
37:    }
38:
39:    super.processRequest(context);
40:}
```

In this version of processRequest(), we haven't done anything with the channel profile; the only thing we're interested in are the log entries. The most important method in this respect is the getLogEntries() method in line 3, which takes one argument: the request context passed into the processRequest() method when it's called. The getLogEntries method returns a Vector object with all the log entries in it. You can then use an Enumeration object to read over each one. (Both Vector and Enumeration are standard Java classes for linked-list–like entities.)

Note that for this particular instance of the plug-in, there will only be one entry because the channel calls update immediately after calling appendLog(). That's not necessarily true for any other plug-in; most of the time, the channel stores up log entries and sends them over as a group, and you have to process each one in turn. The code I used to process those log entries in lines 6 through 12 deals with multiple log entries in case an immediate update didn't happen; you can also use it in your own plug-ins.

Note the line 7 where you cast the log entry to an instance of the class LogEntry. The LogEntry class is part of the marimba.plugin package; it's a simple class that splits up the actual log entry into its time stamp and its data. (If you're interested in the tuner ID, you can get it from the context.getTunerID() method.) And finally, lines 9 through 11 increment the values in the Result object based on the votes that were in the log entries.

The second part of the processReqeust() method ships the updated results back to the tuner. The addFile() method is responsible for adding a new file to the list of files the tuner will receive, and there are several ways of using it (all of which you learned about previously in this chapter). In this case, because the data isn't already in a file, we'll package it as an array of bytes (lines 15 to 19) and call addFile() with the name of the file ("results.txt"), the byte array, and a disposition of IF_NEEDED (line 20).

Why IF_NEEDED? The IF_NEEDED disposition only sends the file if the checksum of the new data is different from the checksum of the results file the tuner already has. If the tuner has done a regular update (not in response to a vote) and the results haven't changed, the channel won't need the new data, so there's no reason to send it. (Note that if the results have changed since the last time the tuner updated, the checksums won't match and the file will be downloaded anyhow.) The IF_NEEDED file disposition is probably the most commonly used disposition.

The final section in processRequest() cleans up after the request is finished—basically by saving the new results out to the local results.txt file. The data still remains in memory for the next request; saving it out to the file is a useful backup maneuver. The contents of this part of the method should look familiar, except for the first few lines at 24 through 27. These lines are used only the very first time the plug-in saves the request file, and they simply make sure that the full path name to the file exists (including the channel directory).

To finish, don't forget to call `super.processRequest()` (as shown in line 39). The default version of this method is what logs the data to the default channel logs (in the transmitter's channel directory, inside `logs`).

Got it all? Listing 12.6 shows the final code.

Listing 12.6. The code for `SurveyPlugin.java`.

```java
import java.io.*;
import java.util.*;
import marimba.plugin.*;
import marimba.io.*;
import marimba.util.*;

public class SurveyPlugin extends Plugin {

String results = "results.txt";
Results rdata;
File rFile;

public void init() {
    super.init();
    /* plug-in's copy of the results file */
    rdata = new Results();
    rFile = getDataFile(results);
    if (rFile.exists()) {
    try {
        FastInputStream fs = new FastInputStream(rFile);
        rdata.yestotal = Integer.parseInt(fs.readLine());
        rdata.nototal = Integer.parseInt(fs.readLine());
        rdata.nooptotal = Integer.parseInt(fs.readLine());
        fs.close();
    }
    catch(IOException e) {
        e.printStackTrace();
    }
    }
}

public void processRequest(RequestContext context) throws IOException {
        /* grab log entries */
        Vector logs = getLogEntries(context);

        /* update results */
        for (Enumeration e = logs.elements() ; e.hasMoreElements() ; ) {
            LogEntry le = (LogEntry)e.nextElement();
            String s = new String(le.data, 0);
            if (s.equals("yes")) rdata.yestotal++;
            else if (s.equals("no")) rdata.nototal++;
            else if (s.equals("noop")) rdata.nooptotal++;
        }

        /* ship results back to tuner */
        String s = rdata.yestotal + "\n" + rdata.nototal + "\n" +
            rdata.nooptotal + "\n";
```

```
            int len = s.length();
            byte[] b = new byte[len];
            s.getBytes(0,len,b,0);
            context.addFile(results,b,IF_NEEDED);

        try {
            /* write the new data back to the local file */
            if (rFile.exists() == false) {
                File dir = new File(rFile.getParent());
                if (dir.exists() == false)
                    dir.mkdirs();
            }
            FastOutputStream rf = new FastOutputStream(rFile);
            rf.println(rdata.yestotal);
            rf.println(rdata.nototal);
            rf.println(rdata.nooptotal);
            rf.close();
        }
        catch (IOException e)
        { e.printStackTrace();
        }

        super.processRequest(context);
    }

}
```

Finishing Up

The final step is simply to compile all the files, make sure the channel directory is arranged right, and publish the channel.

The final channel directory for this survey channel contains the following things:

- survey.gui, the Bongo presentation for the survey's interface.
- SurveyApplication.class, the main channel class.
- question.txt, a file containing the current question.
- bongo.zip, the Bongo library that must be included with all channels that use Bongo.
- plugin, a subdirectory, which in turn contains the SurveyPlugin.class, Results.class, and properties.txt files. Plug-in files *must* be contained in a directory called plugin in order to be recognized as plug-ins by the transmitter.

Don't forget to set the properties.txt file inside the plugin directory; this file always contains one line, which points to the main Plugin class, like this:

```
main=SurveyPlugin
```

The final step is, of course, to publish the channel. I'll use the general properties shown in Figure 12.3, which include the name of the channel and its Bongo presentation. For the update properties, the inactive properties are set to daily for the frequency and ignore for the action. (There's no point in starting the channel for new data; when the reader is interested, he'll start it himself.) For the active properties, I've set the update to `hourly`, and the action to `"install"`, which will make sure the new data gets incorporated into the running channel.

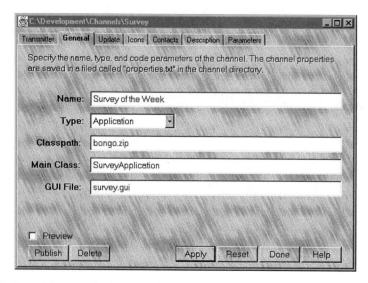

Figure 12.3. *The General properties for the Survey channel.*

The result is a channel that allows the reader to vote for the current question of the week, and also keeps a running update about everyone else's vote for that channel.

There's one other point to note: What happens when you, the channel administrator, update the survey and add a new question? You can simply edit the `question.txt` file to ask a new question and then republish; the channel gets the new question on the next update. However, even though the channel gets the new question, the plug-in continues to keep the old results data and use it to update the results for each channel. So don't forget when you update the questions file to also delete the transmitter's result file (stored in the transmitter root's data directory). This resets everything so that the results of the survey are truly updated on a weekly basis.

Debugging Plug-Ins

One of the first things you'll discover when you start experimenting with plug-ins is that they're really hard to debug. Unlike presentations or channels, where you at least have the bongo to the tuner console to which you can send a call to `System.out.println()`, with plug-ins there isn't any easy place where you can send debugging information. This can make debugging transmitter plug-ins seem a lot like groping around in the dark. (For that survey example, I did a *lot* of groping around in the dark.)

If something goes wrong with your plug-in, the first sign you'll get is when you try to update your channel in the tuner, and you get an "EOF in HTTP Response" Error (and your channel won't update). The first place to look for information on what went wrong is in the transmitter error log, which is stored in your transmitter root directory in the directory logs (for example, C:\channels\logs\errorlog). At the end of that file is the stack trace from your plug-in; you can often get at least a hint of what's going on from that stack trace.

If the plug-in isn't crashing but isn't behaving quite right, then things are even more difficult to diagnose. The best solution in this case is to set up a debugging file in your plug-in's local data directory. You can create and open this file in much the same way that you do the local data files for your plug-in, using getDataFile() to build a File object for that directory.

Listing 12.7 shows an example of a processRequest() method that opens a debugging file with the same name as the tuner ID that made the request, stores some values, and then closes it at the end of the request. You can then view the information by opening that file. (Remember that data files are stored in your transmitter root, in the data directory.)

Listing 12.7. A debugging file for a plug-in.

```
public void processRequest(RequestContext context) throws IOException {

    /* debugging;  no console for plugins (argh!) */
    File debuggingFile = getDataFile("debug.txt");
    try {
       if (debuggingFile.exists() == false) {
          File dir = new File(debuggingFile.getParent());
          if (dir.exists() == false)
             dir.mkdirs();
       }
       FastOutputStream ds = new FastOutputStream(debuggingFile);
       ds.println("Debugging output....");

       //  write various debugging things here

       ds.close();
    }
    catch (IOException e) {
       e.printStackTrace();
    }
    super.processRequest(context);
}
```

Note

Just as I was finishing up this book, there was word that Marimba is working on a better way to debug transmitter plug-ins; however, there wasn't time to include that information here. Check Marimba's Web site, on the Developer's page (http://www.marimba.com/developer/) for more information about debugging plug-ins.

Summary

Most actions between a developer, a transmitter, and a tuner—from publishing channels, to the tuner downloading files and updates—involve getting data down to the user's local disk. Transmitter plug-ins are a mechanism for data to flow the other way: They allow the channel to send information about the user or his actions back to the transmitter during a channel update.

The plug-in has the ability to not only read that data and do with it what it will (log it to a file, or process it in some other way), but also to customize the files that will be returned to the tuner. In this way, transmitter plug-ins can change what occurs during an update based on the user's preferences or what they may have already done while executing the channel. The plug-in provides an enormously powerful mechanism for creating dynamic channels and for tracking what's going on with your channels.

If you've grasped the information in this chapter, congratulations! With a background in transmitter plug-ins, you've now learned everything there is to know about developing channels for Castanet. In Chapter 13, "Inside Wordsmith," you'll work through a much more complex example (which also uses transmitter plug-ins, so if you didn't get it this time, you'll have another chance). Chapter 14, "An Overview of the Marimba Classes," finishes up by giving a bigger overview of the Marimba packages and how they can help you construct channels.

thirteen

Inside WordSmith

At this point in the book, you've explored various concepts for building channels and examined the source code to various small examples that demonstrate those concepts. But sometimes it's difficult to figure out how to combine those smaller concepts into a larger one. For just that reason, in this chapter you'll finish up the meat of this book by exploring a complete, running example of a complex channel. The channel in question is a game called WordSmith. WordSmith combines Bongo presentations and very sophisticated custom widgets with Java channel code to handle automatic updates, save local data, and use a transmitter plug-in as well. We won't cover all aspects of this channel here—just those that relate specifically to channel development—but you can explore the source code on your own to get a feel for how the channel was put together.

WordSmith was written by Carl W. Haynes III, a Marimba employee who has written a number of excellent channels (including the extremely popular SameGame channel). He has graciously released the source code for other channel programmers to see. You can get this source code on the CD-ROM for this book, or from the Marimba Web site at `http://www.marimba.com/developer/samplecode.html`. The version I discuss here—the one that comes with this book—is the version current as of this writing; by the time you read this, WordSmith may have new features or updates added to it, and to see and explore those, you'd need to get the source code from the Web site.

Note

There are two versions of the WordSmith software: one with a dictionary file, and one without. You'll need the dictionary to play the game; but if all you're interested in is the source code, you can download the smaller of the two versions. The version that comes on the CD-ROM with this book has the dictionary.

The Game

The first step towards understanding how any channel or program works is to play with the final version (or, if the program isn't written yet, to have a general plan for how the program will operate).

When you subscribe to and start the WordSmith channel, the main WordSmith window appears and a new game is set up. Figure 13.1 shows that initial window.

Game play works like this: You can drag and drop tiles from the tops of the columns in the main part of the screen to the top of the screen to form words (you can only use the letters at the top of each column; the letters underneath are unavailable until uncovered). Once you've spelled a word of at least three letters, click the Check button. WordSmith compares your word against a dictionary, and if you've created a real word, those tiles are cleared and you're given a score for that word. (Scoring works exponentially based on the number of letters in the word; you don't get extra points for the Zs and Qs like you do in scrabble.) You can also choose the Clear button to put the letters back in the columns where they were before.

Continue building words until you've used all the letters on the screen (you can also create nonsense words to get unusable letters out of the way, but you won't get any points for those letters).

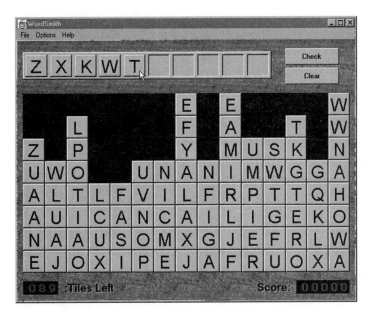

Figure 13.1. The WordSmith channel.

The part of WordSmith that makes it more than just a simple game is the management of high scores. WordSmith keeps track of two lists of high scores: a local list for the version of the channel running on your system and a global list for everyone who is running that same channel. The WordSmith channel keeps track of the global high scores through the use of channel feedback and updates so that the global high scores will always reflect the top WordSmith players in the world (if you feel particularly competitive about it).

Note

The WordSmith channel has a lot in common—both in game play and in underlying infrastructure—with the SameGame channel, which I mentioned earlier on in this book as an example of a channel to play with. (It's available from trans.marimba.com.) If you've played SameGame, you'll most likely recognize many of the same features.

Channel Organization

Let's start exploring the WordSmith channel by looking at the channel directory and its organization. Figure 13.2 shows the contents of the WordSmith channel directory.

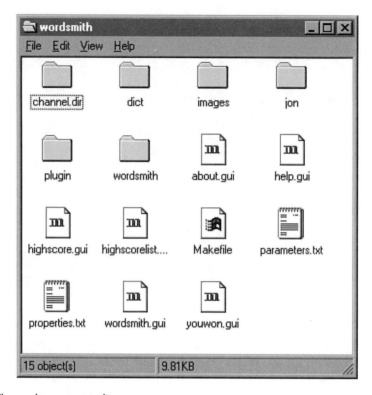

Figure 13.2. *The complete* wordsmith *directory.*

The channel directory contains the following files and directories:

- A set of presentation (.gui) files for the various windows and dialogs in the game
- wordsmith, a directory containing all the Java class files for the game
- plugin, containing the files for the channel's transmitter plug-in
- dict, a directory that contains the dictionary file for the game
- images, a directory of images relating to the game and its icons
- jon, a directory of images for the famous (infamous?) Jonathan Payne spinning head animation (used as part of the dialogs for the channel)
- Other channel files (properties.txt, parameters.txt, and a Makefile for building the channel)

An important aspect of this channel organization: the Java class files for this channel are not arbitrarily placed in the wordsmith directory. Instead, that directory is serving as a package for all the WordSmith code; each of the Java files inside the wordsmith directory are defined to be part of the wordsmith package. For the most part, this doesn't affect how you develop your channel; it's simply a good habit to get into as your create groups of interrelated classes.

The Presentations

WordSmith uses a number of Bongo presentations for the various windows and dialogs in the game. Each of these presentations is stored in the top-level channel directory as a `.gui` file. Those presentations are

- `wordsmith.gui`: The main presentation for the WordSmith channel
- `highscorelist.gui`: A window to display the current local and global high scores
- `help.gui`: A window to display online help for the channel
- `about.gui`: A window to display information about the channel
- `highscore.gui`: A dialog to prompt the user for his or her name and e-mail address if his or her gets a high score
- `youwon.gui`: A dialog to congratulate the user on winning

I'm not going to go over the contents of each of these presentations here; you can use Bongo to view them and their scripts. The main presentation—`wordsmith.gui`—however, is worth at least a glance, as it uses a custom widget called `WordSmithWidget`.

In fact, if you open the `wordsmith.gui` presentation and browse it, you'll notice that most of the basic functionality of the game is contained in this presentation through the `WordSmithWidget` class. The tiles are created and laid out in columns, and you can move them to the rack at the top of the screen or choose the Check or Clear buttons to register the word or to reset the tiles back to normal.

The `wordsmith.gui` presentation is, for the most part, just a display surface for `WordSmithWidget`. `WordSmithWidget` is the heart of the WordSmith application and controls the vast majority of the game play, including choosing and laying out the tiles, animating the tiles when you move them, handling checking your word against a dictionary file, and keeping track of the score as you play.

The code for this widget is contained in the Java file `WordSmithWidget.java`, stored in the `wordsmith` directory. This large file is worth examining, particularly from the standpoint of creating sophisticated custom widgets (a topic that is outside the scope of this book; see the *Official Marimba Guide to Bongo* for more information). I won't go into detail on this file, but there are a few parts I do want to mention.

The `WordSmithWidget` code uses two utility classes, `Rack` and `Dict`, the source of which is also contained in the `wordsmith` directory. `Rack` keeps track of which tiles can be moved and how many tiles are left in the game; `Dict` manages the dictionary and does the testing to see if the word you've spelled is actually in the dictionary. It also has a handle to an instance of the class `HighScoreManager` for dealing with high scores—we'll go into this class later on in this chapter.

One of the more important parts of the WordSmith widget, which links it to the rest of the application is the `checkForWin()` method, which is called periodically during the game to check to see whether the game is over yet. Listing 13.1 shows the code for this method.

Listing 13.1. The `checkforWin()` method in WordSmith widget.

```
 1:public void checkForWin() {
 2:    if (tilesLeft > 2)
 3:        return;
 4:    try {
 5:        int place = -1;
 6:        if ((place = highScores.place(score, HighScoreManager.LOCAL)) != -1) {
 7:            new HighScoreFrame(getFrame(), new
               URL(getPresentation().getBase(),"highscore.gui"),
 8:                highScores, score, getPresentation.show();
 9:        }
10:        else {
11:            new PlayerDialog(getFrame(), new URL(getPresentation().getBase(),
12:                "youwon.gui")).show();
13:        }
14:    }
15:    catch (MalformedURLException e) {
16:        e.printStackTrace();
17:    }
18:}
```

Here's a general overview of what's going on:

- Line 2 checks to make sure it is indeed the end of the game. (There should be fewer than three tiles left on the board for the game to end.)

- Line 6 checks to see whether the score of the current game places it in the current list of local high scores (using methods defined in the `HighScoreManager` class—we'll look at this class in the next section). If so, it launches a dialog to prompt you for your name and e-mail address and to save your high score. This set of lines is the connection between this widget and the parts of the channel that manage high scores.

- Even if the score isn't a high score, you still get a nice congratulatory window (an instance of the Bongo class `PlayerDialog`), in lines 10 through 13.

You see how the `checkForWin()` method connects the WordSmith custom widget to the rest of the channel as this chapter progresses.

Managing High Scores

A significant part of the WordSmith application is dedicated to the management of high scores: reading them, storing them, displaying them in their own window, testing to see whether a current score qualifies as a high score, and logging them back to the transmitter for the plug-in to process.

The WordSmith application keeps track of two sets of high scores: a local set, for the local version of the channel; and a global set, which contains scores for everyone who is subscribed to the WordSmith channel. When you win at WordSmith, the application tests to see whether your score counts as a high score in either the local or global lists and stores your score, accordingly. If you've been good enough to merit a spot in the global list, the application logs your high-score information to be sent to the transmitter at the next update. WordSmith also provides a way for you to display the current lists of global and local high scores.

There are four class files for managing and displaying high scores:

- HighScore.java: A utility class to describe an individual high score (with your name, e-mail address, and score)
- HighScoreManager.java: The central class for reading, writing, and logging local and global high scores, testing to see whether a current score merits placement in the list, and inserting the high score in the right slot
- HighScoreFrame.java: A class to display the high-score dialog and process the name and e-mail the user enters from there
- HighScoreListFrame.java: A class to display the list of the current local and global high scores

Let's start with the HighScoreManager class because that's the central class to manage high scores.

The HighScoreManager Class

The core of high-score management is the HighScoreManager class, which is responsible for

- Reading the stored high scores from a file into memory.
- Testing to see whether a current score needs to be listed.
- Logging global high scores.
- Writing the score files back to disk when the program exits. A new instance of HighScoreManager is created when the application is started, and this object is used both by the main application and the WordSmith widget throughout the execution of the game.

Let's work through the basic life cycle of the HighScoreManager. When the class is first instantiated as the application starts up, the HighScoreManager creates Vector objects to store the local and global high scores and initializes them with empty HighScore objects. Then, two methods are called: readLocalHighScores() and readGlobalHighScores().

The local high-scores file is a file called highscores.txt and is contained in the local data directory for the channel, so the readLocalHighScores() method uses get getDataDirectory() method to locate it. The remainder of the readLocalHighScores() method simply opens that file (if it exists), and parses the scores into a HighScore object and then inserts that object into the vector in the right spot. (All high scores are sorted by score, highest to lowest.)

The readGlobalHighScores() method performs essentially the same operations as readLocalHighScores, except that the global high-scores file is part of the channel's data; you'll use context.getBase() to locate that file and read its values into the vector for the global scores. 279

With the initialization of the existing scores files done, the HighScoreManager class doesn't do anything else until the game has been played and a new score is available. WordSmithWidget, given a new score, uses the HighScoreManager's place() method to determine whether a score counts as a high score or not. All place() does is determine whether a score can be placed in the high-score list (if the score is higher than the lowest score in the list). If it can, the widget uses HighScoreFrame to get the user's name and address, and HighScoreFrame in turn calls the insert() method to actually put the new score into the high-score list.

The insert() method in the HighScoreManager is shown in Listing 13.2:

Listing 13.2. The insert() method.

```
1:public void insert(HighScore hs) {
 2:   int i = place(hs.getScore(), LOCAL);
 3:   if (i != NOT_IN_TOPTEN)
 4:       insertAt(hs, i, LOCAL);
 5:
 6:   i = place(hs.getScore(), GLOBAL);
 7:   if (i != NOT_IN_TOPTEN) {
 8:       insertAt(hs, i, GLOBAL);
 9:       logGlobal(hs);
10:       context.update();
11:   }
12:}
13:
```

There are two steps in the insert() method: First, insert the score in the local high-score list, insert() calls place() to find out where to insert the score (line 2), and then call the insertAt() utility method to actually put it in that spot (line 4). The second step is to do basically the same thing for the global high-score list: Find out where to place it, and if it actually merits entry in the global high scores (which are generally higher than the local high scores), then it does three things:

1. Uses insertAt() to insert the score in the global high score list (line 8).
2. Calls a method called logGlobal() (line 9), to log the score as feedback data to the transmitter (the logGlobal() method simply calls appendLog() with a string representation of the score).
3. Calls the context.update() method (line 10), which forces an update of the channel to send the new global high score to the transmitter for processing. (More about the update later on.)

The only other main operation the HighScoreManager class does is to save the local high scores as a local data file when the application is ready to quit. A method called writelocalHighScores() will do this, opening the local data file and writing each of the local scores to that file (the application doesn't need to write global high scores; those come from the transmitter as part of the channel update).

HighScoreFrame

The second of the major classes for managing high scores is HighScoreFrame. HighScoreFrame is an instance of the PlayerFrame class for displaying the highscore.gui presentation and interpreting the data you get from that window. The highscore.gui dialog is shown in Figure 13.3.

Figure 13.3. *The High Score dialog.*

The WordSmithWidget class is responsible for creating and showing this dialog, once the game has been won and the widget has determined that the new score merits being added to the high score list. After entering his or her name and e-mail address into this window, the user clicks OK, an event which is trapped by the handleEvent() method in the HighScoreFrame class, which calls the handleOKButton() method. The contents of handleOKButton() is shown in Listing 13.3.

Listing 13.3. The handleOKButton() method from HighScoreFrame.

```
1:public void handleOKButton() {
2:    TextBoxWidget name_tbw =
3:      (TextBoxWidget)player.getPresentation().getWidget("name");
4:    String name = name_tbw.getText().trim();
5:    hsm.lastNameUsed = name;
6:    if (name.equals(""))
7:        name = "<empty>";
8:    TextBoxWidget email_tbw =
9:      (TextBoxWidget)player.getPresentation().getWidget("email");
10:   String email = email_tbw.getText().trim();
11:   hsm.laste-mailUsed = email;
12:   if (email.equals(""))
13:       email = "<empty>";
14:   HighScore hs = new HighScore(score, name, email, new Date());
15:   hsm.insert(hs);
```

continues

Listing 13.3. continued

```
16:
17:    dispose();
18:}
```

The `handleOKButton` is responsible for two main things: First, it builds a HighScore object with the information from the dialog's widgets and the score from the `WordSmithWidget`. Then it calls the `insert()` method in `HighScoreManager` (line 15) to insert the new `HighScore` object in the right spot in the list. That done, it calls `dispose()` to get rid of itself.

HighScoreListFrame

The only high score class left to discuss is the `HighScoreListFrame` class, which uses the `highscorelist.gui` presentation to display the current list of local and global high scores. This class is creates in response to the Show High Scores menu item. All it does is display the `highscores.gui` presentation and fill in the list widget in that presentation with the scores information stored in the `HighScoreManager` class. See the code for `HighScoreListFrame.java` for details.

The Main Application

If the `WordSmithWidget` class is responsible for all the actual game play, and the `HighScoreManager` processes all the high-score data, what's left for the main application to do? The main application ties together all the basic behaviors of the widget and the high-score manager, builds and processes a menubar for various options in the application, and manages live updates from the transmitter.

The file `WordSmithApplication.java` in the `wordsmith` directory contains the source for the WordSmith channel. `WordSmithApplication` is a subclass of `ApplicationPlayerFrame`, and implements all the channel methods you've come to know and love: `setContext()`, `start()`, `stop()`, `notifyAvailable()`, `notifyInstall()`, and `handleEvent()`.

Initializing the Channel

Let's start with the `setContext()` method, as that's the first method that's called when the channel starts up. `setContext()` looks like this:

```
public void setContext(ApplicationContext context) {
    super.setContext(context);

    highScores = new HighScoreManager();
    WordSmithWidget wsw = (WordSmithWidget)util.getWidget("wordsmith");
    wsw.setContext(context);
    wsw.setHighScoreManager(highScores);
}
```

The `setContext()` method does three main things to initialize the channel:

- ● It calls `super.setContext()`, as all channels should, so that the `ApplicationContext` can be saved into the `context` instance variable.
- ● It initializes an instance of `HighScoreManager` and stores it in the `highScores` variable.
- ● It gets ahold of `WordSmithWidget` and passes the context and the high score manager to that widget.

The next step is the `start()` method:

```
public void start() {
    super.start();

    highScores.setContext(context);
    highScores.readLocalHighScores();
    highScores.readGlobalHighScores();
}
```

Here's where the high-score manager gets initialized, and where the local and global high-score lists are read into memory. After `start()` finishes executing, the game is ready to be played.

Note

> The `start()` method actually contains two more lines I've edited out here: a call to a method called `readState()` and a call to `show()`. The former is a local method that is not implemented in this version of the channel (or rather, it's implemented empty), and the latter is actually already called in `super.start()` so it's redundant to call it here.

Handling Updates

Live updates to the WordSmith channel happen in the form of updated global high-score lists. An update can occur both because the update interval for the channel has passed, and also in response to a high score being logged by the `HighScoreManager`. (Remember that `HighScoreManager` calls the `context.update()` method explicitly.) To handle the new high-score data, the `WordSmithApplication` channel overrides both `notifyAvailable()` and `notifyInstall()`.

Both these methods should look extremely familiar to you; I used similar versions in the Weather channel class from Chapter 11, "Managing Updates and User Information." Listing 13.4 shows both `notifyAvailable()` and `notifyInstall()`.

Listing 13.4. Update methods in `WordSmithApplication`.

```
1: public void notifyAvailable(String dir) {
2:     if ("restart".equals(context.getParameter("update.action"))) {
3:         context.restart();
```

Listing 13.4. continued

```
 4:     }
 5:
 6:         context.installData(dir);
 7: }
 8:
 9: public void notifyInstall(String dir) {
10:     highScores.readGlobalHighScores();
11: }
```

The notifyAvailable() method, as you know, is called after an update has occurred, and there's new data to be installed. In this method, if the channel has been published with the Data Available property as restart(), the channel will be restarted. In any case, however, we'll want the new data to be installed, so context.installData is called at the end of that method.

The notifyInstall() method processes the new data. In this case, the high-score manager is responsible for managing the global high scores that have arrived as part of the update, so you call the readGlobalHighScores() method in that class to re-read the list of high scores.

The combination of these two methods, in addition to the methods in the HighScoreManager class, ensure that the running channel has the most up-to-date version of the high-score list at all times.

The Menubar

The WordSmithApplication also has one other feature we haven't covered in this book: It has a menubar with several menus and menu items.

Adding menus and menubars for a channel that uses a presentation is extremely similar to adding a menubar to a normal Java application, with one significant difference: Instead of using the java.awt classes for handling menus, you use special classes in the marimba.desktop package (part of the bongo.zip library). These special classes include AppMenuBar, AppMenu, AppMenuItem, and AppCheckboxMenuItem and are very similar to their counterparts in the java.awt package. You can find out more about these classes (and about adding menus to presentations) in the *Official Marimba Guide to Bongo*.

The WordSmithApplication adds the menubar to the channel as part of the constructor for the class; because it's initialization code for the window itself and doesn't fit into setContext() very well, this is a good place for it. You can see the actual code in the Java file for the WordSmith application.

The handleEvent() method for the WordSmithApplication class also manages menu events, calling different methods in different objects for each different menu item. Listing 13.5 shows the part of the handleEvent() method that deals with menus. Note in particular the "Playing WordSmith" and "About WordSmith" menu items in lines 11 through 29, which display the help.gui and about.gui presentations in their own frames, respectively.

Listing 13.5. A partial `handleEvent()` to handle menu events.

```
1:if ((""+evt.arg).equalsIgnoreCase("quit")) {
2:   context.stop();
3:}
4:else if ((""+evt.arg).equalsIgnoreCase("high scores...")) {
5:   showHighScoreList();
6:}
7:else if ((""+evt.arg).equalsIgnoreCase("New Game")) {
8:   WordSmithWidget wsw = (WordSmithWidget)util.getWidget("wordsmith");
9:   wsw.newGame();
10:}
11:else if ((""+evt.arg).equalsIgnoreCase("Playing WordSmith...")) {
12:   try {
13:     PlayerFrame pf = new PlayerFrame();
14:     pf.util.setPresentation(new URL(context.getBase(), "help.gui"));
15:     pf.show();
16:   }
17:   catch(MalformedURLException e) {
18:       e.printStackTrace();
19:   }
20:}
21:else if ((""+evt.arg).equalsIgnoreCase("About WordSmith...")) {
22:   try {
23:     PlayerFrame pf = new PlayerFrame();
24:     pf.util.setPresentation(new URL(context.getBase(), "about.gui"));
25:     pf.show();
26:   }
27:   catch(MalformedURLException e) {
28:       e.printStackTrace();
29:   }
30:}
```

Stopping the Channel

Once users gets bored playing the game, they select Quit from menu channel's menu, the channel stops, and the `stop()` method is called. Here's that `stop()` method, which called the `writeLocalHighScores()` method in `HighScoreManager` to save the state of the local high scores. The `hide()` and `dispose()` methods are part of the `super.stop()` implementation of this method; you could just as easily have called `super.stop()` here instead:

```
public void stop() {
   highScores.writeLocalHighScores();
   hide();
   dispose();
}
```

Note

As with the `start()` method, I've deleted references called `writeState()` from this method. In the version of WordSmith I used for this chapter, `writeState()` doesn't do anything.

The Plug-In

When a user scores well enough in the WordSmith game to merit being listed in the high scores file, the high-score manager logs the score he or she got and calls `update()`. That log data is sent to the transmitter as feedback data; a plug-in on the transmitter site will then process that global high score data.

The plug-in for the WordSmith channel is contained in the `plugin` directory of the channel, as it should be. The code itself for the channel, the file `WordSmithPlugin.java`, is in the `wordsmith` directory inside `plugin`; the code is defined as inside the `wordsmith` package, so it needs to be in that directory. The `properties.txt` file for the plug-in takes that package into account:

```
main=wordsmith.WordSmithPlugin
```

The `WordSmithPlugin` class follows all the basic rules for a plug-in that you learned in the last chapter, including implementing `init()` and `processRequest()` events. In addition, because the procedures the plug-in uses to insert scores into the transmitter's version of the high-scores list are very similar to those the high score manager uses to insert scores into its version of the list, a lot of the code is very similar to that of the `HighScoreManager` class. I'll point out the similarities as they appear.

Let's start with `init()` shown in Listing 13.6.

Listing 13.6. The `init()` method from `WordSmithPlugin.java`.

```
1:public synchronized void init() {
 2:    highScoreFile = getDataFile(HIGHSCOREFILE);
 3:    // initialize array
 4:    for (int i = 0 ; i < HighScoreManager.MAXHIGHSCORES ; i++) {
 5:        HighScore hs = new HighScore();
 6:        highScores.addElement(hs);
 7:    }
 8:    readHighScores();
 9:
10:    highScoreChecksum = calculateChecksum(scoresToBytes());
11:    }
12:
```

The `init()` method here does essentially the same thing the `HighScoreManager` class does to initialize itself: it sets up a vector object to store the scores, initializes it, and then reads the `highscore.txt` file into that vector (using the `readHighScores()` method). Notice that the plug-in only has one set of high scores to deal with, and it stores that file in the local data directory for the plug-in (line 2).

To finish up, the `init()` method calculates a checksum for the existing high-score data (the plug-in will keep a running checksum throughout the channel). The `scorestoBytes()` method is a utility method that converts the scores vector into a byte array.

One important point to note here is that the init() method uses the HighScore class for each entry in the high scores list. Although this may not seem surprising, it does demonstrate a feature of plug-ins: the CLASSPATH for a plug-in includes both the plug-in directory and the channel directory itself—so you can share files such as HighScore between the channel and the plug-in.

With the plug-in initialized with the current high scores, the plug-in waits for an update request. processRequest(), shown in Listing 13.7, handles each request:

Listing 13.7. processReqeust() from WordSmithPlugin.java.

```
 1:public synchronized void processRequest(RequestContext context)
 2:    throws IOException {
 3:    Vector logs = getLogEntries(context);
 4:    for (Enumeration e = logs.elements() ; e.hasMoreElements() ; ) {
 5:      LogEntry le = (LogEntry)e.nextElement();
 6:      String s = new String(le.data, 0);
 7:      add(s);
 8:
 9:      highScoreChecksum = calculateChecksum(scoresToBytes());
10:    }
11:
12:    byte b[] = scoresToBytes();
13:    context.addFile(HIGHSCOREFILE, b, highScoreChecksum, PERSISTENT);
14:
15:    try {
16:      if (highScoreFile.exists() == false) {
17:        File dir = new File(highScoreFile.getParent());
18:        if (dir.exists() == false) {
19:          if (dir.mkdirs()){
20:          }
21:        }
22:      }
23:      FastOutputStream fos = new FastOutputStream(highScoreFile);
24:      for (Enumeration e = highScores.elements() ; e.hasMoreElements() ; ) {
25:        HighScore hs = (HighScore)e.nextElement();
26:        fos.println(hs.toString());
27:      }
28:      fos.close();
29:    }
30:    catch(IOException e) {
31:        e.printStackTrace();
32:    }
33:    super.processRequest(context);
34:}
```

This method should look familiar; it's almost identical to the processRequest() method I used in the last chapter for the survey channel. Here are the most important parts of this method:

● Lines 3 through 7 read the log entries from the reqeust context and process them into HighScore objects. (Actually, the add() method, which I haven't shown here, processes each entry into a HighScore object and then inserts that HighScore object into the current list of high scores at the right spot.)

- Line 9 calculates the new checksum each time a new high score is added.

- Lines 12 and 13 add the new high-score list to the channel index using the `context.addFile()` method. Note that the file disposition for this file is `PERSISTENT`, which means that proxies will cache this file for requests that happen immediately after this one, to speed things up a bit.

- Lines 15 through 32 simply save out the new list of high scores to the local data file.

After the plug-in is finished processing the request, the data for the new high-scores file is sent back to the channel, which uses `notifyInstall()` to install the new data. In this way, a central high-scores list can be updated from each running channel and the changes can be pushed back out to each one.

Functional Flow

Got all that? The WordSmith channel is fairly complicated, involving several different classes and widgets, all interacting, to accomplish its purpose. Now that you have a basic idea of the various parts, here's an overview of how the typical flow of control works in the WordSmith channel as it's played:

- The channel starts up, and the `setContext()` and `init()` methods are called in the `WordSmithApplication` class. The menubar for the application is initialized, the high score manager reads in the local and global high scores, and game play starts in the `WordSmithWidget`.

- The user plays the game until the end. `WordSmithWidget` checks with the high score manager to see if the current score is a local high score (using the `place()` method). If it isn't a high score, the widget displays a congratulatory message.

- If the score is indeed a high score, the widget launches the `HighScoreFrame` to prompt the user for their name and e-mail address. After the user clicks the OK button, the `HighScoreFrame` class packages up that data into a `HighScore` object and send it to the high score manager via the `insert()` method.

- The high score manager inserts the high score into the local high-score list and, if the score merits being added to the global high-score list, logs it as feedback data and calls `update()`.

- The feedback data is sent to the transmitter plug-in via the update request (let's assume the WordSmith channel continues running at this point). The plug-in processes the new high score, inserts it into the high-score list, and returns the new high scores to the channel.

● The WordSmithApplication class handles the update by instructing the high score manager to re-read the global high score list.

● When the user quits the channel, the high-score manager saves the local high scores to a file, ready to be used again the next time WordSmith starts up.

Channel Properties

The last part of the WordSmith channel to go over are the actual properties for this channel. Figure 13.4 shows the general properties.

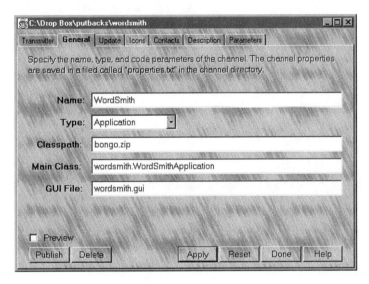

Figure 13.4. *General Properties for WordSmith.*

The only new thing here is the name of the main class for the application—because the channel is contained in the WordSmith package and inside the wordsmith directory, you'll have to include the name of that package here so that the right class can be launched.

The icon properties for the channel, shown in Figure 13.5 are also worth examining.

There are four icons for this channel: the GIF and BMP icons are each a 64-pixel square icon that is used as the icon for the channel (there are two different formats, one for Windows and one for UNIX), and two thumbnail icons for the channel in the tuner. All of these icons are stored in the image directory.

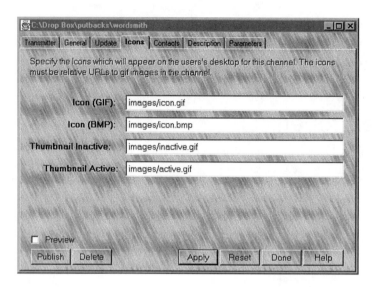

Figure 13.5. Icon properties.

Summary

WordSmith is a reasonably complex channel that makes use of most of the features of the Castanet and Bongo technologies: Bongo presentations, custom widgets, channel classes, local state, automatic updates, and channel feedback (whew!). Throughout this chapter you've explored how this channel uses all these features, and how the various different parts of the channel interact. At this point, you should be able to create your own Java channels that use any of these features. Good luck!

fourteen

An Overview of the Marimba Classes

Many of the classes you've been using to create channels and plug-ins throughout this book have been part of the standard Marimba APIs. Both Castanet and Bongo come with a suite of new Java classes that not only help implement the Castanet and Bongo tools themselves, but can help you create channels, plug-ins, and other tools.

This chapter provides a general overview of many of the classes contained in the Marimba classes and tells you in which library they are located. I'm not going to cover every possible Marimba class here—many of the classes in the `marimba.gui` package, for example, are covered in detail in the *Official Marimba Guide To Bongo*. And I'm going to go into more detail about the classes specific to Castanet and channel development than I am for other classes. After reading this chapter, however, you should have a good idea of all the possible classes and how they can be used.

For more information on any of these classes, API documentation is available online from the Marimba site at `http://www.marimba.com`, as a set of channels from `trans.marimba.com`, and on the CD-ROM for this book. *Official Marimba Guide To Bongo* also contains documentation for many of these classes.

The `marimba.channel` Package

The packages you've used most often throughout this book and the classes you will use time and time again as you develop your own channels are the classes contained in the `marimba.channel` package. These classes include the interfaces for creating applications and for managing the application context; they also include classes for treating applets as channels and for incorporating Bongo presentations into channels.

The `marimba.channel` classes are split amongst multiple .zip files, which you'll need to add to your `CLASSPATH` or to the search path for your development environment before you can use them. The `Application` and `ApplicationContext` interfaces are contained in the `marimba.zip` file for either Bongo or the Castanet Transmitter. For the other four channel classes, you'll need Bongo's `bongo.zip` library, or the Transmitter's `transmitter.zip` class.

The `Application` Interface

The `Application` interface defines the standard channel methods and events; implement this interface in your own classes to convert them into channels. The `Application` interface defines four event types for handling updates:

● `DATA_UPDATE_EVENT` is called just before the channel is updated, allowing you to save channel feedback data that may be sent along with the request.

● `DATA_AVAILABLE_EVENT` is where new channel data is downloaded and ready to be installed. Call the `installData()` method on the application context to install it.

● `DATA_INSTALLED_EVENT` is called in response to `installData()` to allow you to process the newly installed data.

● `DATA_NOTIFY_EVENT` is sent to inactive channels whose Data Available property has been set to "notify." The channel is instantiated, `setContext()` is called, and this event is posted.

The `Application` interface also defines the following methods:

    `public abstract void handleEvent(Event)` processes events.

    `public abstract void setContext(ApplicationContext)` is called at startup with an instance of the current application context. This method should save that context and perform any very basic initialization tasks.

`public abstract void start()` is called when the channel is first started.

`public abstract void stop()` is called when the channel is stopped.

The `ApplicationContext` Interface

The `ApplicationContext` interface defines the environment in which the channel runs and provides a mechanism for accessing Castanet Tuner and channel features. An object that responds to the `ApplicationContext` methods is passed to the channel through the `setContext()` method; usually you'll store that object in an instance variable and call its methods later on as the channel executes.

The `ApplicationContext` defines the following methods:

`public abstract boolean appendLog(byte[])` stores an array of bytes as a channel log entry, to be sent to the transmitter as feedback data during the next update. Returns false only if there was an error writing the log entry.

`public abstract boolean appendLog(String)` is the same as the previous method, except the argument is `String`.

`public abstract boolean channelFileExists(String)` returns true if the given relative path exists in the channel.

`public abstract URL getBase()` returns the base URL for this channel.

`public abstract String getChannelDirectory()` is an older version of `getDataDirectory`; this method is obsolete and will be removed from a later release.

`public abstract String getChannelName()` returns the full name of the channel.

`public abstract String getChannelStatus(String)` returns the current channel status (one of `"unsubscribed"`, `"subscribed"`, `"running"`).

`public abstract URL getCodeBase()` returns the URL of the directory for the channel's code (might be the same as `getBase()`, used most often with applets).

`public abstract URL getDataBase()` returns the URL for the data directory for this channel, which is used to store persistent local files.

`public abstract String getDataDirectory()` returns the path name to the data directory for this channel.

`public abstract String getParameter(String)` returns the value of an application parameter, as stored in the `properties.txt` file for the channel (and set in the Castanet Publish).

`public abstract Updates getPendingUpdates()` returns an `Updates` object representing the changes that will be made to the channel in the course of the update. Returns null if there are no updates to be made.

`public abstract byte[] getProfile()` returns an array of bytes representing the profile data for this channel. Will return empty if there is no profile data for this channel.

`public abstract String getServerName()` returns the name of the server (transmitter) for this channel. The transmitter name is of the form `hostname:port`.

`public abstract void installData(String)` requests the tuner to install all or part of newly arrived data. The argument is the relative path name of the file or directory to install.

`public abstract String[] listChannelDirectory(String)` returns an array of strings representing the names of files in the given directory. To list the entire channel, use `"."` as the argument. Returns null if the path does not exist.

`public abstract String[] listChannels()` returns an array of strings representing all the subscribed channels.

`public abstract long publishTime()` returns the time that has passed since this channel was last published.

`public abstract void removeChannel(String)` removes this channel.

`public abstract void restart()` restarts the channel.

`public abstract boolean setProfile(byte[])` stores the array of bytes as profile data for this channel to be sent to the transmitter as feedback data during the next update. Returns false only if there was an error writing the profile.

`public abstract void startChannel(String, String)` starts some other channel. The first argument is the same as the transmitter; the second is the name of the channel.

`public abstract void stop()` stops the channel.

`public abstract void subscribeChannel(String, String)` subscribes to a channel (don't start it). The arguments are the name of a transmitter and the name of the channel.

`public abstract void unsubscribeChannel(String)` unsubscribes from the named channel.

`public abstract void update()` updates the channel.

`public abstract long updateTime()` returns the time that has passed since this channel was last updated.

Updates

The Updates class represents the changes that will be made to the channel as part of an update. You can get an instance of this class using the `getPendingUpdates()` method from the application context. Using these methods in the Updates class, you can get a collection of strings representing path names to files that will be created, deleted, or changed as part of the update.

public Enumeration getDeletes() returns an Enumeration object, consisting of Strings which represent paths to any files which will be deleted as part of this update.

public Enumeration getCreates() returns an Enumeration object, consisting of Strings which represent paths to any files that will be created as part of this update (new channel files).

public Enumeration getUpdates() returns an Enumeration object, consisting of Strings that represent paths to any files which will change as part of the update.

ApplicationFrame

ApplicationFrame is a subclass of the standard java.awt.Frame class that implements a basic form of the Application interface. You can use this class to implement your own channels.

In addition to the methods defined by both the java.awt.Frame class and the Application interface, ApplicationFrame provides the instance variable context, which holds the application context for this channel, and the following methods:

public void notifyAvailable(String) is called in response to the DATA_AVAILABLE_EVENT event. The argument is the path name to the top-level directory that needs installing. By default, this method calls context.restart() if the Data Available property is set to restart, and context.install is the property set to install.

public void notifyInstall(String) is called in response to the DATA_INSTALL_EVENT event. No default implementation.

ApplicationPlayerFrame

ApplicationPlayerFrame is a subclass of the marimba.gui.PlayerFrame class that implements the Application interface. Use it to create channels that use Bongo presentations for their user interface.

ApplicationPlayerFrame supports all the PlayerFrame methods, all the Application methods, and also has the same base implementation as ApplicationFrame.

AppletContext and AppletViewer

The AppletContext interface extends the java.applet.AppletContext interface and is used to gain access to the application interface when applets are run as channels. Use the getApplicationContext() method to get that context object from inside an applet.

AppletViewer is a part of ApplicationFrame that implements AppletContext and java.applet.AppletStub. It's used by the Castanet Tuner to play applets as channels and to support most of the common applet context methods (showDocument(), showStatus(), and so on).

The `marimba.plugin` Package

The classes in the `marimba.plugin` package are used to create transmitter plug-ins, including the standard `Plugin` class and the `RequestContext` interface, which provides information about the update request the plug-in is processing.

The `marimba.plugin` classes are available only in the `transmitter.zip` class that comes with the Castanet Transmitter. You'll need to add that file to your `CLASSPATH` or to the search path for your development environment before you can use them.

Plugin

The `Plugin` class provides the basic behavior for a transmitter plug-in; subclass this class to create your own transmitter plug-ins. Your class will be instantiated when an update request is made to your channel; with an object that supports the `RequestContext` interface that gets passed along in the `processRequest()` method you can get information and data from that update request and process it.

When you subclass the `Plugin` class, you'll generally override three methods: `init()`, `destroy()`, and `processRequest()`.

The `Plugin` class provides four static variables for setting the disposition of files that you add to the channel's index using `addFile` (you learned about all these dispositions in Chapter 12, "Creating Transmitter Plug-Ins"):

- ● `ALWAYS` sends the byte array to the tuner on every request.
- ● `ASK_ME`: When this data is requested, the plug-in should handle the request.
- ● `IF_NEEDED` sends the byte array to the tuner only if the tuner doesn't already have that data.
- ● `PERSISTENT` treats the data is if it were a file (so it can be cached by proxies).

The `Plugin` class also provides these methods:

Note

> This is not a complete list of methods in the `Plugin` class. Many standard `Plugin` methods are intended to be called by the transmitter to start or to interact with the plug-in and are not useful to you for your subclasses. See the API documentation for the full set of methods.

`public Checksum calculateChecksum(byte[])` returns a checksum for the array of bytes.

`public Checksum calculateChecksum(String)` returns a checksum for the file referred to by the argument (a relative path to a channel file).

`public void destroy()` is called when the plug-in object is unloaded. Override this method to clean up after your plug-in.

`public File getChannelFile(String)` returns a File object representing the path to a channel file.

`public String getChannelName()` returns the name of the channel this plug-in operates on.

`public File getDataFile(String)` returns a file object pointing to the path name for the plug-in's local data directory. You can safely read and write files to this directory.

`public Vector getLogEntries(RequestContext)` returns all the log entries sent to the transmitter as part of the request.

`public void init()` is called by the transmitter when the plug-in is first started. Override to provide your own initialization behavior.

`public void processRequest(RequestContext)` processes a subscribe or update request for this channel. Override this method to process logging or profile data or to customize a channel.

`public void processUnsubscribe(RequestContext)` processes an unsubscribe request for this channel. There will be no profile data, nor will any data be sent back to the tuner.

RequestContext

The `RequestContext` interface defines methods that allow a plug-in to get information about the channel making and update or subscribe request. Usually those methods are used in the `Plugin` class, which is passed an instance of `RequestContext` object by the transmitter.

The `RequestContext` interface provides the following methods:

`public abstract void addFile(String, byte[], int) throws IOException` adds the file data in the byte array to the channel file list with the name given by the string argument, and with the given integer file disposition.

`public abstract void addFile(String, byte[], Checksum, int) throws IOException` is the same as the previous method but also allows you to specify the checksum of the data.

`public abstract void addFile(String, File) throws IOException` adds the file referred to by the File to the file list with the path name given in the string argument.

`public abstract void addFile(String, File, Checksum) throws IOException` is the same as the previous method but also allows you to specify the checksum of the file.

`public abstract void deleteFile(String)` deletes the specified file from the channel file list.

`public abstract byte[] getLoggingData()` returns the data logged by the channel as an array of bytes. Returns null if there is no logging data.

`public abstract String getLogPrefix()` returns a string representing the IP number and date and time of the request.

`public abstract int getMinutesGMT()` returns the number of minutes off the GMT for the system that made the request.

`public abstract getOSarch()` returns the OS architecture of the system that made the request.

`public abstract getOSname()` returns the OS name of the system that made the request.

`public abstract getOSversion()` returns the OS version of the system that made the request.

`public abstract byte[] getProfileData()` returns the profile data for the channel as an array of bytes. Returns null if there is no profile data.

`public abstract int getProtocolVersion()` returns the transmitter protocol version number.

`public abstract String getRequestComment()` returns the request comment (sent as part of the request) and null if there is no comment.

`public abstract long getTunerID()` returns a long integer representing the ID of the requesting tuner.

`public abstract String getTunerIDString()` returns a string object representing the ID of the requesting tuner.

`public abstract void redirect(String, int)` redirects this request to another transmitter. The string argument is the name of the transmitter, and the `int` is the port number.

`public abstract void renameFile(String, String)` renames the file from the channel list specified in the first string argument to the name or path of the second string argument.

`public abstract void setRequestDelay(int)` sets the delay in minutes before the tuner should make a second update request.

LogEntry

The `LogEntry` class is a simple class for dealing with channel log entries. The `Vector` object created by the `getLogEntries` method (from the `Plugin` class) contains a `LogEntry` object for each of the log entries.

The LogEntry class has two instance variables:

● timestamp: The time and date the log entry was made.

● data: The data that was logged for this entry.

The marimba.io Package

The marimba.io package provides classes for input and output to supplement the standard java.io classes. The most significant of those classes are the FastInputStream and FastOutputStream classes, which provide optimized unsynchronized buffered input and output streams.

The marimba.io package is part of the marimba.zip library (in either the Castanet Transmitter or Bongo releases).

FastInputStream and FastOutputStream

The FastInputStream and FastOutputStream classes, as I mentioned, provide input and output streams that are fast versions of a combination of the buffered, byte array, and data and print streams from the standard java.io package. Use FastInputStream and FastOutputStream for reading to and writing from files or arrays of bytes.

FastInputStream

FastInputStream extends the java.io.FilterInputStream class and implements the DataInput interface. You can create FastInputStream in a multitude of different ways:

FastInputStream(byte[]) creates a stream that reads from a byte array.

FastInputStream(byte[], int, int) creates a stream that reads from a byte array (the two integers are the offset and length of the array).

FastInputStream(String) opens a file.

FastInputStream(File) opens the given file.

FastInputStream(InputStream) combines two streams.

FastInputStream(InputStream, int) combines two streams given a buffer size.

FastInputStream(RandomAccessFile) accesses a RandomAccessFile stream.

In addition to the standard methods available from its superclasses and the DataInput interface, FastInputStream includes the following additional methods:

public boolean backup(int) backs up by a given amount (usually just one character or a small amount near the beginning of a stream).

public boolean getError() sees if there has been an I/O error. (I/O errors are only reported when the stream is closed.)

public `PropertyObject` `readObject()` reads a persistent object into a `PropertyObject` instance. (See the section on `marimba.persist` in this chapter for more information about persistent objects.)

FastOutputStream

`FastOutputStreams` are analogous to `FastInputStreams`; the `FastOutputStream` class inherits from `java.io.FilterOutputStream` and implements the `DataInput` interface. `FastOutputStreams` combine the best features of `DataOutputStream`, `PrintStream`, and `BufferedOutputStream`.

You can create a new `FastOutputStream` using one of these constructors:

`FastOutputStream()` creates a memory-output stream.

`FastOutputStream(int)` creates a memory-output stream with a given size.

`FastOutputStream(byte[])` creates a memory-output to the given byte array.

`FastOutputStream(File)` opens the given file for writing.

`FastOutputStream(String)` opens a file for writing.

`FastOutputStream(OutputStream)` combines two output streams.

`FastOutputStream(OutputStream, int)` combines two streams given a buffer size.

`FastOutputStream(RandomAccessFile)` opens using a random access file.

In addition to the standard methods available from its superclasses and the `DataInput` interface, `FastOutputStreams` also implement all the printing methods from `PrintStream` and the following methods:

public `boolean` `getError()` returns true if there has been a write error. (Write errors are not reported until the stream is closed or flushed.)

public `void` `justClose()` is a version of the `close()` method that doesn't throw an exception.

public `void` `writeObject(PropertyObject)` writes a `PropertyObject` object to the stream. See the section on the `marimba.persist` package for more information.

Other Classes

The `marimba.io` package also contains the following classes, which you may find useful:

- ⬤ `RAFInputStream` (inherits from `java.io.InputStream`) creates an input stream to interface to a `RandomAccessFile`.
- ⬤ `RAFOutputStream` (inherits from `java.io.OuputStream`) creates an output stream to interface to a `RandomAccessFile`.
- ⬤ `ScannerInputStream` (inherits from `FastInputStream`) is a fast, efficient string parser.

The `marimba.gui` Package

The `marimba.gui` package contains the classes that constitute Java support for Bongo and its widgets. Although this is a very large package, I'm not going to cover all of it in this chapter; here I'll focus on the parts we've covered throughout this book and that are useful to channel developers. See the API documentation or *Official Marimba Guide to Bongo* for more information.

The `marimba.gui` package is part of the `bongo.zip` library. Because this library will not be part of the standard tuner distribution (it was in previous beta releases of the tuner), you should include it with every channel that uses any of its classes.

PlayerUtil

The `PlayerUtil` class allows you to manipulate the widgets in a presentation from the class that uses that presentation. For channels built from the `ApplicationPlayerFrame` class, you can get to the `PlayerUtil` object for the current presentation via the `util` instance variable.

The `PlayerUtil` class provides the following methods:

Note

> Many of these methods only apply to specific widget classes in the presentation, and others are only meaningful on specific widgets. You should be familiar with the widgets you use so that the values you get and set from those widgets do not surprise you.

`public void addList(String, ListItemWidget)` adds the `ListItemWidget` in the second argument to the `ListWidget` named in the first argument.

`public void addSortedList(String, ListItemWidget)` adds a `ListItemWidget` to a named `ListWidget`, sorted by the key.

`public void appendText(String, String)` appends the string in the second argument to the `TextWidget` or `TextAreaWidget` named in the first string argument.

`public void clearList(String)` clears the `ListWidget` named in the argument.

`public void clearText(String, long)` clears the `TextWidget` or `TextAreaWidget` named in the first argument, after the number of milliseconds in the second argument.

`public String currentPage(String)` returns the current page of the `FolderWidget` named in the argument.

`public boolean getBoolean(String)` gets the value of the `CheckBoxWidget` or `OptionWidget` named in the argument.

`public String getChoice(String)` gets the value of the `ChoiceWidget` named in the argument.

`public PlayerPanel getPlayerPanel()` returns the `PlayerPanel` object for this presentation. (The `PlayerPanel` is a subclass of `java.awt.Panel` that displays a presentation.)

`public Presentation getPresentation()` gets the current presentation.

`public String getText(String)` gets the text of the widget named in the string argument.

`public Object getValue(String)` gets the value of the widget named in the argument.

`public synchronized Widget getWidget(String)` returns the widget object referenced by name in the argument.

`public void gotoPage(String)` goes to the page named by the argument.

`public void setBoolean(String, boolean)` sets the value of the `CheckBoxWidget` or `OptionWidget` named in the first argument to the value of the second argument.

`public void setChoice(String, String)` sets the value of the `ChoiceWidget` named in the first argument to the value of the second argument.

`public void setFPS(String, int)` sets the frames per second for the `AnimatedWidget` listed in the argument to the speed in the second argument.

`public synchronized void setPresentation(String)` sets the current presentation, located at this path and filename.

`public synchronized void setPresentation(URL)` sets the current presentation, located at the given URL.

`public void setText(String, String)` sets the text of the widget named in the first string argument to have the value of the second string argument.

`public void setValue(String, Object)` sets the value of the widget named in the string argument to the value of the object argument.

`public void show(String)` shows the widget named by the first argument.

`public void show(String, boolean)` shows or hides the widget named by the first argument. If the second argument is true, this shows the widget; if false, it hides the widget.

Widget and its Subclasses

The `Widget` class is the generic class for all Bongo widgets and includes a set of standard properties and behaviors for all widgets. All the widget classes in the `marimba.gui` class inherit from this class.

`Widget` is a large class and contains many of the same methods available from `PlayerUtil` to get and set various values of a widget. For more information on the variables and methods in `Widget` and its subclasses, see the API documentation or *Official Marimba Guide to Bongo*.

PlayerFrame

The `PlayerFrame` class is a subclass of `java.awt.Frame` that displays a Bongo presentation in a window. Usually with a channel, you'll subclass `ApplicationPlayerFrame` so that your Java program can respond to channel events; however, if your channel uses subwindows with separate Bongo presentations, you'll want to subclass `PlayerFrame` instead.

The `marimba.persist` Package

The `marimba.persist` package contains classes that help freeze the state of objects—which usually means saving them to files. These classes are used as part of Bongo to help widgets store themselves and their properties. If you're interested in learning more about widget persistence, *Official Marimba Guide to Bongo* has details.

The `marimba.persist` classes are stored in the marimba.zip class, available from either the Castanet Transmitter or Bongo releases.

The `marimba.desktop` Package

The `marimba.desktop` package contains classes that allow Bongo widgets and classes that use Bongo to interact with the native desktop. These classes are, for the most part, used internally by Bongo, with a few notable exceptions: four classes for adding a menubar and menus to presentations being displayed in `PlayerFrame` or `ApplicationPlayerFrame`. These classes behave nearly identically to the `java.awt` classes for menus (in fact, they inherit from those classes and are effectively Bongo-based wrappers for that AWT functionality) and include

- `AppMenuBar` (inherits from `java.awt.MenuBar`) is used to add a menubar to the frame playing this presentation.
- `AppMenu` (inherits from `java.awt.Menu`) is an individual menu, which can be added to a menubar.
- `AppMenuItem` (inherits from `java.awt.MenuItem`) is an individual menu item that can be added to a menu.
- `AppCheckboxMenuItem` (inherits from `java.awt.CheckBoxMenuItem`) is a specialized menu item that can be checked or unchecked.

The `marimba.text` Package

The `marimba.text` package contains classes for implementing a rich text editor—used by Bongo for its script editor. These are utility classes that you generally won't use in your own classes. `marimba.text` is part of the `bongo.zip` library and includes the following.

- The `marimba.text.editor` package, with classes for the actual Bongo editor.
- The `marimba.text.keymap` package, with classes to handle special keyboard combinations and key mappings.
- `ByteString`, a structure representing a collection of bytes.
- `DeviceFont`, a subclass of the `java.lang.Font` class for device-specific fonts.
- `Mark`, to mark and go to a place in the text.
- `Style`, a representation of a text style.
- `StyleChange`, a position in the text where the style should change to something else.
- `StylePool`, a class that maintains an array of styles and their positions in a document.
- `Text`, a class for managing styled text.
- `TextView`, abstract view of a `Text` object (for example, a single or multiline text widget).

The `marimba.util` Package

The `marimba.util` package provides assorted utility classes for the other Marimba classes. Although these classes are generally only useful to the Marimba software, they are worth a mention here.

The `marimba.util` package is contained in the `marimba.zip` library, in either the Castanet Transmitter or Bongo distributions, and includes the following classes and interfaces:

- `Checksum` is a class that represents a 128-bit MD5 checksum. You can create a checksum from a variety of sources including files and strings.
- `Environment` is an interface to native desktop capabilities (for example, loading URLs and copy/paste).
- `Password` is a class that encrypts and decrypts passwords, using base64 encoding.
- `Props` is a subclass of `java.util.Properties` that provides features including headers, filenames, and case insensitivity.
- `PWEncoder` is a subclass of `sun.misc.BASE64Encoder` that doesn't add a newline.
- `QuickSort` is a class to sort things using a `QuickSort` algorithm (optimized for strings).
- `ThreadUtil` is a helper class for threads, mostly to find the current thread group.
- `Sortable` is an interface for sortable things.

Summary

Do any work developing Castanet channels, and you'll end up touching the classes in the various Marimba packages. (Often you'll end up putting your hands all over them, actually.) In this chapter you got a general overview of the classes available to you in the marimba packages, in which zip libraries they can be found, and, in the case of the more important classes, the sorts of things you can do with them.

Congratulations! You've reached the end of *Official Marimba Guide to Castanet*. After slogging through all 14 chapters in this book, you've now learned nearly everything you'll need to know about using the Castanet software and creating channels. Stay tuned to the Marimba home page and to the mailing lists for new information and details on further releases, and good luck!

IV

Appendixes

Tuner Reference

In this appendix you'll find a quick reference to the menus and panels in the Castanet Tuner.

Tuner Menu

The Tuner menu contains operations that apply to the tuner itself or to channels in general.

New Channel (Ctrl+N): Subscribe to a new channel on a new transmitter.

Listing Page (Ctrl+L): Show the Listing page (for getting a listing of channels on a transmitter).

Channels Page (Ctrl+T): Show the Channels page (for starting and stopping subscribed channels).

Cancel Transfers (Ctrl+C): Stop any current network connections (channel subscriptions, updates, or transmitter listings).

Show Console: Display the Java console; errors and other output will appear here.

Update Tuner: Get the latest version of the Tuner software from Marimba's site.

Quit (Ctrl+Q): Quit the tuner.

Channel Menu

The entries in the Channel menu usually apply to selected channels listed on the Channel page.

Channel Description (Ctrl+D): Show the long description of the selected channel.

Channel Properties (Ctrl+P): Show the full properties (the author, update frequency, date last updated, and so on) for the selected channel.

Create Shortcut (Windows only): Create a shortcut to this channel on the desktop.

Subscribe (Ctrl+S): Subscribe to the selected channel.

Update (Ctrl+U): Request an update of the selected channel.

Start (Ctrl+X): Start (run) the selected channel.

Stop: Stop the selected channel.

Unsubscribe: Unsubscribe from the channel. (Unsubscribed channels are still installed on the local disk but are not updated.)

Remove (Ctrl+R): Delete the channel from the local disk.

Help

Display the online help for the Tuner (requires a Web browser). The online help is stored as Web pages on Marimba's Web site or as the Tuner doc channel from trans.marimba.com.

Marimba: Go to the Marimba Web site.

License Agreement: Display the license agreement for this tuner.

Index: Show the index to the inline help.

User Guide: Show the user guide.

Browsers: Instructions on using channels from a Web browser or Web page.

Support: How to get support and help from Marimba.

Release Notes: Information about this release of the Tuner.

Pages

The Castanet Tuner contains several pages with different functionality in each. Those pages include

Marimba: The opening screen for the tuner. Choosing the Marimba button displays the Marimba home page in the user's Web browser.

Channels: Display the currently subscribed channels, sorted by transmitter.

Listing: Display the channel listing for a transmitter. The Browse button shows the list in a Web browser; the Refresh button updates the channel listing.

Hot: Available transmitters with channels that might be interesting.

Configure: Configure the tuner.

Configuration

The configuration page in the tuner contains several subpages:

Loading: Configure the time and frequency of automatic channel updates.

User: Configure user information (all optional).

Network: Configure an HTTP or Marimba proxy, if needed.

Options: Configure your connection options (direct or dialup; the speed of your connection determines how frequently updates will be made) and channel options.

Transmitter and Publish Reference

In this appendix you'll find a quick reference to the menus and panels in the Castanet Transmitter and Castanet Publish, as well as the options for the command-line versions of these programs.

Castanet Transmitter

The transmitter itself doesn't have any menus, but it does have screens for setting up the configuration.

Basic Configuration

Transmitter Channels Directory: The directory on the transmitter's system where channel files and logging information are stored.

Transmitter Host and Port: The name of the host and the port on which the transmitter runs. By default, the port number is 80. Make sure that there isn't a Web server already running on that port, and if there is, use another port. (5282 is a common substitute.)

Transmitter Access: The hosts that will be allowed to publish channels on this host and the password they must use to do so. If no hosts are specified, any host can publish channels.

Publish Notifications: The e-mail address of the announcement service at Marimba for new channels. (Leave blank to avoid announcing channels.) The value of SMTP host is the default mail server.

After the basic configuration is complete, you have the following options:

Advanced: View the advanced configuration properties.

Back: Return to the basic configuration.

Launch: Start the transmitter.

Start/Stop: Start or stop the transmitter.

Help: View the online help for the transmitter (requires a Web browser).

Exit: Exit the transmitter.

Advanced Configuration

Transmitter Concurrency: Set the total number of processes and the number of initial threads per process. The total number of concurrent connections equals the number of processes times the number of threads; increase these numbers to allow more concurrent connections. Use the value of Max threads to limit the number of concurrent connections.

Transmitter Cache: A memory cache for storing channels. The optimum size of this cache should be the total size of all the channels you publish on the transmitter.

Command-Line Transmitter (Solaris Only)

After you've configured the transmitter at least once, you can start it from the command line using the transmitter command and the name of the transmitter's channel directory:

```
% transmitter /usr/local/channels
```

Castanet Publish

The Castanet Publish tool is used to publish channels to a transmitter. This section describes the various properties and buttons available in the Castanet Publish tool, and the options for the command-line version of Publish.

Channels Under Development Screen

The main Castanet Publish screen shows a list of local channels being developed and ready for publishing.

Proxy: Set the proxy information for accessing the transmitter.

Add: Add a local channel directory to the list.

Remove: Remove a local channel directory from the list.

Edit: Edit the properties for that channel. (See "Properties," below.)

Quit: Quit the Publish tool.

Help: Display the online help for channel configuration (requires a Web browser).

Properties

The properties screens allow you to set or change the properties for the channel and to publish it.

Publish: Publish the channel to the transmitter listed in the transmitter properties.

Delete: Delete the channel from the transmitter listed in the transmitter properties. This command does not delete the channel from the local disk.

Preview: When selected, choosing Publish saves all properties but does not actually move any files to the transmitter.

Apply: Save the values for each properties screen.

Reset: Revert to the save properties for each screen.

Done: Return to the Channels under Development screen.

Help: View the online help (requires a Web browser).

Transmitter

Properties for the transmitter and for which files to publish.

Host: The host name of the transmitter. Use localhost when the transmitter is running on the same system as the Publish.

Port: The port number of the transmitter.

Password: The transmitter password, if any.

Ignore: Filenames to ignore when publishing channels (for example, source or backup files).

Password: The channel password, if any.

General

Properties for the overall makeup of the channel and how it will be handled in the tuner.

Name: The name of the channel as it will appear in the tuner.

Type: The type of channel (application, applet, HTML, or presentation).

Classpath: The directories in addition to the channel directory in which to look for class files.

Main class: The first class to start when the channel is launched.

Code: The main applet class for applet channels.

Code base: The value of the CODEBASE attribute from the <APPLET> tag, for applet channels.

GUI file: The name of the presentation associated with this channel.

Width: The width of the applet channel window.

Height: The height of the applet channel window.

Index page: The home page of an HTML channel.

Update

Properties for how the channel will manage updates. For inactive channels:

Update Frequency: How often to update a non-running channel.

Data Available action: How the channel will handle an update: ignore, start, or notify. (The latter requires special code in the channel.)

For active channels:

Update Frequency: How often to update a running channel.

Data Available Action: How the channel will handle an update: ignore, restart, or install. (The latter requires special code in the channel.)

Icons

Properties for custom channel icons.

Icon (GIF): A 64-pixel square icon in GIF format for the channel.

Icon (BMP): A 64-pixel square icon in BMP format for the channel.

Thumbnail Inactive: A 16-pixel square icon for how an inactive channel looks in the tuner.

Thumbnail Active: A 16-pixel square icon for how an active channel appears in the tuner.

Contacts

Contact information for the channel.

Author: Name and e-mail address of the channel's author.

Administrator: Name and e-mail address of the channel's administrator (might be the same person as the author).

Description

Copyright and summary information for the channel.

Copyright: Copyright information for the channel (such as Copyright © 1996 Laura Lemay).

Description: A summary paragraph of what the channel is for.

Parameters

Parameters or options for how the channel should behave. Especially useful for applet channels.

Parameters are indicated by name value pairs, one per line, for example:

```
name=Laura
age=29
```

The publish Command

You can also publish channels using the command-line version of the Publish tool, which does not pop up a GUI. Each channel you publish should already have its properties set (should have a properties.txt file in its channel directory).

In Windows, you must use the publish.exe tool from the command directory, not the publish.exe tool from the top level of the tuner installation directory.

The command-line Publish tool works like this, where the brackets ([]) are optional commands:

```
publish [-host hostname[:portnum] [-ignore wildcards] [-quiet] -[n] directory
```

The options are

> **-host:** Publish to the named transmitter *hostname*. Use the port in *portnum*.
>
> **-ignore:** A list of *wildcards*, surrounded by single quotes, of files to ignore while publishing—for example '*.java'. The default is to ignore core, *~,*.java,*.bak'.
>
> **-quiet:** Operate without output. (Normally, the publish command prints what it's doing.)
>
> **-n:** List the operations to perform, but don't do any of them.
>
> *directory*: The full or relative path name to the channel directory.

You can also use publish to delete a channel from a transmitter, like this:

```
publish -delete [-host hostname[:portnum] directoryOrChannel
```

> **-delete:** Delete the channel.
>
> *directoryOrChannel*: Either the full or relative path name of the channel directory, or the name of the channel. If you use the name of the channel, you must also include the -host option. Note that this command deletes only the channel from the transmitter; it does not effect the local copy of that channel.

Tuner Extensions

A newer feature of Castanet (as of this writing) is the ability to allow Windows or Solaris native-code libraries (DLLs or .so files) to be installed on the local client system (that is, on the system on which the tuner runs) and used by channels that run on that system. Tuner extensions are not downloaded and installed automatically, as normal channel files are; instead, the tuner extension files must be intentionally downloaded by the user for your channel to take advantage of them. In this way, tuner extensions are somewhat analogous to browser plug-ins: they extend the capabilities of channels to include specific functionality.

This appendix gives a quick overview of tuner extensions; more information will appear on Marimba's Web site at http://www.marimba.com/developer/.

When to Use Tuner Extensions

If at all possible, your channel should be written entirely in Java so that it has all the cross-platform and security features of Java and can be updated and provide channel feedback as all normal Java channels can. However, there may be instances where you need to include access to native libraries for select parts of your channel, for example:

● To access specific system features such as CD-ROM drives or special display systems that might not be accessible from within Java.

● To speed up very processor-intensive parts of a channel—for example, to do complex 3D rendering or mathematical equations.

● To leverage large amounts of existing code that has not (yet) been ported to Java.

Tuner extensions provide a way of gaining access to native capabilities and speed while still maintaining the flexibility of channels. Tuner extensions accomplish this by combining the channel code written in Java with a set of native libraries.

Tuner extensions are not a mechanism for getting around Castanet's use of Java; in fact, because they require the user to install the libraries, they don't provide any advantage over a regularly downloaded and installed program. Keep in mind also that tuner extensions are not cross-platform (you'll have to port them for each system that needs to run your channel), and are not updated automatically as part of the channel.

Creating Tuner Extensions

Tuner extensions are created using Java's native method capabilities. If you don't know how to create native methods, any good Java book will have instructions on using native methods and developing the native code to implement those methods. (In fact, there's a good book that will teach you just that on the CD that comes with this book: *Teach Yourself Java in 21 Days.*) Your extension will generally be made up of a single Java class definition with a set of native methods, and then any number of native-code libraries to implement those methods. Try and keep the parts of your code that use native methods and the bulk of your channel separate from each other; this will make it easier to install, to update, and to manage the channel.

Keep in mind that because native code libraries must be downloaded and installed before they can be used by your channel, there is a strong possibility that a user might subscribe to your channel and NOT have those libraries installed. You can test for this case by catching the `NoClassDefFound` exception the first time you instantiate the Java class that uses the native code. If your channel runs and the native code is not yet installed, your channel will throw that exception. In the catch clause, you can then show an alert to tell the user where to download and install your native libraries (or, perhaps, work around the fact that they don't exist by running a slower or less efficient Java version of that code).

Installing Extensions

On the client system, the native DLL file and your Java class with native methods must be installed in the top-level Tuner folder, in a directory called `etc` (for example, `C:\Marimba\Castanet Tuner\etc\` or `/usr/local/castanet/tuner/etc`). You might have to create this directory if it does not exist. You or the user must download and install those libraries manually; for security reasons they cannot be automatically installed by the channel itself.

Once you or your user has installed the extensions, restart the Tuner for the changes to take effect. On restart the `etc` directory will be added to the Java classpath for channels so that your channel can find any native libraries it needs.

Summary

The intent for tuner extensions is to provide a simple mechanism for a channel to access native code functionality where it is required. It is not a mechanism for allowing native code to substitute for Java. Extensions are not part of the Castanet channel mechanism; they are not automatically updated, their libraries are not shared between channels, nor do they have access to the application context to be able to start or restart the way regular channels can. Also, because extensions are not subject to the security restrictions that channels are, they must be intentionally installed by each user.

For these reasons, its a good idea to keep the channel and the extension as separate as possible and to include only the bare minimum in the extension itself. Keep the bulk of the Java code for your channel in the channel itself so it can be updated and shared.

Marimba will provide more examples of tuner extensions on their Web server at `http://www.marimba.com/developer/`.

index

Official Marimba Guide to Bongo

—Danny Goodman

Designed for programmers and non-programmers alike, Bongo is Marimba's visual tool for designing and implementing graphical user interfaces for Java applications and Castanet content. Written by best-selling author Danny Goodman, this hands-on guide teaches users how to create sophisticated, well-designed applications with this powerful tool.

CD-ROM contains special versions of Bongo, the Castanet Tuner and Transmitter, all from Marimba, as well as examples from the author and additional tools and utilities.

Covers Marimba Bongo

$39.99 USA/$56.95 CDN 1-57521-254-4 *500 pp.*
Casual–Accomplished *Internet/General/WWW Applications*

Teach Yourself Java in 21 Days, Professional Reference Edition

—Laura Lemay & Michael Morrison

Introducing the first, best, and most detailed guide to developing applications with the hot new Java language from Sun Microsystems.

Provides detailed coverage of the hottest new technology on the World Wide Web

Shows readers how to develop applications using the Java language

Includes coverage of browsing Java applications with Netscape and other popular Web browsers

CD-ROM includes the Java Developer's Kit

Covers Java

$59.99 USA/$84.95 CDN 1-57521-183-1 *900 pp.*
Casual–Accomplished–Expert *Internet/Programming*

Laura Lemay's Web Workshop: Netscape Navigator Gold 3, Deluxe Edition

—Laura Lemay & Ned Snell

Netscape Gold and JavaScript are two powerful tools to create and design effective Web pages. This book details not only design elements, but also how to use the Netscape Gold WYSIWYG editor. The included CD-ROM contains a fully licensed edition of Netscape Navigator Gold 3!

Teaches how to program within Navigator Gold's rich Netscape development environment

Explores elementary design principles for effective Web page creation

Covers Web Publishing

$49.99 USA/$56.95 CDN 1-57521-292-7 *400 pp.*
Casual–Accomplished *Internet/General*

Laura Lemay's Web Workshop: Graphics and Web Page Design

—Laura Lemay, Jon M. Duff, & James L. Mohler

With the number of Web pages increasing daily, only the well-designed will stand out and grab the attention of those browsing the Web. This book illustrates, in classic Laura Lemay style, how to design attractive Web pages that will be visited over and over again.

CD-ROM contains HTML editors, graphics software, and royalty-free graphics and sound files

Teaches beginning and advanced level design principles

Covers the Internet

$55.00 USA/$77.95 CDN	*1-57521-125-4*	*500 pp.*
Accomplished	*Internet/Online/Communications*	

Laura Lemay's Web Workshop: ActiveX and VBScript

—Paul Lomax & Rogers Cadenhead

ActiveX is an umbrella term for a series of Microsoft products and technologies that add activity to Web pages. Visual Basic Script is an essential element of the ActiveX family. With it, animation, multimedia, sound, graphics, and interactivity can be added to a Web site. This book is a compilation of individual workshops that show the reader how to use VBScript and other ActiveX technologies within their Web site.

CD-ROM contains the entire book in HTML format, a hand-picked selection of the best ActiveX development tools, scripts, templates, backgrounds, borders, and graphics

Covers ActiveX and VBScript

$39.99 USA/$56.95 CDN	*1-57521-207-2*	*450 pp.*
Casual–Accomplished	*Internet/Programming*	

Java Unleashed, Second Edition

—Michael Morrison, et al.

Java Unleashed, Second Edition is an expanded and updated version of the largest, most comprehensive Java book on the market.

Covers Java, Java APIs, Java OS, just-in-time compilers, and more

CD-ROM includes sample code, examples from the book, and bonus electronic books

Covers Java

$49.99 USA/$70.95 CDN	*1-57521-197-1*	*1,200 pp.*
Intermediate–Advanced	*Internet/Programming*	

Teach Yourself Web Publishing with HTML 3.2 in a Week, Third Edition

—Laura Lemay

This is the updated edition of Laura Lemay's previous bestseller, *Teach Yourself Web Publishing with HTML in 14 Days, Premier Edition*. In it readers will find all the advanced topics and updates—including adding audio, video, and animation—to Web page creation.

Explores the use of CGI scripts, tables, HTML 3.2, the Netscape and Internet Explorer extensions, Java applets and JavaScript, and VRML

Covers HTML 3.2

$29.99 USA/$42.95 CDN	*1-57521-192-0*	*624 pp.*
New–Casual–Accomplished	*Internet/Web Publishing*	

Web Publishing Unleashed, Professional Reference Edition

—William Stanek, et al.

Web Publishing Unleashed, Professional Reference Edition is a completely new version of the first book, combining coverage of all Web development technologies in one volume. It now includes entire sections on JavaScript, Java, VBScript and ActiveX, plus expanded coverage of multimedia Web development, adding animation, developing intranet sites, Web design, and much more!

Includes a 200-page reference section

CD-ROM includes a selection of HTML, Java, CGI and scripting tools for Windows/Mac-plus Sams.net Web Publishing Library, and electronic versions of top Web publishing books!

Covers HTML, CGI, JavaScript, VBScript, ActiveX

$59.99 USA/$84.95 CDN	*1-57521-198-X*	*1,200 pp.*
Intermediate–Advanced	*Internet/Web Publishing*	

Add to Your Sams.net Library Today
with the Best Books for Internet Technologies

ISBN	Quantity	Description of Item	Unit Cost	Total Cost
1-57521-254-4		Official Marimba Guide to Bongo (Book/CD-ROM)	$39.99	
1-57521-183-1		Teach Yourself Java in 21 Days Professional Reference Edition (Book/CD-ROM)	$59.99	
1-57521-292-7		Laura Lemay's Web Workshop: Netscape Navigator Gold 3, Deluxe Edition (Book/CD-ROM)	$49.99	
1-57521-125-4		Laura Lemay's Web Workshop: Graphics and Web Page Design (Book/CD-ROM)	$55.00	
1-57521-207-2		Laura Lemay's Web Workshop: ActiveX and VBScript (Book/CD-ROM)	$39.99	
1-57521-197-1		Java Unleashed, Second Edition (Book/CD-ROM)	$49.99	
1-57521-192-0		Teach Yourself Web Publishing with HTML 3.2 in a Week, Third Edition	$29.99	
1-57521-198-X		Web Publishing Unleashed, Professional Reference Edition (Book/CD-ROM)	$59.99	
		Shipping and Handling: See information below.		
		TOTAL		

Shipping and Handling: $4.00 for the first book, and $1.75 for each additional book. If you need to have it NOW, we can ship product to you in 24 hours for an additional charge of approximately $18.00, and you will receive your item overnight or in two days. Overseas shipping and handling adds $2.00. Prices subject to change. Call between 9:00 a.m. and 5:00 p.m. EST for availability and pricing information on latest editions.

201 W. 103rd Street, Indianapolis, Indiana 46290

1-800-428-5331 — Orders   1-800-835-3202 — FAX   1-800-858-7674 — Customer Service

Book ISBN 1-57521-255-2

MACMILLAN COMPUTER PUBLISHING USA

A VIACOM COMPANY

Technical ---- Support:

If you need assistance with the information in this book or with a CD/Disk accompanying the book, please access the Knowledge Base on our Web site at **http://www.superlibrary.com/general/support**. Our most Frequently Asked Questions are answered there. If you do not find the answer to your questions on our Web site, you may contact Macmillan Technical Support **(317) 581-3833** or e-mail us at **support@mcp.com**.

Installing the CD-ROM

The companion CD-ROM contains all the source code and project files developed by the author, plus evaluation versions of the Marimba products for Windows 95, Windows NT 4, and Solaris 2.x:

- Castanet Tuner

- Castanet Transmitter

- Bongo

The CD-ROM also includes an electronic version of *Teach Yourself Java in 21 Days* in HTML format. To view this book, open the file **TYJFM.HTM** in a Web browser such as Netscape Navigator or Microsoft Internet Explorer.

To install the Marimba products, please follow these steps.

Windows 95 / NT 4 Installation Instructions

1. Insert the CD-ROM into your CD-ROM drive.
2. From the Windows 95 or NT 4 desktop, double-click the My Computer icon.
3. Double-click the icon representing your CD-ROM drive.
4. Double-click the icon titled README.txt to read detailed installation instructions for the Marimba products.

Sun Solaris 2.x Installation

Most of the Solaris files on the CD are stored in tar/zip archives. You must uncompress the files to your hard drive before you can use them. Be sure to read the file README.txt in the root directory of the CD-ROM; it includes important information about how to install the files on the disc.

Technical Support

If you need assistance with the information in this book or with a CD/disk accompanying the book, please access the Knowledge Base on our Web site at http://www.superlibrary.com/general/support. Our most Frequently Asked Questons are answered there. If you do not find the answer to your questions on our Web site, contact MacMillan Technical Support at (317) 581-3833 or e-mail us at support@mcp.com.